# Taxes, Spending, and the U.S. Government's March Toward Bankruptcy

What's in a word? Plenty, when it's a word such as "taxes," "spending," or "deficits" that pervades Washington political debate despite lacking coherent economic content.

The United States is moving toward a possible catastrophic fiscal collapse. The country may not get there, but the risk is unmistakable and growing. The "fiscal language" of taxes, spending, and deficits has played a huge and underappreciated role in the decisions that have pushed the nation in this dangerous direction.

Part of the problem is that, by focusing only on the current year, deficits permit politicians to ignore what is looming down the road. The bigger problem lies in the belief, shared by people on the left and the right alike, that "tax cuts" and "spending cuts" lead to smaller government, when in fact the characterization of any new policy as a change in "taxes" or "spending" is purely a matter of labeling.

This book proposes a better fiscal language for U.S. budgetary policy, rooted in economic fundamentals such as wealth distribution and resource allocation in lieu of "taxes" and "spending," and in the use of multiple measures (such as the fiscal gap and generational accounting) to replace misguided reliance on annual budget deficits.

**Daniel N. Shaviro** is Wayne Perry Professor of Taxation at New York University Law School, where he has taught since 1995. He previously served on the faculty of the University of Chicago Law School from 1987 to 1995. Professor Shaviro was a Legislation Attorney for the U.S. Congress's Joint Committee on Taxation from 1984 to 1987, and he worked on the landmark Tax Reform Act of 1986. His previous books include *Who Should Pay for Medicare?* (2004), *Making Sense of Social Security Reform* (2000), *When Rules Change: An Economic and Political Look at Transition Relief and Retroactivity* (2000), and *Do Deficits Matter?* (1997). Professor Shaviro has served as a Visiting Scholar at the American Enterprise Institute and chaired the Tax Section of the American Association of Law Schools and the American Law and Economics Association. He has published articles in the *Harvard Law Review, University of Chicago Law Review, Michigan Law Review, University of Pennsylvania Law Review*, and *Tax Law Review*. His blog, Start Making Sense, may be found at http://danshaviro.blogspot.com.

# TAXES, SPENDING, AND THE U.S. GOVERNMENT'S MARCH TOWARD BANKRUPTCY

## Daniel N. Shaviro

New York University Law School

**CAMBRIDGE**
UNIVERSITY PRESS

CAMBRIDGE UNIVERSITY PRESS
Cambridge, New York, Melbourne, Madrid, Cape Town, Singapore, São Paulo

Cambridge University Press
32 Avenue of the Americas, New York, NY 10013-2473, USA

www.cambridge.org
Information on this title: www.cambridge.org/9780521869331

© Daniel N. Shaviro 2007

First published 2007

Printed in the United States of America

*A catalog record for this publication is available from the British Library.*

*Library of Congress Cataloging in Publication Data*

Shaviro, Daniel N.
Taxes, spending, and the U.S. government's march toward bankruptcy /
Daniel N. Shaviro.
   p.   cm.
Includes bibliographical references and index.
ISBN 0-521-86933-1 (hardback) – ISBN 0-521-68958-9 (pbk.)
1. Fiscal policy – United States.   2. Taxation – United States.   3. Budget deficits – United
States.   I. Title.
HJ257.3.S53   2006
336.973 – dc22        2006008552

ISBN-13   978-0-521-86933-1 hardback
ISBN-10   0-521-86933-1 hardback

ISBN-13   978-0-521-68958-8 paperback
ISBN-10   0-521-68958-9 paperback

*For the late David F. Bradford,*

*a colleague and friend whose untimely*

*loss I still mourn*

# Contents

# Contents

## Part 4. Conclusion

# Acknowledgments

I am grateful to Lily Batchelder, Thomas Firey, Jason Furman, William Gentry, David Kamin, Edward McCaffery, Margaret Shulman, and four anonymous reviewers for their comments on earlier drafts of the manuscript or on particular chapters.

An earlier version of Chapter 2 appeared in *Regulation Magazine*. An earlier version of Chapter 8 appeared in the *Tax Law Review*. Some of the ideas in Chapters 2, 4, and 5 were earlier articulated in Daniel Shaviro, "Reckless Disregard: The Bush Administration's Policy of Cutting Taxes in the Face of an Enormous Fiscal Gap," *Boston College Law Review* 45 (2005): 1279, copyright © 2005 by Boston College Law School.

# PART 1

# LABELS AND CONSEQUENCES

## THE FAILURE OF OUR FISCAL LANGUAGE

*Language, the greatest human invention, helps us to understand the world, but also to misunderstand it. We use it to inform other people, but also to deceive them. It connotes more than it directly says, increasing the amount communicated but adding a subliminal element that we may not consciously appreciate even when it sways us.*

*Fiscal language, or the set of terms such as "taxes," "spending," and "budget deficits" that we use to categorize the government's dealings in cash, exemplifies the bad side much more than the good. Our fiscal language depends on form, yet seems to connote real substance. The result is confusion and deliberate manipulation that increasingly endanger our national economic welfare.*

# 1

## Fiscal Language and the Fiscal Crisis

*Words enable us to behave like human beings, but also to behave more stupidly than dumb beasts.*

— Laura Huxley

**Language,** *n. The music with which we charm the serpents guarding another's treasure.*

— Ambrose Bierce, *The Devil's Dictionary*

### The Fiscal Crisis and Its Roots in Fiscal Language

The United States is presently moving toward a possible catastrophic fiscal collapse. We may not get there, but the risk is unmistakable and growing. Whether we get there or not depends on whether our political system can generate responsible decisions. Like a car headed for a cliff, our present course is clear, but the driver could still turn the wheel.

It might seem that our economy is too strong, and our political system too stable, for us ever to face the sort of discredited–debtor purgatory that has recently plagued nations such as Brazil and Argentina, complete with hyperinflation, high unemployment, and recurrent bank failures. We can indeed afford a lot of mistakes, and our political system has never entirely failed us since the Civil War. But if our policies are foolish enough for long enough, default or hyperinflation can and will happen here.

Our march toward government insolvency is a complex historical event with multiple causes. The central causes involve health care technology and demographics, and are being faced by countries around the world. Improved but costlier health care and the aging of our population have made Social Security and Medicare ever more expensive, and are expected to keep on doing so. Recent tax cuts and spending increases, however, have made the problem much worse. And worse still are the dim political prospects for a course correction any time soon. Tax increases and entitlement cuts are both effectively off the table. Democrats advocating the former, or Republicans the latter, would risk dire political consequences. Nor does a bipartisan deal, combining both poisons but inoculating both parties against the attacks they would face if acting alone, seem plausible today. The Republican leaders and the party's "base" are adamantly opposed to any such deal, and the Democrats might turn them down even if offered it.

The current political impasse reflects the Republicans' march to the right, starting in the aftermath of the first President Bush's defeat in the 1992 presidential election, and cemented in place by the 1994 "Contract With America"–led congressional takeover. During the ten years before 1992, major bipartisan budget deals promoting fiscal responsibility were almost an annual event. Not any more. Nowadays, even the return of enormous budget deficits has failed to prompt any movement toward revival of the earlier pattern.

Bipartisanship is bound to be harder when the parties are further apart ideologically. But Ronald Reagan and Tip O'Neill, who were not especially close either, nonetheless worked together when necessary in the early 1980s. The key difference this time has been the rise of a conservative anti-tax movement that relied ideologically on basic misperceptions and misunderstandings that were shared across the political spectrum. These errors, in turn, depended importantly on the language that we use to organize events into a coherent narrative. Failures of fiscal language – the set of terms we use to describe government and categorize programs that deal in cash – have played a vital role in the recent rush toward default, and will continue to need correction even if the budget crisis passes.

The defects in our preexisting fiscal language have mattered on two levels. First, they have helped to supply the ideological motivation for the anti-tax crusade, by encouraging the mistaken belief that the tax cuts of recent years actually advanced conservative small-government principles. Second, the defects in our fiscal language have contributed to grave and often bipartisan misunderstanding of the long-term implications of our current budgetary course.

We can start with the policy choice to cut taxes. For many decades, a dominant theme in American conservative thought and politics has been battling "big government." While in part waged on the regulatory front, the main action for at least three decades has centered on tax policy, and is well conveyed by Ronald Reagan's famous, oft-repeated charge that Democrats like nothing better than to "tax and spend." Conservative Republican advocacy of tax cuts, after premiering nationally in Reagan's 1980 presidential campaign and the ensuing 1981 tax act, became a core ideological and policy aim with the promulgation in 1994 of the "Contract with America," and then bore fruit in the recent tax cuts.

Controversial though the tax cuts have been, their supporters and opponents alike generally agree that they are steps toward smaller government. While merely reducing the government's tax take for now as spending continues to rise, they are likely to require much tighter spending controls in the future. Indeed, down the road they will require, not only offsetting tax increases, but also substantial Social Security and Medicare cuts, since that is where the money is.

The effort to make future spending less affordable was deliberate, reflecting antigovernment sentiment. While the Bush Administration was circumspect about this goal (and has largely ignored spending discipline for the present), its close political allies were more forthcoming. Tax-cutting advocate Grover Norquist, for example, stated that his "goal is to cut government in half in twenty-five years," and thus "to get it down to the size where we can drown it in the bathtub."

The English writer Saki once observed: "When one's friends and enemies agree on any particular point they are usually wrong." So it was this time. The point of agreement between supporters and opponents of President Bush's tax policy, that the tax cuts were a step toward smaller government, reflected a shared misunderstanding of what "smaller government" means. More specifically, it rested on spending illusion, or confusing the amount of the nominal dollar flows between individuals and the government with the actual size of government. Once we really examine the idea of government size, we can see that the tax cuts may well, on balance, prove to have been a step toward *larger* government, because their main effect may be to increase economic distortion, along with wealth redistribution from younger to older Americans.

The flawed fiscal language that encouraged the Bush Administration to view large-scale wealth transfers to older generations as a march to smaller government was as vital to its fiscal policy as faulty intelligence information was vital to its Iraq policy. However, the truly Enron-style aspect related to the long-term fiscal picture. And here the misunderstandings, while equally bipartisan, have been more deliberate. Both parties are averse to long-term fiscal measures that would make the unsustainable character of their preferred policies more evident. Better to rely on annual cash-flow deficits and surpluses, even though they reflect the use of an accounting method that would lead to jail time for any corporate executive who tried to use it.

What is the rationale for computing deficits and surpluses? We might think of them as trying to measure the government's annual departure from the no-free-lunch principle, which holds that everything must ultimately be paid for. Deficits seem to indicate a lack of full financing, while surpluses seem to indicate that the government is accumulating more cash than it needs. Unfortunately, however, both are highly defective as measures of departure from the no-free-lunch principle. In particular, while they take account of changes to explicit public debt, such as that occurring when the government sells bonds to finance a deficit, they ignore rising implicit liabilities, such as those under Social Security and Medicare, that most consider almost as sacred a commitment as repaying the national debt.

Economists have recently developed a long-term measure, called the fiscal gap, of our government's long-term departure from the no-free-lunch principle. In effect, this is current public debt plus the present value of all future debt that would have to be issued if we continued on our current course. As we will see, this measure is far from perfect, and can itself be gamed in certain ways, but it does avoid the myopic time frame that constitutes the chief shortcoming of annual or even ten-year budget deficits.

The fiscal gap has recently been estimated at $68.6 trillion, or alternatively $85.5 trillion, with the main difference lying in whether the tax cuts of recent years are assumed to be permanent. In 2003 alone, it increased by more than $20 trillion, reflecting the nearly simultaneous adoption of tax cuts and of an unfunded Medicare prescription drug benefit that the Medicare trustees subsequently estimated would cost $18.2 trillion over the long run. This was quite a spree by any imaginable yardstick. And while it was entirely done by Republicans, Democrats might have made the Medicare portion larger still, given their support for a more generous drug benefit.

The fiscal gap admittedly uses a more ambitious system of projecting the government's long-term finances than anything a company is required to use in financial reporting. It takes into account expected future cash flows that have not yet, in an accounting sense, accrued. This difference reflects the fact that an elected government has a commonly understood, if legally unenforceable, commitment to its citizens to keep doing certain things, such as paying retirement benefits and providing national defense, in sharp contrast to a company's mere expectation (without any sort of commitment) that it might want to hire new workers in the future. So corporate executives would not go to jail for failing to publish fiscal gap–style measures of their companies' long-term net revenue projections. But they most assuredly would go to jail if they published financial statements that ignored accruing liabilities, like those owed by Social Security to current workers. By one recent estimate, the consequence of this omission for Social Security in 2002, a reasonably typical year, was that the system reported a $165.4 billion increase in assets, whereas it should have reported a $467.5 billion loss (Jackson 2004). This might have been grounds for jailing the responsible officials, if not for the fact that for decades the U.S.

Congress has mandated the misreporting, and is not about to send itself to jail.

Short-term measures for long-term issues are inherently a recipe for mischief. They have encouraged budgetary game-playing for decades, practices such as back-loading the costs of proposed changes to arise outside the official budget window, or scheduling tax cuts for expiration even though everyone knows the plan is to extend them. But the worst blow of all, planned and expected by no one, was the short-lived emergence of budget surpluses in the late 1990s, encouraging the view that fiscal discipline no longer mattered. As we soon learned, a measure that gives the wrong sign, relative to the actual long-term picture, is even more damaging than one that has been lowballed through "smoke and mirrors" gamesmanship. By the time annual budget deficits were back, the rules and habits that had aided fiscal responsibility despite all the games had vanished, and to date irretrievably.

Throughout all this, most experts recognized that we faced a long-term fiscal gap. But this understanding lacked a sufficient political voice, in part because focus on the surplus was so inescapable. So our fiscal policy was powerfully pushed in the wrong direction – away from sustainability, and often explicitly premised on the idea that "if we don't blow the surplus our way, the other guys will do it their way."

By fostering confusion about how "taxes" and "spending" relate to the size of government, along with the view that a temporary surplus was meaningful, fiscal language has played a major role in the U.S. government's march toward bankruptcy. This book is therefore dedicated to two vital agendas, one short-term and the other long-term. The short-term agenda is correcting the misguided beliefs that tax cutting is bringing us smaller government and that annual deficit measures adequately show what we are doing. I explain, moreover, why the threat of bankruptcy or hyperinflation is so real and potentially so dangerous to our economic welfare.

The book's long-term agenda is to improve our fiscal language so that similar episodes of confusion and irresponsibility will be less likely in the future. This long-term agenda, in turn, has both a destructive and a constructive side. I aim both to show in detail just how bad our fiscal language currently is, and to sketch a better one that is rooted in such fundamentals as resource allocation, wealth distribution, and policy transparency.

## Fiscal Language in the Labeling Sense

Again, by "fiscal language" I mean the set of terms we use to describe and categorize government programs that deal in cash. Its use and abuse occur at two different levels, distinguishable by their degree of generality.

At the superficial level, politicians give nice names to policy instruments they like, and not-so-nice names to those they dislike, with "niceness" being defined by the same sort of intensive research with focus groups that underlies the choice of brand name for a new toothpaste. Thus, potentially controversial law enforcement legislation is named the "Patriot Act" (who in politics would want to oppose patriotism?), while a Bush Administration plan to increase permissible air pollution is dubbed the "Clear Skies" initiative.

Recently in the fiscal policy realm, the "estate tax," an accurate name for a tax levied on decedents' estates, suddenly got renamed the "death tax," an inaccurate name given that death without a requisite estate would not trigger it. The labeling change was pushed by proponents of repeal, who determined that it would make the tax politically more vulnerable. But this was just bold marketing, not misleading or mistaken reliance on formal categories to mischaracterize the policy effects of estate tax repeal.

Also in the fiscal policy realm, Republicans in Washington never speak of "tax cuts," a term that might run afoul of status quo bias, or the view that changes in current policy require affirmative justification. Rather, the term of choice is "tax relief," conveying that "there must be an affliction, an afflicted party, and a reliever who removes the affliction and is therefore a hero" (Lakoff 2004, 3).

These word games are reasonably entertaining and undeniably important, and I will examine them in a number of cases, such as the recent Social Security debate. However, my main interest in writing this book is to look at the fundamental categories that we use in describing the federal budget and its parts. Here there are basic organizing terms, more stable and far-reaching than the name of a given proposal. To describe a whole range of fiscal institutions as "taxes" means more than simply changing a particular tax's name or demanding "relief" from all the rules that are called taxes.

## Fiscal Language in the Structural Sense

The fundamental subatomic particles of our prevailing fiscal language are "taxes" and "spending," defined as cash flows to and from the government, respectively, leaving aside those from voluntary consumer transactions (such as paying for mail service or a subway fare). Taxes and spending, ostensibly, are the main things governments do, along with regulation. The budget deficit, our third core fiscal language term, builds on the first two by comparing annual taxes to annual spending as officially defined, with the aim of measuring – well, whatever it is that budget deficits and surpluses are supposed to measure, a topic that I address in Chapter 4.

The account I will offer in this book of the fiscal language that is built on these core terms may initially remind some readers of postmodernism, which emphasizes the power and artificiality of words and their "texts" while also denying that there is an outside, objectively describable reality. The important thing about fiscal language, however, is that, postmodern though the players' writhings may be, there really is an objectively describable reality. For example, a given government policy actually has some set of effects in the world, which a better language could be used to describe – even if we face irreducible uncertainty about exactly what these effects are, along with normative controversy about how to evaluate them.

Unfortunately, the prevailing structural fiscal language creates a backward world where "up" may mean "down" and "green" may mean "red." The good news (such as it is) is that we are not in the linguistic world of George Orwell's *1984,* where the authorities decide that war is peace and freedom is slavery. Our structural fiscal language, rather than being dictated from on high by Big Brother, involves formal rules of the game that participants can manipulate but not openly flout. It tilts and constrains real policy choices, and induces political actors to befuddle themselves even as they labor to befuddle constituencies whose support they need.

Since most political actors are trying to win, not to engage in reflection or genuine dialogue, our current fiscal language inevitably has a dual character. It is both a purportedly objective descriptive tool and a weapon of political combat. However, its use as a political weapon is parasitic on its claim to offer objective and meaningful description. For example, if calling a proposed rule a "tax" were recognized as merely a matter of convention, rather than being thought to reflect something important about the rule's substance, then any inference we were invited to draw from the label, such as that the rule is an example of "big government," would be unlikely to persuade.

Classifications must seem not only objective but meaningful, if broader inferences are to be drawn from them. Thus, suppose Congress created a special budgetary category for all spending that was done with red dollar bills. While this would involve objective description, the charge that a politician favored spending too much red rather than green money would likely have no bite.

Our current fiscal language is largely on a par with talking about green versus red dollar bills. Its inadequacy starts with the fundamental subatomic particles of "taxes" and "spending." Each is defined by looking at a specific cash flow, generally in isolation from all other cash flows. When a dollar goes to the government, we generally call it a "tax." When a dollar comes from the government, we generally call it "spending."

The direction of a given cash flow, by itself, means nothing because it depends on the contours of a single, arbitrarily defined transaction between the government and the private party. For example, if you paid the government ten dollars in the late morning, and it paid you ten dollars in the early afternoon, would it really make sense to discern taxes and spending of ten dollars each, rather than a net outcome of almost nothing? Everyone engages in innumerable transactions with the government, and a label that depends on how the separate transactions are defined cannot be meaningful. Anyone who has ever had a job, or even buys a stick of gum, is likely to make some payments to the government. Indeed, nearly everyone ends up making net payments to the government, since it provides goods and services rather than just rebating cash. Against this background, it makes no economic difference whether, at any given point, you get a dollar back ("spending") or pay a dollar less ("taxation"). A dollar is a dollar. But "taxes" and "spending" are both ostensibly higher if offsetting cash flows travel in both directions, even though they may add up to precisely nothing.

Why should it seem to matter whether a ten-dollar improvement in one's net position is labeled as a tax cut (or better still, tax relief) or as spending? While I further discuss this issue in Chapter 2, an initial general point is worth making here. The choice of labels involves framing (Lakoff 2004, 3), or the use of language to evoke underlying worldviews that people find emotionally compelling. Thus, a tax connotes "theft" or "punishment" (Lakoff 2002, 30), while spending ostensibly gives people things they have not earned and that make them dependent (Lakoff 2004, 9).

While this may capture the lay view, there also are important intellectual claims associated with the tax/spending distinction. This is well illustrated by the op-ed writings of leading conservative economists such as Milton Friedman, who says that "I have never met a tax cut I didn't like" (Friedman 2003). What appears to have blinded Friedman to the potential equivalence between "tax cuts" and "spending increases" is that he has in mind particular types of fiscal instruments that differ in more than just the direction of cash flow. On the tax side, he has in mind rules such as the income tax, which even liberal economists would agree inefficiently deters economic production. On the spending side, he has in mind the provision of particular goods and services – say, a highway demanded by a powerful congressman, or a federal bureaucrat's salary – that he suspects are worth less to society than their cost.

Friedman is entirely right to think that, from his perspective on markets and government, reducing income tax rates is a lot better than building more highways, even though both reduce the government's net cash. What makes these two proposals so distinct, however, is the fact that this spending proposal, unlike this tax proposal, directly has what economists would call allocative effects. That is, it steers societal resources to a particular use. By contrast, the income tax rate cut gives people more money to spend as they like. While this is an important distinction between the two proposals, it emphatically is *not* a function of the direction of cash flow. After all, if the tax cut had been a credit for solar-powered homes, while the spending increase had involved unrestricted cash grants, then it would have been the tax cut that directed societal resources to a particular use. As we will see, there simply is no substitute for looking at the economic substance of government rules, rather than using the direction of a given cash flow as a proxy for other characteristics.

## Road Map

The rest of this book proceeds as follows. In the remainder of this Part One, covering basic concepts, Chapter 2 discusses the terms "taxes" and "spending" and their relationship to the size of government, while Chapter 3 examines the adequacy of deficits as a measure relevant to long-term budgetary considerations.

Part Two discusses long-term budgetary issues in greater detail. Chapter 4 examines what we have in mind when we discuss the issues that are thought to be associated with the deficit measure. Chapter 5 evaluates alternative long-term measures, such as generational accounting and the fiscal gap. Chapter 6 examines the politics of creating a huge fiscal gap and of restoring fiscal responsibility.

Part Three shifts the direction of fiscal language inquiry from looking across time to looking across the groupings that we use at any one time to make sense of the federal budget. Chapter 7 discusses the recent fiscal language wars concerning Social Security, waged in connection with President Bush's ill-fated 2005 proposals. Chapter 8 returns to the distinction between taxes and spending, by examining the "tax expenditure" concept that has often played a major role in debates concerning tax reform. Chapter 9 explores how fiscal language, through the distinction between taxes and spending, has thwarted designing sensible welfare policies that aid the poor without harshly punishing attempts to escape poverty through productive work.

Finally, Chapter 10 offers a brief conclusion, including ten concrete suggestions for improving both public reporting about the budget and its components, and the specific budgetary rules that shape and constrain our fiscal policies.

# 2

## Taxes, Spending, and the Size of Government

*Fanaticism consists in redoubling your efforts when you have forgotten your aim.*

– George Santayana

*Alice came to a fork in the road. "Which road do I take?" she asked. "Where do you want to go?", responded the Cheshire cat. "I don't know," Alice answered. "Then," said the cat, "it doesn't matter."*

– Lewis Carroll, *Alice's Adventures in Wonderland*

### Which Way Is Which?

Advocates of smaller government invariably call for tax cuts. If they are honest and principled, rather than just playing politics, they also advocate spending cuts. Advocates of a larger and more active government oppose them on both counts. It rarely occurs to either side that they may misunderstand the basic relationship here between means and ends – that is, between tax and spending cuts and the size of government. Stand-alone tax cuts, in particular, may actually lead to what is in substance a larger and more invasive government, even if fewer dollars observably travel back and forth.

Both sides ought to think back to the old childhood game Pin the Tail on the Donkey. In this game, you start out facing the donkey, pin and tail in hand, but, before you can go anywhere, you are blindfolded and rapidly spun around. You lose your bearings, and thus cannot simply plunge straight ahead with any confidence that you are going the right way.

In the fiscal version of Pin the Tail on the Donkey, existing federal programs point in so many directions that, whatever your stance in the smaller-versus-larger-government debate, you cannot really know which way a given change would take you until you have fully oriented yourself. No simple rule of thumb, such as "tax cuts good, spending bad" (or the reverse) can be adequate.

As a case in point, the enormous tax cuts of recent years, although presumably designed to "starve the beast," may actually end up increasing the size of government, as defined in terms of substance rather than mere form. More specifically, they may increase both redistribution and government-induced economic distortion. If that is not larger government, it is hard to say what is.

If such a possibility appears surprising, it is only because of what I call "spending illusion," or confusion between the actual size of government and the gross amounts of the nominal dollar flows that are denominated as "taxes" and "spending." This illusion is so pervasive, among expert as well as casual observers of government policy, that the effort to dislodge it cannot begin soon enough. I start with three examples, two of them hypothetical but one actually historical.

## Example 1: Reducing the Budget Deficit through "Spending Cuts" while Also Enacting "Tax Cuts"

David Bradford, a prominent economist who shared and helped stimulate my interest in fiscal language issues, once described his pretended "secret plan" to eliminate a budget deficit by formally cutting spending rather than by raising taxes. In Step 1, $60 billion of defense spending on weapons procurement is eliminated. In Step 2, a new $60 billion "weapons supplier tax credit" (WSTC) is enacted. "To qualify for the WSTC, manufacturers will sign appropriate documents prescribed by the Secretary of Defense (looking much like today's procurement contracts) and deliver to appropriate depots weapons systems of prescribed characteristics. The WSTC, which may be transferred to other taxpayers without limit, may only be used in payment of income tax. Step 2 is, apparently obviously, a tax cut" (Bradford 2002, 8). As it happens, the money goes to exactly the same companies that would have gotten the weapons appropriations, in exchange for exactly the same weapons.

Step 3 (modifying the Bradford plan) is an income tax rate increase that raises $50 billion. In form, tax revenues are still down by $10 billion overall (the excess of the WSTC "tax cut" over the money from the new rates), while spending has dropped by $60 billion. Thus, $50 billion worth of deficit reduction has been accomplished while actually (in form) cutting taxes. In substance, however, all that really has happened, beyond relabeling the unchanged weapons procurement, is the enactment of a $50 billion income tax increase.

Why wouldn't the labeling game work? I see only two obstacles to public acceptance of the claim that this really is, on balance, a spending cut rather than a tax increase. First, the fact that a preexisting "spending" program is being converted into an identical "tax" program makes it a bit too obvious that nothing is really happening apart from the increase in income tax rates. This, however, merely means that the proposal comes a bit too late in the day. Proponents of new programs may not be similarly inhibited from using tax credits instead of direct appropriations right from the start, so that they can call their proposals "tax cuts."

Second, the folk definition of "taxes" that governs our fiscal language apparently holds that favorable tax attributes, such as credits and deductions, cannot properly be traded. Evidence comes from the past history of United States income tax legislation. In 1981, under the influence of President Reagan, Congress enacted sizable tax cuts that included generous depreciation and other benefits for various industries. It was understood, however, that many of the intended corporate beneficiaries would be unable to use all of the deductions. The problem was that the depreciation and other cost recovery rules were so generous that many companies, even if they were doing well (and there was a recession at the time), would zero out their taxable incomes and still have plenty of extra deductions and investment tax credits that they could not use.

One possible solution might have been to make the extra tax credits, along with the tax-reducing value of the extra deductions, directly refundable from the U.S. Treasury. This, however, would have violated the folk definition of taxes as payments *to* the government rather than *from* the government. So Congress decided instead to make the deductions and credits effectively transferable, for an arm's-length fee, from companies that could not use them to those that could. It did so by enacting what were called the "safe harbor leasing" rules.

These rules did not literally permit deductions and credits to be sold. What they allowed instead was transactions in which Company A, which actually was investing in depreciable property, would purport to sell the property to Company B, which immediately (and by simultaneous prearrangement) would lease the property right back to Company A. This would have the effect of giving the deductions to B because, under long-standing income tax rules, only the owner of property, as distinct from a lessee, is allowed to claim the tax benefits. Companies had already been doing tax-motivated sale-leasebacks of this kind for many decades. But the transactions that the safe harbor leasing rules newly blessed as effective for tax purposes could more fully and transparently involve nothing beyond mere paper shuffling, as opposed to being required to meet some minimum standard of genuine economic effect on the companies' investment positions.

Unfortunately for the proponents of safe harbor leasing, the fact that it was effectively a method of deduction selling (and indeed expressly rationalized on this ground) proved too transparent. Prominent newspaper stories started to appear describing cases in which millions of dollars worth of deductions and credits were effectively sold. In response to mounting public outrage about the fact that safe harbor leasing actually was working as intended, Congress decided that it was shocked, shocked, and hastened to repeal the rules the very next year. The lesson was clear. Provisions that are labeled "tax benefits" are not supposed to be tradable, any more than they are supposed to be directly refundable by the government beyond the amount of taxes otherwise due from the same taxpayer at the same time under the same set of tax rules.

Returning to our hypothetical example involving the WSTC, why did we need to make it tradable to begin with? The only reason is that some of the target companies might not otherwise have had enough income tax liability to enable them to use the full benefit. For example, a freestanding weapons supplier would end up with zero income if its only source of revenue was defense procurement contracts and it was being paid purely in tax credits. Suppose, however, that all weapons suppliers were owned by enormously profitable corporate conglomerates with multiple lines of business. Now tradability would no longer be necessary, so long as the companies otherwise owed enough federal income tax from their other operations to use all of their WSTCs. It is hard to see, however, why the use of corporate affiliates to soak up the extra credits should be considered any different from the outright sale of tax benefits (though evidently, in the public mind, it is different).

What is the bottom line here? In fact, the WSTC proposal probably would not be politically feasible. But this would not be for any reason of programmatic substance. Rather, it would be because, as a matter of defense industry structure, meeting the accepted folk definition of taxes as nontradable and nonrefundable just happened to be impractical. One lesson we learn is that, while the underlying fiscal language is arbitrary (why should industry structure matter here?) and can potentially be gamed in some situations, its built-in rigidities do potentially limit its manipulability.

## Example 2: Taxing Social Security Benefits: "Big Government" Tax Increase, or "Small Government" Spending Cut?

In 1993, President Clinton sought to reduce the federal budget deficit through a package that combined spending cuts with tax increases. Mindful of years of Republican attacks on Democrats' claimed proclivity to "tax and spend," his Administration started out by promising a 3:1 ratio of spending cuts to tax increases. However, this gradually dropped to 2:1 and finally to 1:1. Congressional Republicans, however, insisted that the Clinton plan, by the time it passed the House of Representatives, had $6.35 in tax increases for each dollar of spending cuts. One of the biggest disputes concerned a proposal (subsequently enacted) to increase the income taxation of Social Security benefits. The Clinton Administration called this a spending cut, but the nonpartisan Congressional Budget Office agreed with Republicans that it was actually a tax increase.

Was President Clinton's classification wrong? The Congressional Budget Office was not alone in thinking that it was. He also captured third place in the 1993 Doublespeak Awards, administered by the National Council of Teachers of English, for this maneuver plus his insistence on "using the word 'investment' as a substitute for the word 'spending' in his rhetoric on economic policy" (Ackerman 1993). The storm blew over a bit, however, when word came out that the Reagan Administration had gotten away with classifying income taxation of Social Security benefits as a benefit cut (Greenhouse 1993).

The Clinton Administration argued that its proposal really was a spending cut because its effect was to reduce seniors' net Social Security retirement benefits. It was "wrong," apparently, because the Social Security checks that seniors got in the mail were not affected. Instead, the change affected their computations of taxable income, and thus the income tax payments they sent to the federal government. So apparently it "really" was a tax increase within the accepted conventions.

Suppose, however, that there had been a politically acceptable way to give the Social Security Administration information from seniors' tax returns that it could use to reduce all benefit checks by exactly the amount of the tax increase under the actual proposal and enactment. Then, despite identical economic effects, there would have been a generally accepted "spending cut" rather than a "tax increase." Under this scenario, however, a brand new concern would have arisen. The United States would have been means testing Social Security benefits – a gross violation, in some people's view, of the sacred social compact under which Social Security is a universal program, but one that evidently was not a concern under the actual Reagan and Clinton enactments.

In sum, the Clinton and Reagan proposals "really" were tax increases, under prevailing conventions, due to mere cash flow details. Yet only administrative details distinguish (1) reducing a given senior's Social Security checks by $X given her income, from (2) making her pay $X more in income tax given her Social Security benefits. Surely the size of government, in any meaningful sense, is the same in both cases.

## Example 3: The Social Security Program That Wasn't

To approach size-of-government issues from another angle, let's consider Social Security. In 2004, the basic U.S. Social Security retirement system was projected to receive inflows of $543.8 billion and to pay out $406 billion, almost all of it directly for benefits. Surely this is "big government" at its most grotesquely bloated.

The answer is: not so fast. While Social Security is an important government intervention in our economy, the gross dollar flows that it involves are hopelessly uninformative about its real magnitude. To make this clear, suppose that Social Security were twice as big, in terms of the nominal cash flows involved, but that it differed from the actual program in the following respects. First, suppose that it was actuarially fair, in that each participant's retirement benefits equaled the value of her tax contributions. Second, suppose that all participants were farsighted enough to plan the lifetime personal spending paths that they preferred, and that financial markets were complete enough that they could always borrow and lend at will. Stripped of economics jargon, this means that all of us would save exactly as much as we wanted for retirement, no more and no less, Social Security's provision of mandatory retirement benefits be damned. People would save outside Social Security if it did not give them enough retirement income. And if it gave them more retirement saving than they wanted, they would simply borrow against the value of their expected future retirement benefits and use the money earlier anyway.

We now would have a program that was twice as large as the actual one – taking in more than $1 trillion per year and spending more than $800 billion – and yet that was completely vacuous, in the sense of having no aggregate effect on anything. Since it was actuarially fair, no redistribution would result from it. In addition, its trivial administrative costs aside, Social Security would have no allocative effect on the economy. For example, workers would be totally indifferent to the payroll tax, since they would realize that, for every dollar they paid, they would be earning benefits that were worth a dollar and that they could consume whenever they liked. Seniors would have and spend exactly the same amounts of disposable income during their retirement years as they would have if the program had not existed.

Needless to say, actual Social Security is by no means so vacuous. For example, it has resulted in vast wealth redistribution, in particular from younger to older age cohorts. In addition, since people generally can't and don't borrow against the value of their future Social Security benefits, it really does require a minimum level of retirement saving (Shaviro 2000, 29–31). Moreover, workers probably do treat the payroll tax as reducing their incentive to work, even in cases where a dollar paid actually earns them a dollar's worth of extra retirement benefits (12–13). On the other hand, my hypothetical story is not entirely false either. For example, surely many beneficiaries would save for retirement anyway, and understand that Social Security reduces the amount of direct retirement saving that they need. Moreover, some workers may currently understand that, under the Social Security benefit formula, they really do earn extra benefits (in addition to accruing extra tax liabilities) by working more.

While Social Security therefore does matter, unlike my hypothetical program that does not, its dollar flows are still no measure of how much it matters. For example, since it pays cash that retirees can spend as they like, it surely affects resource allocation far less than would a program that spent the same amount of money on specific assets (such as roads and office buildings) that the government chose. Moreover, increasing its cash flows does not necessarily make its total effects bigger, and reducing them does not necessarily make them smaller. We would have to ask how the actual effects that matter were being changed – and we will shortly see a real life case where reducing some people's Social Security benefits makes the program's total impact greater.

## Why Do the "Tax" and "Spending" Classifications (Seem to) Matter?

Again, this chapter is arguing that "taxes" and "spending" are arbitrary categories, defined by the direction of a particular cash flow considered in isolation, when the overall pattern is what really matters. And it is arguing that policy changes denominated as "tax cuts" can actually make the government larger. However, we need to look more carefully at why people think the terminology matters.

Why might the "secret plan" to substitute the WSTC for military spending be politically appealing if one could actually get away with it? And why would President Clinton and the congressional Republicans have been so motivated to battle about the ratio of "tax increases" to "spending cuts" in Clinton's deficit reduction plan, and thus about the classification of reducing net Social Security benefits through the income tax? This, by the way, was no isolated incident. As Martin Sullivan (2000, 1188) recounts:

> During the 1990s, President Clinton...perfected a political tactic that [did] wonders for the Democratic party, but at the same time... complicated the tax code. Tax-and-spend liberalism [was] replaced with "tax expend" liberalism. Rather than directly funding new government programs, the president [knew] that politically it [was] far easier to implement social programs through the tax code.

The reasons for preferring "spending cuts" to "tax increases," and "tax cuts" to "spending increases," even when the difference is purely a matter of form, arise at two different levels. One involves universals of human psychology, while the other involves cultural particulars of American ideology.

## Behavioral Economics and the Endowment Effect

There is an old story about a man who drops his house keys on the street while staggering around drunk one night, and is spotted looking for them by a lamppost. "Is that where you dropped them?" he is asked. "No, but the light is good here," he replies.

## The Failure of Our Fiscal Language

At one time, many leading economists, if asked to explain why people might prefer "tax cuts" to identical "spending increases" even though a dollar is a dollar, would have committed a version of the drunk's fallacy. Since narrowly defined rational (in the sense of profit-maximizing) behavior is easiest to model, economists long had a strong preference for using it to explain all phenomena, even where, as a matter of common sense, it plainly was not operating. Thus, voters and consumers alike would be assumed at all times to act as if a dollar is always a dollar, unless and until this assumption became totally untenable. And anyone sufficiently ingenious to keep on devising new "rational" explanations could postpone this dire event indefinitely.

Over time, however, a great deal of empirical research, in a field known as behavioral economics or decision theory, has changed the predominant view even among rational choice–loving economists. A large body of evidence, derived from a variety of settings, shows that people do not always honor the principle that a dollar is a dollar. Rather, they follow a set of "irrational" preferences, decision strategies, and rules of thumb – albeit possibly rational ones from the standpoint of evolutionary brain design, given the cost of solving all problems perfectly. These departures from strict rationality may work well a lot of the time, but in some settings they lead to decisions that are systematically erroneous, inconsistent, or manipulable.

Among other departures, people tend to be highly sensitive to the benchmarks or starting points that they use in evaluating a given cash flow. One well-known illustration involves the choice between paying for gasoline with a credit card or with cash. "When a gas station charged a 'penalty' for using credit cards ($2.00 versus $1.90, say), people paid cash; when a gas station across the street gave a 'bonus' for using cash ($1.90 versus $2.00), people used credit cards" (McCaffery and Baron 2005, 1751). The price structure is exactly the same either way, but people dislike being "penalized" more than they like receiving "bonuses," even though the only difference lies in the arbitrary choice of baseline. Indeed, the state of California, within a single statute of just two sentences, first prohibits retailers from imposing surcharges on customers who use credit cards in lieu of cash, and then permits them to offer discounts for using cash in lieu of credit cards (California Civil Code, section 1748.1).

Such distinctions between alternative presentations of the same choice reflect the endowment effect, which induces people to underweight opportunity costs relative to other costs (Thaler 1991, 8). Consumers apparently conceptualize forgoing a "bonus" as merely involving an opportunity cost, whereas a "penalty" is paid out of pocket once one has adopted the stated regular price as one's baseline. Recent empirical research confirms the applicability of this phenomenon to fiscal policy. For example, research subjects prefer child "bonuses" in the tax system to childless "penalties," and marriage "bonuses" to single "penalties," in instances where the alternatives are arithmetically equivalent (McCaffery and Baron 2005, 1758–1759).

Under the endowment effect, taxes require people to pay over money that is seen as theirs. The Treasury merely has an opportunity cost if its tax receipts are lower rather than higher. By contrast, government spending has an out-of-pocket cost to the Treasury (and thus to all taxpayers), while forgoing spending merely imposes an opportunity cost on the person who would have benefited from it. Reliance on the baseline overrides straight dollar comparisons, even though the distinction between particular cash flows is arbitrary if cash is going back and forth all the time.

## American Anti-Tax Sentiment

If the endowment effect were the only factor inducing departures from rational, dollar-is-a-dollar style fiscal thinking, one would not expect the level of anti-tax sentiment to be higher in the United States than anywhere else. The mental structures that help give rise to such sentiment are presumably universal. In fact, however, anti-tax sentiment clearly is more powerful here than in European countries that are economically and culturally similar. Indeed, the degree of divergence appears to have increased in recent decades, given the prominence and recent political success of the American anti-tax movement.

This divergence reflects the fact that, whether here or abroad, proponents of higher taxes do not lack tools to sweeten the medicine.

## The Failure of Our Fiscal Language

As George Lakoff (2004, 25–26) notes, taxes may be "framed" positively as investments in the future (a favorite Clintonian device) or as membership dues that we rightly owe for the benefits of citizenship. Moreover, tax cuts are not nearly as "good," from the standpoint of the endowment effect and status quo bias, as tax increases are "bad." So a high-tax baseline for defining changes can increase people's tax tolerance. Thus, while people in all countries share the mental structures that support the perceptual distinction between "tax increases" and identical "spending cuts," it is not surprising that countries would differ with regard to the distinction's political significance.

The American tradition of anti-tax sentiment goes way back (consider the Boston Tea Party, or the anti-tax Whiskey Rebellion of 1794), and has frequently been at center stage in our politics since the late 1970s. The sociological and ideological reasons for the tradition are surely complex, and may reflect, if not the influence of the frontier, then at least the fact that a powerful central government emerged much later here than, say, in England or France.

In terms of how anti-tax sentiment appeals to Americans today, perhaps the best "deep" explanation is George Lakoff's widely noticed claim that the American divide between progressives and conservatives reflects alternative moral worldviews that he connects to basic concepts of the family. Conservatives, he argues, lean more toward a "Strict Father" view, while progressives lean more toward a "Nurturant Parent" view (although most of us feel the pull of both). Under the Strict Father view, in his account, economic success is deemed a reward for hard work and personal virtue, while taxation of the rich is deemed "punishment for doing what is right and succeeding at it" (2002, 189). Cash payments by the government, by contrast, "immoral[ly] . . . give people things they have not earned" (2004, 8–9), thereby encouraging dependence and lack of self-discipline.

Acceptance or rejection of the Strict Father worldview is not a matter of logic, as it depends on one's initial moral premises. What can be questioned logically, however, is its application (or rather misapplication) to base the moral coding of particular cash flows on whether they are arbitrarily labeled as "taxes" or as "spending." People of all political views have been prevented by arbitrary framing from seeing accurately how particular government policies really ought to be viewed given one's underlying political and moral preferences. Both sides evaluate the size of government, the key issue on which they differ philosophically, by reacting to form rather than substance. This leads to the question: how should people think about the size of government in applying their underlying worldviews?

## What Is the "Size of Government"?

Any society with a set of institutions or other means for exercising continuous political authority has a government. When we speak of the size of government in a society, we presumably are interested in how much of what happens in the society is publicly or politically controlled, rather than reflecting decisions by individuals acting in a private capacity or through what we classify as private institutions.

As a first blow against using a simplistic dollar measure, consider outsourcing, or the use of government rules to affect what private individuals end up doing. Suppose that employees in fast food restaurants are getting six dollars per hour, and that a political decision is made to ensure that they get at least seven dollars per hour. One way to accomplish this would be to levy a tax on fast food restaurant owners equal to one dollar times the number of hours of work by these employees, and to use the proceeds to pay the employees a wage subsidy of one dollar per hour. Alternatively, one could enact a seven-dollar-per-hour minimum-wage law. Either way, one would have raised the employers' hourly cost and the workers' hourly return from six dollars to seven dollars (possibly at the cost of reducing low-wage employment levels). As between the two alternatives, it would be a mistake to think that the government must be smaller in the minimum-wage example, simply because it uses an off-budget regulatory mandate in lieu of formal taxes and spending, thus avoiding any moment where money actually passes through the government's coffers.

The minimum wage example involves a regulatory command. But the same point about outsourcing can be made using an example where the government merely changes market prices, and thereby alters private incentives by means that fall short of command. Suppose, for example, that the government wants to accomplish a specified increase in the use of solar heating in private homes. However, rather than either constructing solar heating units or affirmatively requiring their use, the government simply offers special income tax deductions to the units' manufacturers or purchasers, thereby lowering solar heating's after-tax cost by just enough to have exactly the same quantitative effect. The government's choice between these different means of intervening in the market should not affect our ability to recognize that a market intervention is taking place.

We therefore are driven to assessing the size of government in terms of the effects of many different kinds of government action, without being limited to the use of cash or the size of particular discrete cash flows. Once we are focusing on effects, however, we face the question: Compared to what state of affairs is the government having effects? What is the baseline or counterfactual?

A familiar response would be the state of nature, where government is assumed not to exist. Yet this response raises more questions than it answers. The state of nature is a mere hypothetical or thought experiment, remote from anything we observe in our society or would consider implementing, making it of little use in a size-of-government measure. Suppose, for example, that, in the tradition of Thomas Hobbes, we think of the state of nature as involving a war of all against all, where life is solitary, poor, nasty, brutish, and short, and thus where the world population is likely to be billions of people lower, and the economy and physical environment unrecognizably different from what we actually observe. How can we possibly evaluate the relative proximity to this state of affairs of, say, the actual U.S. economy with, as compared to without, a minimum wage law?

Libertarians, who offer the most coherent intellectual expression of what Lakoff calls the Strict Father view, sometimes respond by assuming instead the state of nature described by John Locke. Locke's state of nature features a recognizable social order based on general acceptance of the principle that "no one ought to harm another in his life, health, liberty, or possessions." (Locke, section 6). Property rights are therefore viewed as pre-political, rather than as merely a "legally constructed social relation" (Holmes and Sunstein 1999, 59). Libertarians have thus been accused of "imagin[ing] life roughly as it is now, with jobs, banks, houses, and cars, and lacking only the most obvious government services such as Social Security, the National Endowment for the Arts, and the police" (Murphy and Nagel 2002, 16).

Reliance on the state of nature to support observed pre-tax property relations invites a logical challenge, however. Even without Hobbesian chaos, people's talents would not have similar, or even the same proportionate, value in a world without existing institutions. Barbara Fried (1999, 176), for example, notes "the enormous gains society bestows on those whose natural talents have little use value on [a] Crusoeian island." An example is "Wayne Gretzky alone on a desert island, thinking of inventing a game called hockey if he could ever find ice, eleven other players, and an audience to pay to watch" (177), so that (as in actual late-twentieth-century America) he could earn $20 million per year. It is hard to accept, therefore, that in the state of nature Wayne Gretzky would have been earning the same $20 million, only without the obligation to pay taxes on this money.

Does this challenge rebut making any practical use of the "size of government" concept? If it did, then rejecting the libertarian view of the state of nature would mean that one could not distinguish between, say, the government's level of intervention in the 1880 United States economy as compared to the 1980 Soviet economy. From the standpoint of equipping ourselves with useful tools for evaluating public policy, this would amount to throwing out the baby with the bathwater.

The size-of-government debate ranges from libertarianism at one pole to what might be called socialism at the other pole (although "socialism" is a dirty word in contemporary United States politics). At the libertarian pole, the government, at most, polices force and fraud, enforces contracts, and protects property rights. At the socialist pole, government decision makers do not just establish background institutions, but exert ongoing control over the determination of what is produced and who ends up with how much. Between the two poles, where all countries with market economies find themselves, governments attempt to varying degrees, through government production, regulatory commands, and fiscal tools such as taxes, transfers, and subsidies, to exert some influence over market outcomes. The deeper underlying question in steering between the two poles goes to the relative merits and defects of market and government processes, and to the value or disvalue of government intervention to redistribute wealth (relative to the libertarian pole) – from rich to poor, for example, or from healthy to sick.

Given this debate, even the harshest critics of libertarianism commonly speak of the government as being larger or smaller, depending on where its policies fall along a continuum.[1] Even if this baseline is sufficiently clear, however, no single comprehensive measure of the size of government is likely to be feasible, if only because the issues involved are so multidimensional. For example, how would one integrate, in a single composite measure, the degree of government intervention in the economy with the scope of civil liberties protections? Thus, a more promising approach than seeking any such measure is to evaluate the size of government on particular dimensions, one at a time.

In evaluating the effects of fiscal rules, or those that involve cash flows or something close thereto, we can simplify things a bit. The effects most often and directly implicated by such rules can be divided into two categories. First, there are *allocative* effects, or those relating to the level and use of our society's resources. Second, there are *distributional* effects, or those relating to whom among us has what claims on society's resources. This typology dates back at least to Richard Musgrave's classic 1959 book, *The Theory of Public Finance,* which has done much to shape economic thinking to this day about how we should conceptualize the issues in fiscal policy.

## The Allocative Size of Government

Conservatives are not alone in thinking that government spending provides a good measure of the government's allocative interventions in the economy. To similar effect, on the political left, Liam Murphy and Thomas Nagel (2002, 76) offer the following description of what I would call the allocative side of government policy:

> It determines how much of a society's resources will come under the control of government, for expenditure in accordance with some collective decision procedure, and how much will be left in the discretionary control of private individuals, as their personal property. Call this the *public-private division.*

This way of putting it ignores the continuum between issuing commands and changing the prices that affect people's discretionary decisions. No less than many conservatives, Nagel and Murphy describe the allocative size of government as a function of how much it taxes and spends as opposed to leaving in people's pockets. But again, the round trip of cash between private and government hands is not what really matters. Suppose again that I buy solar heating panels for my home because a special income tax benefit makes the after-tax price attractive. The money I spend in this way reflects a collective decision procedure even though it has remained in my private discretionary control. The government would not have been any bigger had I ended up in the same place, after paying higher income taxes but paying less at the store for the panels because of the price effects of policy-equivalent cash subsidies paid by the U.S. Treasury to the solar heating industry.

Consider as well a tariff on importing French champagne. Suppose that, if the tariff is set at ten dollars per bottle, ten million bottles will be imported and the tariff will raise $100 million. If it is set at $100 per bottle, however, no bottles will be imported, and the tariff will therefore raise zero revenue. Is the government necessarily smaller in the case where it raises zero revenue through the higher tariff but imports of French champagne have been totally eliminated?

Finally, suppose I receive a cash transfer, or equally, a benefit (such as food stamps) that I would have spent the same way even if offered cash in the amount of the benefit's cost to the government. Here we have money that the government "spent," in the sense of directly or indirectly handing it to me, thus relying on collective decision procedures. However, the ultimate use of the cash either was under my private discretionary control, or else might as well have been for all the difference it made. In a sense, therefore, while the government may have changed wealth distribution in the society by giving me the benefit, it did not meddle allocatively at all. I did exactly what I wanted to with the money, once it was given to me.

In another sense, however, the government may indeed have changed allocative outcomes. Perhaps the people who paid for my benefit would have spent the money differently than I did, had it not been taken away from them. So the government, by making the transfer and then sitting back and letting market forces do the rest, really did change the use of resources in our society. In economic parlance, this was an income or wealth effect, defined as the change in market supply or demand at a given price that occurs when people's income or wealth changes. The tougher question is whether we should consider this part of the allocative size of government.

The answer to this question depends on what we actually care about when we debate the proper size of government. Weighing against counting wealth effects is the consideration that surely the government would in a sense be bigger still if, in addition to giving me a transfer, it made me spend the money differently than I wanted to. While a wealth change is clearly a distributional effect, why should we count as a distinct allocative change the consequences of the ordinary functioning of consumer preferences? But on the other hand, perhaps in some cases we have reasons apart from straight consumer preference for caring about how money ends up being spent. Consider two examples. In the first, the government takes money from people who do not happen to like ice cream, and gives it to people who do. As a result, even though ice cream lovers are free to spend the transfers however they like, more ice cream ends up being sold, simply through the normal operations of our market economy. So the main point of interest about the government's interventions is simply the redistribution.

In the second example, tracking the actual operation of Social Security, the government takes money from young people and gives it to old people. This reduces national saving because older people, having less of an extended future to worry about, tend not to save as much of an extra dollar that comes their way. The well-founded (though not uncontroversial) view that Social Security has historically done exactly this is prominent in the debate concerning Social Security reform (Shaviro 2000, 86, 131–132). Logically, it is exactly parallel to the ice cream example, but there is a big difference. We may care more about national saving than about national ice cream consumption – perhaps due to a belief that saving has positive externalities, such as its effect on future generations. When it comes to ice cream, leaving aside the health effects of calories and cholesterol, there is really no reason for anyone but the consumer to care how much ice cream she consumes. Let her tastes determine the answer. But increased national saving, if it makes society more affluent, may benefit people other than the savers themselves.

Suppose someone therefore complains that the government, by creating a huge, unfunded Social Security system in 1935, reduced national saving to our detriment today. To say that this is not really part of the "size of government" because it merely reflected market forces at work given the underlying wealth transfer would seem strained at best, desperate at worst. The bottom line, unfortunately, can be no clearer than that, from an allocative standpoint, we care about the wealth effects of government action when we care about them, and don't care about them when we don't care about them.

What would an improved measure of the allocative size of government look like? For a very rough first cut that is limited to the fiscal system, one might take government spending as conventionally defined, but with two big changes. First, one would remove from it transfers, or programs that hand out either cash or benefits, such as food stamps, that are cashlike in the sense that the beneficiaries' spending patterns wouldn't change much if they were given cash instead. The ground for this change would be that these programs are mainly distributional. Second, one would add in some measure of the allocative effects of rules that are formally located in the tax system but that are mainly allocative, like the hypothetical WSTC. (These items may be called tax expenditures, a familiar if contested fiscal language category that I discuss in Chapter 8.)

Obviously, this is a crude oversimplification at best. In addition to ignoring the regulatory realm, it treats all fiscal rules as if they were solely allocative or solely distributional, based on an assumption about which type of effect seems primary, whereas in fact nearly all rules have both types of effects. Its great virtue is simply its vast improvement over treating all "spending" as allocatively the same, whether cash-equivalent or not.

Classifying fiscal rules as primarily allocative or not is a matter of judgment, line drawing, and degree. Medicare, for example, is probably a lot more cashlike than building bridges and tunnels, since seniors are highly inclined to spend available resources on health care. Nonetheless, it plainly has significant allocative effects, such as increasing the size of the health care sector. So "either/or" does not really work for Medicare. It must be included in any serious assessment of the government's distribution policy, but is also of great importance allocatively.

## The Distributional Size of Government

For distribution no less than allocation, there appears to be an accepted folk measure of the size of government. Here, rather than the amount of government spending, it involves the standard tax distribution tables that measure tax liability as a percentage of income for people at different income levels. The underlying assumption, one could reasonably surmise, is that a flat-rate tax would be non-redistributive, and that the government gets bigger as progressive redistribution, defined as imposing higher average tax rates on higher-income people, grows greater. I infer this assumption from the facts that libertarians and other conservatives often propose flat-rate taxes, and that much of the prominent literature in the field, going back at least to the renowned 1953 study by Walter Blum and Harry Kalven, *The Uneasy Case for Progressive Taxation,* treats progressive rate graduation as the departure from a neutral benchmark that needs to be explained. Both the use of tax tables and the flat-rate assumption need further consideration.

### Tax Rate Tables

In recent years, tax distribution tables have played a prominent role in debates concerning proposed tax changes. The Treasury Department and the Joint Committee on Taxation regularly issued such tables until recently, but private groups on the liberal side of the political spectrum, such as the Brookings Tax Policy Center and the Citizens for Tax Justice, have stepped into the void.

One reason for conservative hostility to these tables was that, since they estimated only the changes to a prevailing baseline, they seemed to imply that each new enactment should be progressive (Sullivan 2003, 1870). The high-income concentration of distributional benefit from the Bush Administration's tax changes, which the Administration was not eager to acknowledge, made this concern all the more pressing. But the basic complaint had some validity if we accept that the tables carried this implication. After all, even if you favor overall progressivity, it is absurd to think that each enactment must be progressive.

A second complaint about the distribution tables was that they inevitably contained a lot of guesswork, imprecision, and arbitrary assumptions (Graetz 1995; Furchtgott-Roth 1995). This complaint was indeed worth making, since it was true. For some reason, however, those making it drew the conclusion that the best should be the enemy of the good, and thus that the use of the tables should be abandoned because they are imperfect.

Despite these controversies about estimating tax changes and about particular official methodologies, taxes and tax rates are indeed what people generally look at to assess our distributional policy. The one important exception to this rule is a general recognition that transfers to the poor, such as through welfare and food stamps, are distributionally relevant as well. But such transfers are often disparaged as unworthy distributional policy because they are "spending" – notwithstanding that the people getting them generally pay lifetime net taxes on balance, and thus could in theory have ended up in exactly the same position through tax reductions that were resequenced across time.

A recent example of the contortions that can result from distinguishing between "transfers" and equivalent "tax reductions" came in the aftermath of the 2003 tax cuts. At the last minute in the enactment process, Republican leaders, seeking to meet official budget targets without sacrificing any of the tax breaks that they really cared about, eliminated a provision that would have made child tax credits refundable, and thus available to certain low-income working parents who did not owe federal income tax. As controversy swelled, House majority leader Tom DeLay professed himself entirely unmoved by complaints about the last-minute change, although he later permitted a bill restoring the credits to pass the House in a form that was carefully chosen to ensure that it would not actually be enacted. "There are a lot of things that are more important than that," DeLay said. "To me, it's a little difficult to give tax relief to people that don't pay income tax" (Firestone 2003, A-1).

Note the carefully chosen words here: "tax relief" and "income tax." DeLay had to use these words because the working parents who would have gotten the refundable credits were actually paying pay-roll taxes, which are treated as financing Social Security and part of Medicare. This was not the first time that Republican leaders had tried to keep payroll taxes out of the discussion of tax cutting. Counting both the worker and the employer shares of the Social Security payroll tax, it is imposed at a 12.4 percent rate on annual earnings up to about $90,000, and at zero above that. So it is not especially directed at key Republican constituencies.

The Republicans did, however, have a rationale for the view that the Social Security payroll tax is not really a tax. As Lawrence Lindsey, director of the National Economic Council for the first two years of the George W. Bush Administration, put it:

> The way Social Security is set up, is when I pay another dol-lar for Social Security tax, I buy an explicit, legislated amount of benefits. . . . I pay the money in, I get the money out, and that's all there is to it. Now, as a first pass, therefore, it wouldn't make sense to me to call the OASDI contribution a tax, even though we all do. . . . I can't see a logical reason why we should include the Social Security OASDI portion of that, in its entirety, as a tax. I think we should write our [distribution] tables without it there. It is purely a private good. (quoted in Noah 2002)

It is hard to decide which is more absurd: this line of argument or the standard Democratic response rejecting it. The arguments on both sides are fatally compromised by arbitrary line drawing and game playing that reflect a basic limitation of the "taxes versus spending" paradigm.

Let's start with the Republican view that Social Security payroll taxes are not really taxes because you get the money back. This necessarily implies that Social Security spending isn't really spending, but the refund of a deposit. This, of course, is not a conclusion that conservatives frequently draw.

A problem with the Lindsey view is that, within Social Security, taxes do not actually equal benefits. Social Security has historically been an engine for massive wealth redistribution, mainly from younger to older generations. Given the magnitude of these transfers, treating the welfare system as a relevant source of nontax distribution policy but leaving lifetime Social Security transfers out of the calculus is a bit like boldly scaling molehills while ignoring mountains.

What is the Democratic response, however? It is not that the taxes and the benefits both matter. That response would hardly do when many Democrats are eager to treat Social Security and Medicare benefits as politically sacrosanct, and indeed as worth expanding at every opportunity even if wealthy current seniors benefit at the expense of poorer current and future workers. So the usual Democratic response is that the payroll taxes are indeed taxes, and should be on the table when tax cutting brings distributional policy to the fore, but that the benefits can be completely excluded from the calculus.

Let's return our gaze to the Social Security portion of the payroll tax. Considered in isolation, it is indeed wildly regressive, what with its 12.4 percent rate on annual earnings up to about $90,000. But is it wholly irrelevant, as Democrats sometimes appear to assume, that, for the members of a given age cohort, the combined effect of the taxes and the benefits is modestly progressive on a lifetime basis?

For that matter, is it really the mismatch between officially designated Social Security taxes and benefits that makes the Lindsey view so unsatisfying? Suppose Congress passed a law requiring Social Security taxes to equal benefits, but without actually changing distribution overall. This could involve imposing Social Security benefit cuts that were offset, dollar for dollar, by income tax cuts on the very same people. So Social Security would now be actuarially fair, but not a single dollar would actually change hands relative to the prior state of affairs. The broader point is that it is silly to overfocus on the distributional effects merely of some officially designated subset of cash flows involving the government. We should be interested in the overall picture. Thus, Social Security taxes and benefits ought *both* to be on the table whenever we evaluate the government's distributional policy, but not *just* those taxes and benefits. Everything the government does is relevant, everything we can measure should be included, and even things we cannot measure should be kept in mind.

There actually is a tool available for purposes of broader measurement of the government's distributional policy through the fiscal system. While called "generational accounting," because its most prominent uses have involved measuring intergenerational transfers, it is not limited to this use. The basic idea is to measure lifetime net taxes and lifetime net tax rates for the average member of a given group. Lifetime net taxes equal taxes paid minus transfers received, computed in present value terms from birth. Dividing this net amount by one's lifetime income, likewise computed in present value terms from birth, provides a measure of one's lifetime net tax rate. Thus, suppose that on average the members of a given group paid lifetime gross taxes of $3.5 million, received lifetime transfers of $1 million, and had lifetime income of $10 million. The average lifetime net tax payment for members of the cohort would be $2.5 million (the taxes paid minus the transfers received), and the lifetime net tax rate would be 25 percent.

Needless to say, generational accounting does not include everything that we should consider relevant. As an example of its incompleteness, benefits from government outlays other than transfers generally are ignored, as are burdens from government regulation, the military draft of the 1940s through the 1960s, and so forth. In principle, any such items could be incorporated if economists could figure out a plausible way of doing so. In addition, generational accounting unavoidably relies on speculative long-term economic and policy assumptions and projections. Still, its basic underlying structure offers the best currently available way of getting a handle on the government's overall distributional policy through the fiscal system. And because generational accounting treats taxes and transfers symmetrically, it is immune to the framing and labeling games that usually dominate policy debate. For example, if my taxes net of my transfers go up by $50,000, it makes no difference for purposes of the measure whether the change is styled a tax increase or a benefit cut.

Accordingly, insofar as we are using tax rates to offer a gauge (however flawed and incomplete) of the government's distributional policy, the figures of greatest interest are lifetime net tax rates or lifetime net taxes paid. These measures at least offer a whole-life perspective and allow the netting of transfers against gross taxes paid.

## Flat-Rate Assumption

It may seem natural to assume that a non-redistributive fiscal system would have a flat lifetime net tax rate, whereby everyone paid the government the same percentage of lifetime income (or whatever was being used as the metric). In fact, there is no reason why this has to be so, and indeed it surely is not generally so. Keep in mind that the big reason nearly everyone is shown as paying lifetime net taxes is that we cannot measure the value of in-kind benefits from public goods such as national defense spending. The tax rates that are being compared therefore depend on a missing term in the equation, that is, the value of those benefits.

How should we think that benefits from government outlays generally relate to income? This depends on the program. Social Security and Medicare benefits, which are included in generational accounting computations of lifetime net tax rates, generally increase with income because more affluent people tend to live longer and to get more intensive medical treatment (Shaviro 2004, 34–36). Public support for education has mixed effects, because higher-income people are less likely to attend public elementary or secondary schools, but get greater subsidies when they go to college (Steuerle 2003, 1187). For the benefits of military and police protection, relative benefit is highly debatable. Might we think of it as proportionate to the income or wealth that is being protected? Or is it uniform because everyone's life has the same worth? Might the protection be more valuable to low-income people, if they would have a harder time procuring it for themselves? These questions lack clear answers.

Still, suppose we observe two groups, one of which pays significantly higher lifetime net taxes, both absolutely and as a percentage of lifetime income, than the other. If we have no reason to think that the difference in net taxes is being systematically offset by differences in in-kind benefits, it is plausible to infer that redistribution is afoot, going from the high-tax to the low-tax individuals.

## Summing Up the Allocative and Distributional Aspects of the Size of Government

We now have a very rough basis for evaluating how a given set of fiscal policy changes would affect the size of government. Allocatively, the question is whether the changes increase or reduce the government's impact on the economy. Non-cash-equivalent outlays and allocatively targeted tax rules are important inputs in evaluating this. Distributionally, the question is whether the changes increase or reduce wealth transfers through government policy, which can be roughly gauged by differences in lifetime net taxes or tax rates if we have no reason to think that any such differences are being offset on the benefit side.

## Transition Problems in Making the Government Smaller

One more step remains before we turn to a concrete illustration of how tax cuts plus spending cuts can increase the size of government. While it relates most closely to Social Security and Medicare, we can illustrate it initially using nothing more than debt financing. Suppose that Jill and Bill live in a two-person, two-period society. In Period 1, the government spends ten dollars supplying a public good that benefits Jill and Bill equally. It finances the expenditure by borrowing the entire ten dollars from Jill at the market interest rate of 10 percent per period. In Period 2, when the government owes Jill eleven dollars (and does not supply any further public goods), it must choose between (a) levying a uniform head tax of $5.50 in order to raise the money it owes her, and (b) reneging on the debt.

Suppose first that the government reneges. Using formal, conventional definitions of taxes and spending, this means that it will have levied taxes of zero in both periods while spending ten dollars in Period 1 and zero in Period 2. By contrast, if it levies the head tax, Period 2 taxes rise from zero to eleven dollars and Period 2 spending rises from zero to one dollar. (Payments of interest on government bonds, but not repayments of bond principal, are treated as spending when computing official budgetary measures such as the deficit.) So reneging appears, from the standpoint of spending illusion, to lead to smaller government. In fact, however, it would mean that the government over the two periods engaged in substantial redistribution from Jill to Bill, rather than zero redistribution, while supplying the same public goods.

Many people who favor small government might not like the decision to renege in Period 2, because they would recognize that it involved the expropriation of a contract right, and thus a government taking that was equivalent to taxation. However, the conclusion that Period 2 reneging would make the government bigger, rather than smaller, did not rely upon the fact that Jill may have been told in Period 1 that she had a contract right to repayment. Suppose that the government had simply levied a ten-dollar tax on Jill in Period 1. Then, in Period 2, suppose it had to choose between (a) doing nothing and (b) levying a tax of $5.50 on both Bill and Jill and handing the eleven dollars to Jill. The allocative and distributional consequences of (b) would generally be the same as those of honoring the bond in my example. Thus, despite the absence of a Period 1 promise to Jill to even out the distribution in Period 2, option (b) would continue to imply a smaller government overall. From the standpoint of nominal cash flows, however, option (b) would look like it involved even bigger government than did my earlier example. It would cause Period 2 taxes and spending to be eleven dollars each.

The key to this example is that the Period 2 decision comes in midstream. It is easy to accept that government would have been smaller if taxes and spending had been zero in both periods. Once the government has sprung into action, however, an immediate shutdown – or even one constrained by honoring express contractual commitments already in place – does not necessarily lead to a smaller government. It may instead lead to increased wealth redistribution over time if the alternative in Period 2 would have been to even things out on an all-periods basis.

## The Recent Tax Cuts and the Size of Government

Adopting a substantive, rather than formalistic, view of the size of government can have startling effects on how one thinks about given policies. Perhaps the most striking recent illustration concerns the huge tax cuts enacted during President Bush's first term. Despite the proponents' goal of "starving the beast," the tax cuts may actually end up increasing, rather than reducing, the size of government.

An initial problem in evaluating this question is that the tax cuts were only part of the relevant story. Over the long run, under the no-free-lunch principle, the present value of government inflows and outlays must be equal. Only resources on hand can be spent, and everything must ultimately be paid for (even if through default, which effectively taxes the bondholder). Accordingly, reducing cash inflows through tax cuts implies compensating changes, in the form of reduced outlays and/or offsetting future tax increases. What ought to be evaluated, then, is the full package, not just the tax cuts standing alone. But the rest of the package has not yet been specified.

While the details of future offsetting changes are impossible to predict, some general points are already clear. The U.S. government faces a long-term fiscal gap, defined as "current federal debt held by the public plus the present value of all projected federal non-interest spending, minus all projected federal receipts." This measure indicates "the amount in today's dollars by which fiscal policy must be changed in order to be sustainable: A sustainable fiscal policy requires [the fiscal gap] to be zero" (Gokhale and Smetters 2005, 2), under the no-free-lunch principle.

One recent estimate (Gokhale and Smetters 2005) places the fiscal gap, as of 2006, at $68.6 trillion. Another (Auerbach, Gale, and Orszag 2004, 1051) places it at $85.5 trillion, with the greater size largely reflecting rejection of budgetary tricks such as purporting to "sunset" tax cuts and ignoring the probable need to curtail the fast-growing alternative minimum tax. Different though these two estimates are, their implications are quite similar. It is difficult for anyone to grasp the difference between such huge numbers anyway. Both estimates agree that at least $50 trillion of the fiscal gap is attributable to Medicare, and about $10 trillion to Social Security.

The fiscal gap as a whole illustrates a counterfactual: what would happen if current policy were continued indefinitely? Since this is impossible under the no-free-lunch principle, the implication is that actual future policy will not match currently announced future policy. At some point, cash inflows to the government will have to increase, and/or outlays will have to decline. Moreover, to the extent that outlays decline, "discretionary" domestic spending, such as that on schools, bridges, and national defense, is too small a component to bear the major brunt. Social Security and Medicare cuts will almost certainly have to do most of the heavy lifting on the spending side, given the size of these two programs' fiscal gaps.[2]

Accordingly, to specify the full package of changes that would be needed to gauge the size-of-government effects of the recent tax cuts, two main possibilities merit attention. The first is that they are offset by future tax increases. The second is that they are offset by future Social Security and Medicare cuts. Each of these two packages can then be evaluated for its size-of-government effects, keeping in mind that we are likely to get some of each, along with (lesser) discretionary spending cuts.

## Offsetting Future Tax Increases and the Size of Government

The enactment of substantial future tax increases should not be pooh-poohed on the ground that the current political environment is so anti-tax. Things may look very different once the payment of current Social Security and Medicare benefits is visibly at risk. I have suggested elsewhere that, within the next fifteen years, the enactment of a consumption-style value-added tax (VAT) on top of the existing income tax, and the use of inflation as a deliberate policy tool for partly reneging on current obligations, are strong possibilities (Shaviro 2004, 148). This, of course, is just speculation, and we do not really know what the tax increases will be. Two points about them are clear, however. First, since they will not take effect until the future, they will result in the application of higher tax rates to future than to current economic activity. Second, by applying mainly to younger or future taxpayers by today's perspective, they will result in the application of generally higher lifetime net taxes and tax rates to younger than to older generations. The former of these two points matters allocatively, while the latter matters distributionally.

For two reasons, the application of higher tax rates to future than to current activity is likely to increase economic distortion. First, the application of higher tax rates to future than to current activity may induce taxpayers to shift taxable transactions from high-tax to low-tax years, especially as the transition nears and begins to take a more definite and predictable form. Second, even where economic activity cannot shift between years, the application of higher rates to some years and lower rates to others tends to increase total distortion relative to having smooth rates across time. It is a public economics truism that the waste resulting from a tax generally rises much faster than the rate. Thus, "[d]oubling a tax quadruples its [distortionary effect], other things being the same" (Rosen 1999, 294). This suggests that overall waste will be greater if the rates are high in some years and low in others than if they were held constant at the intermediate rate required for long-term revenue equivalence. That is, even without timing shifts, the reduction in waste in low-rate years is more than offset by the increase in high-rate years.

Accordingly, to the extent that the recent tax cuts are offset by future tax increases, the sum total is likely to increase the size of government allocatively. Only if the newly enacted taxes were a great deal less distortionary than those they replaced would this conclusion be likely to change. Distributionally, however, it seems even clearer that the package of current tax cuts plus future tax increases makes the government larger. Indeed, the distributional impact is really the big enchilada – persisting, as we will see next, in the scenario where Social Security and Medicare benefits are cut.

In this regard, it is instructive to consider evidence from generational accounting (GA). GA computations are made under the assumption that current policy will continue indefinitely. Since the fiscal gap is unsustainable, however, its elimination must be reflected somewhere in the accounts to avoid violating the no-free-lunch principle. The usual convention, further discussed in Chapter 5, is to assume that the net tax increases (i.e., higher taxes or lower transfers) needed to eliminate the fiscal gap will be borne entirely by future generations. This is concededly unrealistic, but is meant to provide "an informative counterfactual, not a likely policy scenario" (Kotlikoff 2001, 22), keeping in mind that delay in addressing the fiscal gap does indeed leave it to be met by future generations.

The most recent GA forecasts, pre-dating the policy changes of the George W. Bush Administration, showed lifetime net tax rates of 17.68 percent for the youngest members of current generations, and 35.81 percent for future generations (Kotlikoff 2001, Table 1). Leaving the entire fiscal gap to be borne by future generations, therefore, would cause them to pay more than twice the lifetime net tax rate of current generations. Lifetime net taxes paid would presumably be even more uneven, since lifetime income is expected to continue rising. This pattern strongly implies sizeable transfers from future to current generations. The rate imbalance is the product of our having run Social Security and Medicare on an unfunded basis, with early generations getting free benefits. This does not appear to be a case where the younger people who pay higher lifetime taxes will be compensated by getting greater in-kind benefits from government spending.

The subsequent tax cuts (and Medicare benefit expansion) have greatly exacerbated the redistribution from future to current generations. By lowering current generations' already-low lifetime net tax rates, in exchange for raising such rates for future generations, the package of tax cuts now in exchange for tax increases later unmistakably increases intergenerational wealth redistribution. This effect is so significant that the package has in all likelihood made the government larger in distributional terms, even if the tax cuts reduce redistribution from the rich to the poor.

## Future Social Security and Medicare Cuts and the Size of Government

The conclusion just reached may seem a bit too easy. It should be no surprise if cutting taxes now in exchange for raising them in the future fails to make the government smaller. And surely this is not the scenario that supporters of the tax cuts envision. They are hoping, rather, to "starve the beast" on the expenditure side. Cutting Social Security and Medicare benefits is no easy matter, however – a key reason why "starve the beast" advocates have been reluctant to advocate it directly. Still, these advocates are probably right that entitlements will not be exempted in the future reckoning. Thus, to make the story complete, we should consider the scenario where the tax cuts serve to increase future Social Security and Medicare cuts.

This does surprisingly little to change the conclusion regarding the size of government. This is best shown by analyzing the package's effects in three stages: distributional effects for both programs, allocative effects for the Social Security piece, and allocative effects for the Medicare piece.

### Distributional Effects of Current Tax Cuts plus Future Social Security and Medicare Cuts

Distributionally, substituting future Social Security and Medicare cuts for future tax increases does not change the basic picture. Today's elderly are still benefiting at the expense of younger generations, with the consequence that lifetime net tax rates are being lowered where they were already low, and raised where they were already high. Today's workers, by getting their benefits cut after they have paid decades worth of payroll taxes, simply learn the hard way that Lawrence Lindsey was wrong in arguing that these taxes were not really taxes.

A decision to cut Social Security and Medicare rather than raising taxes might also make the burden sharing less progressive within a given age group. However, this depends on exactly how benefits are cut, and on how, in the alternative scenario, taxes would have been increased. Means testing for Social Security and Medicare, so that affluent seniors get less or pay more, might actually be more progressive than raising flat-rate payroll taxes that apply to even the poorest workers.

## Allocative Effects of Current Tax Cuts plus Future Social Security Cuts

Under the influence of spending illusion, cutting Social Security benefits may seem like a dagger in the throat of "big government." After all, the program currently "spends" close to $500 billion per year, an amount that is expected to grow much faster than the economy as baby boomers retire and life expectancies keep increasing. But things are not quite as they seem, or at least as they seem under the view that all "spending" is the same, be it on cash grants or on highways.

The main allocative complaint about Social Security is that it has reduced national saving through the income effects of its enormous transfers to seniors in older generations.[3] But cutting taxes today, in exchange for cutting Social Security benefits in the future, only makes this problem worse. It gives current taxpayers more money to spend on current consumption, thus magnifying the effect that Social Security has had on national saving to date.

## Allocative Effects of Tax Cuts plus Future Medicare Cuts

When we consider cutting taxes today in exchange for cutting Medicare benefits in the future, at last we find ourselves in arguably smaller-government territory. Medicare has allocative effects that Social Security lacks, because its benefits are in-kind, taking the form of health care services rather than free cash. Yet even this effect can be overstated. Empirical research suggests that health care is an area where consumers' price sensitivity, while not nil, is relatively low. Thus, even if offered as free cash, a significant proportion of the outlays that the government makes through Medicare would likely have been spent on health care anyway.

Even for Medicare, therefore, it is not entirely clear that a package of current tax cuts plus future benefit cuts would make the government smaller on balance. The bottom line would depend on how we compared the reduction in the government's allocative effects to the increase in its redistributive effects. However, when you consider that tax increases and Social Security cuts are likely to be enacted as well, and that these more clearly increase the size of government, the case becomes quite powerful that the recent tax cuts, over time, will make the government larger on balance. The overall package is one of much greater redistribution to older generations, accompanied by only a possibility of reduced net allocative effects.

## Are We Just at an Intermediate Stage?

One common response to the suggestion that recent tax cutting may end up increasing the size of government involves the transition issue, but with a longer time frame than I gave it in the two-period discussion of Jill and Bill. So what, this argument goes, if tax cuts increase the already huge transfers from future generations to current seniors? Once we reach a new steady state, the government will prospectively be smaller because it will no longer be able to afford big programs such as current Social Security and Medicare.

If this scenario of transition to a stable new small-government steady state were credible, this trade-off would indeed be present. The government would be transferring more wealth today, but in the future steady state it might indeed be doing less. So the question would be what time frame you cared about.

Unfortunately, this scenario is speculative at best. I call it the "*mañana* scenario," as in: "We don't dare to rein in entitlements today, and indeed we are expanding them. But fear not, we will do it all *mañana*." Or it might be called the "comes the revolution scenario," as in: "Comes the revolution, we will be able to do all of the tough things that we are too scared to try today."

The question, obviously, is what revolution? And what *mañana*? Why would the politics of the future be so different from politics today? Have "starve-the-beasters" really thought about the political scenarios that the threat of an impending credit collapse by the U.S. government, which seems to be what they are counting on, would actually involve?

It plainly is true that a large fiscal gap creates pressure not to increase outlays, and indeed to reduce them. But again, this is not necessarily the same thing as reducing the size of government. The effect at any time may be to increase generational redistribution, as the elderly in each period play hot potato with younger voters, who generally are less politically well organized, and keep pushing fiscal burdens forward. A scenario of continuously increasing lifetime net tax rates would be far indeed from the small-government, limited-redistribution Valhalla.

Moreover, the revenue pressure on the government may be so great – especially with seniors clamoring against benefit cuts – that it simply cannot be met through the sorts of straightforward, visible, widely distributed net tax increases that are generally most efficient and even-handed. For example, the use of inflation to ease the fiscal crunch may become tempting. Stealth tax increases and ostensibly one-time takings from various groups may also become the order of the day.

Likewise, the use of regulatory mandates will become ever more tempting as a substitute for the government spending that would have been financed (in many cases, more equitably and efficiently) by broad-based taxes. The fiscal-restraint era of the late 1980s through the 1990s provided ample advance warning of this probable future trend. One example was the 1993 Clinton health care plan, which would have relied on employer mandates to provide much of the financing off-budget. As it happened, this effort failed, in part because small business owners were politically well positioned to resist the mandates. But other major new mandates of the era, such as the Americans with Disabilities Act, showed how much could be done this way. A fiscal gap loads the dice in favor of using mandates even when they impose more targeted burdens, are more intrusive, and are less efficient than outlays that are financed through general revenues.

Finally, the sheer uncertainty that results from having a huge fiscal gap with no resolution in sight makes the government in a sense more intrusive. By cutting taxes and increasing spending, Congress has pointed a loaded gun at its own head (or rather, at the heads of future Congresses), but we simply do not know when and how the gun will go off. Thus, anyone engaged in long-term planning, such as for retirement, must deal with considerable uncertainty about future government policy. For example, should you save more for your retirement because you simply cannot count on any specific component of the existing Social Security and Medicare commitments? Or should you instead save less because a big part of narrowing the fiscal gap will probably be to squeeze the people who had enough foresight to plan properly?

Having a huge fiscal gap is also a surefire political formula for making the competing interest groups in Washington continually invest in seeking to influence future government policy. Nothing is really safe, and no government commitment can be taken for granted for more than a few years. With even Social Security and Medicare likely to be on the chopping block, none of the players can afford to rely on political inertia to protect what they now have. This is an enviable setting for fund raising by politicians, but less enviable for those whom Congress tells that they must "pay to play."

Merely having a huge fiscal gap is evidently not enough for Congress, however. In both 2001 and 2003, Congress went out of its way to make the fiscal system even less stable, and unstable sooner, than if it merely had been larding an already immense fiscal gap. The mechanism of choice was to provide that the entire 2001 act, and many of the provisions in the 2003 act, would expire (barring further legislation) within periods ranging from two to nine years.

The main reason for these "sunsets" – which proponents of the two acts insisted would not be permitted to take effect – was to lower the official ten-year estimates of the acts' revenue cost by more than 50 percent (Gale and Orszag 2003, 1553), while also avoiding the procedural need to get sixty Senate votes in support of the measures. Congress was playing a cynical game of "bait and switch." First, it would enact a tax cut with a sunset, estimated (by reason of the sunset) to cost only, say, $350 billion over ten years. Next, when proponents moved to eliminate the sunset, as they had promised in advance to do, they could accuse any critics of the new proposals of trying to "raise taxes." In short, the baseline would be deceptively shifted without an honest accounting at any time.

Deceptive bookkeeping and gaming of the budgetary rules was only part of the sunsets' effect, however. A further effect, unacknowledged but not necessarily unforeseen, was to guarantee that Congress would have to keep on considering major tax legislation again and again for the foreseeable future. For example, would interested parties with billions of dollars at stake really do nothing as the scheduled estate tax repeal in 2011 grew nearer? Indeed, wouldn't lobbying over further extensions of the expiring tax cuts be expected to commence immediately? Congress could hardly have done more to ensure that the resources devoted to trying to influence its ongoing decisions would be as large as possible for years to come.

Finally, consider the message that current policy is sending to future politicians and voters. Present generations are transferring wealth to themselves from future generations, ostensibly so that those in the future will be unable to engage in wealth transfer. The audacity of this puts to shame Saint Augustine's famed wish when he was young that he would stop sinning, only not just yet.

## Summary

Relying on nominal tax and spending levels to discern the size of government can lead to fundamental errors, among liberals and conservatives alike, in evaluating important policy choices, such as whether to cut taxes in the face of a huge fiscal gap. There simply is no substitute for trying to grasp the underlying fundamentals, which for fiscal rules typically involve allocation and distribution.

The flaws in our fiscal language would be bad enough if they simply caused people to head the wrong way, given their underlying policy views, like a disoriented player of Pin the Tail on the Donkey. It gets worse, however, when we turn to the other big issue in the tax and spending debate: the overall relationship between inflows and outlays, commonly misconceptualized in terms of the federal budget deficit. Here the danger is not just ideological disorientation, but the infliction of serious harm on the U.S. economy that could last for decades. I therefore turn next to the fiscal language issues raised by the practice of measuring budget deficits.

# 3

# Fun and Games with Budget Deficits

*Child: We're going to be late!*
**Navy SEAL played by Vin Diesel:** *Not on my watch.*
— From *The Pacifier* (2005 movie and trailer)

*"The question is," said Alice, "whether you can make words mean so many different things." "The question is," said Humpty Dumpty, "which is to be master — that's all."*
— Lewis Carroll, *Through the Looking Glass*

"Deficits don't matter," Vice President Cheney once remarked (Suskind 2004, 291). They are a "threat," warned Alan Greenspan. In stating these very different views, one thing the two men probably had in common was confidence that the term "deficit" offers a meaningful measure of something.

Just what the deficit measures, and how well, is considerably less clear. As we will see more fully in Part Two of this book, the deficit is thought relevant to a number of different concerns, ranging from generational equity to easing recessions to the danger of default. As a multipurpose tool, however, it should immediately be suspect. At least a Swiss Army knife has separate attachments for each of its separate functions. The deficit, by contrast, apparently is meant to serve all of its multiple purposes at once.

To measure the deficit in its simplest form, you compare the government's cash inflows to its cash outlays for the year, disregarding any cash flows that are classified as involving debt principal. An excess of outlays is a deficit, while an excess of inflows is a budget surplus. Debt principal has to be disregarded, since otherwise the deficit or surplus would always (tautologically) be zero.[1]

Sometimes, the lack of deliberate fine-tuning to suit a measure to a given purpose is no big deal. The temperature in a weather forecast, for example, may help us decide how to dress – although possibly the temperature-humidity index in summer or the wind chill in winter, invented to address how weather conditions feel, would be better still. But at least the temperature is not a measure of something arbitrary. Temperature is a meaningful physical attribute of the energy level of matter, and only the units we express it in (such as Fahrenheit or Celsius degrees) are arbitrary, as opposed to the phenomenon itself.

The deficit, by contrast, is an arbitrary measure in two main respects. The first is its bright-line distinction between debt principal and other cash flows. The second is its use of an annual measurement period.

These arbitrary aspects of measurement immediately prompt suspicion that the deficit will not work well as a measure of anything real and substantial. They also prompt suspicion, which on fuller examination proves dismayingly well founded, that self-interested politicians will find ways to manipulate it to death.

Someone once defined the job of a tax planner as finding pinpricks in the law and driving trucks through them. Enron's accountants seem to have approached financial reporting rules in a similar spirit. But tax planners and accountants are pikers compared to government officials who are in a position to play deficit games, if only because the officials don't have to worry about being sent to jail.

## Distinction between Debt Principal and Other Cash Flows

My calling this distinction "arbitrary" may at first seem questionable. After all, everyone knows the difference between buying a government bond and paying a tax. Buying a bond is voluntary, and implies that you reasonably expect to benefit from the purchase. By contrast, paying a tax is involuntary, and presumably makes you worse off, since your share of the extra government benefits it may finance is trivial in a mass society.

What is arbitrary, however, is not the treatment of government bonds as such, but the bright-line distinction between them and everything else. Bonds present only one of many instances in which cash flows go in to the government in one year and back out in other years, and in which focusing only on the current-year cash flow would therefore be misleading. The integrated, multiyear approach that underlies the exclusion of bond principal from the deficit measure makes a lot of sense, but it is not logically restricted to bonds, or applied on a bright-line, either-or basis.

Consider Social Security again, and the Lawrence Lindsey argument (discussed in Chapter 2) that the payroll tax is not really a tax because you get your money back. But suppose we remember, as Lindsey conveniently forgets, that people's Social Security taxes typically do not have the same value as their benefits, giving them an overall gain or loss. Suppose a given individual figures to get benefits that have two-thirds of the value of her Social Security taxes. Ignoring this offset would overlook the fact that, as for two-thirds of her taxes plus all of her benefits, the cash flows really were like those on a bond. Thus, her participation is arithmetically equivalent to buying a bond plus paying taxes equal to just one-third of her observed Social Security taxes. Reporting the cash flows this way, however, would change the budget deficit for each affected year, by requiring that we disregard all cash flows that were classified as bond principal (Kotklkoff 1992).

Why isn't this treatment just as good as the existing convention whereby Social Security taxes and benefits are fully included? Now, it is true that Social Security taxes are paid involuntarily, unlike the purchase of a bond. However, many people would be willing to pay the amount of their Social Security taxes in exchange for actuarially fair benefits. And it is true that benefit payments are not guaranteed. Yet clearly there is a strong sense of political commitment in the United States to paying the benefits as promised. Moreover, from an economic perspective, expected but uncertain future payments should merely be discounted, not treated as worth zero today.

## Use of a One-Year Period

The second arbitrary element in the deficit computation is its use, purely for accounting convenience, of an annual measurement period. We all know that there is next to no economic difference between a payment on December 31 and one that is made the next day, on January 1. For current-year deficit purposes, however, the former is completely included, while the latter is completely excluded. This has frequently inspired "smoke and mirrors" game playing, on both the federal and state levels, such as postponing payments from the end of one year to the start of the next to facilitate meeting official deficit targets.

Time itself does matter, of course. For example, at a 5 percent discount rate, a dollar in a year is worth only about ninety-five cents today. This does not, however, support in effect infinitely discounting cash flows that occur on January 1 of the next year or thereafter.

The arbitrariness of this boundary presents a disconcerting problem for advocates of *any* measurement period short of an infinite horizon. Even if one has good reasons for favoring, on balance, the use of a finite term (whether one or five or ten years, as with typical deficit computations, or even seventy-five years, as in long-term Social Security forecasts), one is doing something at the outer boundary that seems anomalous: shifting suddenly at the end of the period from discounting at some reasonable interest rate, or perhaps not discounting at all,[2] to the equivalent of infinite discounting.

## Significance in Practice of the Problems with the Deficit Measure

To show how the deficit measure's defects can distort actual policy choices, a few illustrations may be in order. As it happens, all of them rely on the use of a too-short time period. Up to now, there has been less inclination in Washington to play deliberate games with the use of debt versus nondebt labels. Indeed, the most recent gambit went in the opposite direction by exaggerating the *similarity* between debt and nondebt commitments. In 2005, proponents of President Bush's private accounts plan for Social Security argued that decades of massively increased public debt issuance to fund the accounts was not a problem because it was merely converting implicit debt (via the promise of future benefits) into explicit debt. This claim might have been reasonable if not for the fact that the conversion seemed likely to make renunciation of the heretofore merely implicit debt considerably more difficult, thus raising the true present value of the government's future obligations.

Examples of how budgetary measurement can go awry when the time horizon is truncated include the following:

## "Sold My Desk!"

The late economist Robert Eisner (1986, 34) once told the story of his father, a lawyer during the Great Depression, who supposedly came home one day and exclaimed mock-excitedly to his wife: "Had a good day in the office. Sold my desk!" The point, of course, was that it wasn't really a good day, because while the father had brought home some cash, he no longer had a valuable asset.

Congress is more than willing to "sell the desk" when this improves the short-term optics of its budgetary policy. A recent example was the Boeing leasing brouhaha of late 2003. Rather than sell an asset, what the Pentagon did here was opt not to buy one, choosing instead to lease Air Force refueling tankers from the Boeing Corporation, even though under the terms of the deal this would increase the long-term budgetary cost. The great advantage of the lease structure was that it permitted official military appropriations to include only the annual lease payments as they became due, rather than the entire purchase price all at once (Jehl 2003).[3]

## Revenge of the Bad Hairpiece

In 1981, to encourage retirement saving, Congress created the individual retirement account (IRA) rules. Under these rules, one could contribute money up to a specified dollar amount to a special tax-free savings account. One's contribution would be deducted from taxable income, and the income earned through the account would not be taxed as long as the money stayed there. Only when one withdrew money from the account would it be taxed. Thus, suppose that you contributed $2,000 in 1982, earned $3,000 of interest in the account, and withdrew the full $5,000 when you retired in 1998. You would have a $2,000 deduction in 1982, $5,000 of taxable income in 1998, and nothing in between.

One political problem caused by IRAs was that their short-term effect on the deficit looked worse than the actual long-term fiscal impact that they had on the government. In particular, the transaction just described would cause the deficit to rise in 1982 by the taxes forgone on the $2,000, even though the revenue was not being permanently lost. The government would get a kind of refund in 1998 when this deduction was effectively reversed by including the full $5,000 (principal as well as interest) in the taxpayer's income. Nothing in the 1982 deficit measure, however, distinguished this case from one where a current tax reduction had permanent effects.

Not to worry, however; bright minds on Capital Hill soon figured out a solution. An economic principle known as the Cary Brown theorem shows that another method of benefiting saving is economically equivalent under specified circumstances (such as constant tax rates across time) to the "deferral" method of traditional IRAs. This alternative method involves yield exemption, instead of deferral. In other words, you do not get a deduction when you put $2,000 into your special savings account, but you also are not taxed on any of the money (principal or interest) that you later withdraw.

While the two types of IRAs are economically similar, there is a major difference in how they affect short-term cash flows and therefore deficit computations. Had Congress enacted exemption-method rather than traditional IRAs back in 1981, it would thereby have avoided increasing the deficit in 1982 in the hypothetical transaction. Only in 1998, when nothing instead of $5,000 was included, would the measurement difference be reversed and the deficit look worse. Congress generally cares a lot more, however, about deficits next year, when it is still in office, than about those occurring much further down the road. (Presumably, the reason for nonetheless using the traditional IRA was that investors and voters were short-sighted or cash-constrained, or else did not trust Congress's pledge to exempt the income in the future.)

By the mid-1990s, it had become clear that both types of IRAs had their political charms. So Congress in 1997 added an exemption-style IRA, dubbed the "Roth IRA" as a monument to the then-chair (by virtue of seniority) of the Senate Finance Committee, a previously back-seat legislator known mainly for his atrocious hairpiece and suspected of being barely (if at all) able to spell "IRA."

The Roth IRA was created at a time when the short-term budget picture seemed relatively favorable. While there was some accompanying game playing, such as encouraging taxpayers to shift to Roth IRAs so that the short-term picture would look better still, a part of the motivation was simply to create a brand new tax benefit that could be named after a congressional leader. Expanding existing benefits is not as much fun for Congress as creating new ones. But once the Roth IRA was there, its potential use as a way of creating tax cuts without increasing short-term budget deficits became clear to Washington's keener political minds. Thus, the Bush Administration, in its 2005 budget, proposed not only expanding Roth IRAs, but inducing taxpayers to shift funds from traditional to Roth IRAs. A commentator noted that the "bait-and-switch nature of the proposal would shift substantial amounts of revenue from future decades into the next five years, allowing the proposal to raise revenue in the five-year budget window that the House now uses, but deferring the much greater and increasing deficits onto the next generation" (Shafroth 2003, 799).

## "Hey, Big Spender"

One ground for relying on the deficit, even accepting that the years outside the budget window do matter, might be that it offers a representative slice of the long-term picture. When we consider the uncertainty of any long-term projections, it may seem quite sensible to restrict our gaze to the short-term picture, which we know best, and treat it as a proxy for the rest. This claim of representativeness is being made implicitly when people argue, for example, that our economy can afford budget deficits at current levels. And if the current-year deficit offers too small a sample, then five- or ten-year deficit projections can be relied on instead.

One problem with relying on representativeness is that we may actually know how things are changing. Thus, the trend of increasing life expectancies, which affects Social Security and Medicare outlays, is expected to continue. But worse still, from the standpoint of representativeness, is that politicians can deliberately exploit a finite budget window in order to distort the picture it gives us.

A good example came in 2003, when the Bush Administration, eager to forestall possible Democratic attacks in the next year's presidential campaign, decided to push hard for a Medicare prescription drug benefit. The effort succeeded, though only by the slimmest of margins in the House, where conservative Republicans, concerned about the new benefit's scope and cost, were ready to join Democratic foes of the measure. A key consideration among the conservatives who grudgingly agreed to go along was that the bill had an estimated ten-year cost of "only" $400 billion.

It later turned out that the Bush Administration had withheld from Congress the news that its updated estimates placed the ten-year cost at $550 billion. But even that number was unrepresentative, given how the benefit had been structured to keep costs outside the ten-year budget window. In particular, it was given a start date of 2006. This ensured that the ten-year estimate used during the enactment process would include only seven years of actual operations, and that the ten-year estimate, once operations started, would be far higher even without any surprises.

The Medicare trustees subsequently projected the infinite horizon cost of the benefit at $18.2 trillion. Quibble as one may about the radical uncertainty of any infinite-horizon estimate, at least it cannot be manipulated like a shorter-term budget window through the use of timing games, and thus potentially conveys more honest and balanced information.

## The Short-Lived and Misleading Emergence of Budget Surpluses

The most powerful recent example of how the deficit measure has failed comes from the dominant political story in federal budget policy during the late 1990s and early 2000s. For decades, the annual budget measure, being a deficit, had displayed the same sign as the long-term fiscal gap. But then, when surpluses emerged in 1997, they offered the main pretext for the enormous tax cuts that were enacted in 2001, and that kicked off the subsequent spree of tax cuts and spending increases.

The fact that the emergence of enormous deficits had no evident effect on this spree, once started, may lead one to wonder whether the surpluses mattered so much after all. In retrospect, it seems likely that, to the Bush Administration, the surpluses were just a pretext for policy preferences that it held in any event. Thus, when the surpluses disappeared, the Administration altered only the rationale for its tax policy, as opposed to the policy itself. Nonetheless, the surpluses were politically essential, and perhaps even indispensable, to the budget policies of the first Bush term. They helped to set the train in motion, aided by the fact that once deficits had reemerged but there were external scapegoats (al Qaeda and a recession attributed to the Clinton Administration), there was no more taboo.

Why budget policy has recently gone so wrong is a complex and multifaceted question, which I address more fully in Chapter 6. But the role played by budget surpluses, which emerged at a critical moment with a misleading long-term sign, cannot be minimized. Live by the deficit (in terms of relying on it to dramatize the long-term problem) and, we have learned, you die by the deficit.

## Ad Hoc Fixes to the Deficit Measure

The problems with the deficit measure are plain enough that various ad hoc fixes have been tried. Unfortunately, each of these, while perhaps better than doing nothing, falls well short of providing an adequate correction. In addition, these fixes have a tendency to inspire new kinds of game playing, akin to the one-day "smoke and mirrors" postponement of an outlay, while also waylaying political discourse so that it is too mired in formalistic mumbo-jumbo for people to keep sight of what they are supposed to be concerned about.

## On-Budget Deficit or Surplus

A good example of the mumbo-jumbo problem is provided by the "on-budget" deficit, which differs from the "unified" or overall budget measure in that it disregards annual cash flows from Social Security (and several other less important sets of cash flows as well).

What could be the rationale for this adjustment, given that all of the federal government's money "goes into the same stomach" (Eisner 1994, 133)? The rationale has a couple of elements. One is that, while Social Security is currently running cash-flow surpluses, making the deficit smaller if these are counted, over the long run it is inadequately financed. So excluding the current Social Security surplus is a step, if only a partial and inadequate one, toward accounting for the long-term problem. In effect, it makes the treatment of Social Security taxes more like that of debt principal, the receipt or payment of which is ignored under deficit accounting.

Adding political cogency to the on-budget measure is the fact that Social Security is supposed to be a self-financing system. So, if there is an on-budget deficit, there may be a feeling that the government has improperly "raided" Social Security and put its grubby mitts on funds that are supposed to be used to pay Social Security benefits only. This underlay the "lockbox" concept of years past, which demanded maintaining not just a unified but an on-budget surplus.

There is something naïve about this formulation. The "raid" is purely notional, since it doesn't matter which dollar bills the government uses for one purpose or another. The long-term concern about Social Security benefits that *does* matter is whether they will be paid. This is almost completely unaffected by the difference between having a one-dollar on-budget surplus or a one-dollar on-budget deficit. Still, the "lockbox" notion had good effects if it helped at the margin to discourage profligacy.

No matter how preferable the on-budget measure might be, it has serious rhetorical and salience problems, in addition to the conceptual ones with deficit measures generally. Try as one may to jawbone Congress and the president by emphasizing one deficit measure instead of another, the difference between the two simply sounds too much like an exercise in insider jargon. Policy makers cannot be forced to emphasize the better measure. Not surprisingly, as deficits grew under the George W. Bush Administration, so did the relative emphasis that official reports placed on the overall as compared to the on-budget measure (Jackson 2004). This sleight of hand was hard to counter. Arguments about this deficit versus that deficit are hardly the stuff of an effective attack ad in a political campaign.

Even when attempted, such arguments can take the political conversation so far away from the real budgetary issues that people lose sight of them completely. An amusing example, at least for those with a sufficiently esoteric sense of humor, came in mid-2001, when the Democrats sought to tighten the political grip of the "lockbox" by arguing that the relevant budget surplus, for purposes of deciding whether President Bush had cut taxes too much, would exclude not only the Social Security surplus but also a specified Medicare surplus.

Here a bit more background about Medicare is needed. Officially, Medicare's main benefits are divided into those provided under Part A of the program, pertaining to hospitalization insurance, and those provided by Part B, pertaining generally to outpatient treatment. (Part C is a relatively minor HMO-type program, and prescription drugs are now Part D.) Part A is financed, like Social Security, through a portion of the payroll tax that is attributed to the Medicare Part A Trust Fund. Part B also ostensibly has a trust fund, but this does not mean much because Part B is funded out of general revenues. Part A, like Social Security, is currently running annual surpluses, but its long-term fiscal prognosis is even grimmer than that for Social Security. Part B is considered to be in long-term trouble simply because it is growing so fast that general revenues cannot easily keep pace.

Against this background, the Democrats in 2001 argued that President Bush would have been caught stealing cookies from the lockbox (to mix the metaphors) if the overall budget surplus fell below the

Social Security surplus *plus* the Part A Medicare surplus for the year. To this, not surprisingly, Mitchell E. Daniels, Jr., director of the White House Office of Management and Budget, vigorously demurred. A *New York Times* news article reported his argument as follows:

> In any case, [Daniels] said, it is meaningless to measure fiscal health relative to the Medicare surplus, which he described as an accounting gimmick.
>
> The Medicare surplus is generated by one part of the Medicare program, its hospital insurance trust fund. The rest of Medicare requires infusions of general tax revenue each year. So there is no Medicare surplus, Mr. Daniels said, when the program is looked at as a whole.
>
> "With respect," he said, "the notion of a Medicare surplus is flawed, it's misleading, and it's dangerous."
>
> He said Mr. Bush's standard for fiscal prudence was the Social Security surplus, which he said the administration would protect at all costs, even if that meant vetoing spending bills passed by Congress. (Stevenson 2001, A-20)

Let's be kind enough here to suppress a chuckle about protecting the Social Security surplus, and about President Bush vetoing congressional spending bills. What is truly extraordinary here is the looking-glass logic of how the argument relates to the conclusion. Things are worse than they seem, Daniels argues. Medicare is not truly in current surplus. Therefore, we must use a less cautious and prudent measure than if it actually were in current surplus. The fact that things are even worse means that we must act as if they were even better, by treating only the Social Security surplus as off-budget. To do otherwise – to admit some tiny portion of the long-term Medicare downside, by treating the Part A surplus as needed to help finance it in the future – would be "flawed." It would be "misleading." Indeed, it would be "dangerous."

Daniels was not being unusually deceptive here. This kind of game playing in budget politics is par for the course. But that is exactly the point. Discussion of all the different surpluses is simply too arcane and specialized for anyone without an extensive background in budgetary issues to have parsed through his argument and seen that he was perversely using bad news to argue *against* greater prudence.

## Full-Employment Deficit

Another popular version is the full-employment deficit, measuring what the budget deficit would have been under the often counterfactual circumstance of full employment. The point of interest about this measure is that it disentangles business cycle effects from other effects. Suppose, for example, that the actual budget deficit is $100 billion, while the full employment deficit is only $20 billion. The implication is that the smaller number may tell us more about what Congress's budgetary policy looks like over the long term. If the economy picks up and everything else stays the same, then indeed the full-employment number does tell us more about what the long-term budget policy really looks like. Unfortunately, however, stripping away temporary business cycle effects on the level of the deficit, while a step in the right direction for some purposes (such as assessing policy sustainability), leaves in place all of the measure's other flaws.

## Deficit with Capital Budgeting

The Robert Eisner idea of using capital budgeting in the official measure, and thus, for example, amortizing the cost of a series of new fighter planes over their expected useful life, likewise may have merit for some purposes. Economically, if one is concerned about the costs the government really incurs in a given year, converting a billion dollars of cash into a billion-dollar asset is not at all the same as simply paying that amount to someone. Depreciation of the assets over time is the true economic expense.

There accordingly is a good case for revising the deficit measure to use capital budgeting, if we think that Congress will not abuse it too much. But once we are thinking about economic accrual rather than cash flows, it becomes harder to justify ignoring the accrual of future liabilities, such as those under Social Security and Medicare. If we make that move as well, we end up with a measure that has more in common with the fiscal gap than the deficit, apart from the issue of just how far ahead we look.

## Five-Year and Ten-Year Budget Forecasts

Congress has for some time recognized, in its official score keeping, that one year is simply too short a period for budget projections. In the 1980s, it began using five-year budget forecasts for major legislation, such as the Tax Reform Act of 1986 (which was supposed to break even in revenue terms over that period). In the 1990s, Congress shifted to ten-year forecasts. The House of Representatives, however, has recently returned to five-year projections, supposedly to permit swifter revenue estimates. As we have seen, however, even ten-year budget deficits can easily be gamed by back-loading costs, as in the Medicare prescription drug and Roth IRA examples.

## Summary

Budget deficits really do measure something: the excess, for the measurement period, of the government's cash outlays over its inflows, disregarding any cash flows that are deemed to be of loan principal. Further adjustments can be made as well, as in the case of the on-budget deficit, which ignores certain sets of outlays such as those associated with Social Security; or the full-employment deficit, a projected measure of what the deficit would have been under full-employment conditions.

The real issue for any measure is what of interest it tells us. This, in the case of budget deficits in all versions, is not so obvious. The use of a limited time window, which is equivalent to infinite discounting outside the window, is one source of problems. The distinction between cash flows denominated as debt principal and other cash flows is another. Further refinements, such as counting only items that are classified as on-budget, can lead to further problems.

Budget deficits' greatest technical virtue as a measure is the flip side of their greatest analytical limitation: the fact that, at least for this year's or next year's deficit, they concern events that have already happened or are about to happen. Thus, we don't need to project very far into the future the underlying variables, such as economic and demographic trends or the adoption of policy changes. For this to be a virtue, however, we need to identify a purpose that relying on the measure can serve. Mere certainty or measurability is not enough, or else we could reasonably use measures based on the number of letters in the secretary of the treasury's last name. We will see in Part Two that there are a couple of purposes for which the deficit concept remains useful, but that for other purposes it should simply be abandoned.

# PART 2

# THE WHY AND HOW OF LONG-TERM BUDGETING

*Fiscal language issues arise both latitudinally and longitudinally – that is, both across time and across program categories. Part Two takes the latitudinal view, examining issues of long-term budgeting. To this end, Chapter 4 examines why budgeting over time, even if poorly measured by deficits, is considered (and is) important. Chapter 5 explores how to address the measurement issues raised by the long-term issues. Chapter 6 discusses why the long-term budgeting outlook in the United States (as well as elsewhere) has grown so dark, and how, as a matter of political economy and rule design, the approaching dangers could be addressed.*

# 4

## What Are We Talking about When We Talk about Budget Deficits?

*"And then," said Mr. Micawber, who was present, "I have no doubt I shall, please Heaven, begin to be beforehand with the world, and to live in a perfectly new manner, if – in short, if anything turns up."*

– Charles Dickens, *David Copperfield*

*A government which robs Peter to pay Paul can always depend on the support of Paul.*

– George Bernard Shaw

We saw in Part One how labels can matter even if they are arbitrary and misleading. Thus, politicians fight about labeling a particular provision as a tax increase or a spending cut, even if substantively the classification makes no difference. Likewise, they play budgetary games to reduce short-term deficits, even if the long-term budgetary picture does not improve. However, for budget deficits, unlike taxes and spending, Part One left open the question of why these machinations would be politically advantageous.

From the politicians' standpoint, asking why they prefer reporting lower deficits might prompt the old retort: "Is this a trick question?" Obviously, no one wants to be accused of running up the tab. However, the other side of the coin, concerning why voters and analysts may care, is considerably more complicated. The underlying concerns are multiple, and are grounded in substance even though the deficit measure is not. In demonstrating this, it is useful to start by reviewing deficits' modern history.

## Budget Deficits – A Capsule History

Concern about budget deficits and resulting national debt has deep roots in Anglo-American history. In the eighteenth century, writers as illustrious as David Hume and Adam Smith were convinced that England and other leading European nations would be ruined by the debt burdens they had incurred through decades of war. These fears actually came true for King Louis XVI, if not for France itself, when a crippling fiscal crisis impelled him to call the Estates General, leading swiftly to the outbreak of the French Revolution (Shaviro 1997, 15–16, 28–31).

In England after the Napoleonic Wars, and again in the United States after the Civil War, the seemingly crippling fiscal burdens that had been left behind dwindled swiftly into triviality due to the rapid economic growth triggered by the Industrial Revolution. America then experienced, in the late nineteenth century, a considerably more extended prequel to the short-lived "surpluses far as the eye can see" era of the late 1990s. The federal budget was in surplus for every year from 1866 through 1892. For the era's Republicans, this posed what now seems the almost comical dilemma of needing to figure out how to spend enough money to fend off pressure for cuts in tariffs, which were the era's main federal tax and which they wanted to keep at high levels in order to protect domestic manufacturing interests from foreign competition (Shaviro 1997, 21).

Deficits did not again figure prominently in American public policy debate until the Great Depression. President Roosevelt, after having pledged in the 1932 presidential campaign to balance the budget, instead more wisely eschewed the tax increases and spending cuts, in the middle of a sustained economic downturn, that budget balancing would have entailed. His policy of tolerating deficits under these conditions came eventually to be understood as a proper Keynesian or countercyclical response to the Depression. The renewed downturn of

1937 was blamed by subsequent economists, if not by contemporary voters, on Roosevelt's ill-timed effort to move toward restoring budgetary balance while the economy was still weak (Savage 1988, 170). Economic dogma for nearly thirty years after the end of the Great Depression held that popular fears about deficits were wholly "imaginary," and even risked subjecting us to "nuclear war and/or totalitarian domination" if the result was to discourage needed spending (Shaviro 1997, 41).

The pendulum swung again beginning in the late 1960s, prompted by the era's Vietnam War/Great Society deficits along with the collapse, under the pressure of "stagflation" or simultaneous recession and inflation, of the belief that Keynesian "fine-tuning" by wise and omnipotent centralized decision makers could keep the economy humming along smoothly like a pampered Rolls Royce. By the 1970s, grim warnings of "democracy in deficit" (Buchanan and Wagner 1977) held that flaws in our political institutions were pushing us inexorably toward default or hyperinflation, a fiscal fate more typical of banana republics.

But then the worm turned once again, in a couple of stages. President Reagan, whose "riverboat gamble" 1981 tax cut (plus increased defense spending) in the face of large deficits was a kind of prequel to the policies of the George W. Bush Administration, belied his reputation as a simplistic ideologue by supporting significant tax increases in 1982, 1983 (for Social Security), and 1984. Congress and the next two presidents, George H. W. Bush and Bill Clinton, then made frequent and (until 1993) bipartisan deficit reduction efforts, reflecting the widely shared view that something had to be done, but seemingly doomed to fall short of ever actually getting the deficit as low as everyone thought it should be.

I personally remember the complacency, in this regard, with which I contemplated the continuing timeliness of a book I had in the publication pipeline at the time, called *Do Deficits Matter?* Writers about public affairs always worry that they are hostages to fortune, in that the topics they are writing about could disappear or be radically transformed while their books are being copy edited or waiting for jacket blurbs. But no such fears had I, since everyone agreed that deficits were with us to stay. My book came out on April 30, 1997, and one day later the Congressional Budget Office announced that the achievement of many years of budget surplus was at hand (Zitner 1997, A-1).

What had happened? Part of the "problem" (from my selfish perspective as an author) was that the politicians really had made progress up to a point, by restraining growth in outlays and raising taxes on several occasions. Part of it was unanticipated revenue growth in the expansionary, stock-market-bubble-enhanced economy of the late 1990s. And the rest of it was that things had not really changed so much after all. The long-term picture of Social Security and Medicare unsustainability, which eventually, down the road, would trigger unsupportably large deficits if nothing was done, was still there even as President Clinton trumpeted surpluses "as far as the eye can see."

By the mid-1990s, however, there had been a political sea change, albeit one that did not immediately change the course of government policy. A conservative Republican revolt against the first President Bush, though quelled in the 1992 primaries, had taken over the party by 1994 and prompted that year's "Contract with America" congressional campaign. Even so noted a pragmatist as Senator Bob Dole found it necessary to embrace large tax cuts in his 1996 presidential campaign, despite an absence of public enthusiasm for them outside of the core Republican base. The budget surpluses that emerged in 1997 then gave renewed political life to Republican tax cutting, by permitting the argument that surely large tax cuts were now affordable.

President Clinton responded, with characteristic political deftness, by moving the goalposts. He used the slogan "Save Social Security First" to argue that nothing of the sort should be done, at least on the Republicans' proposed scale, until Social Security's future had itself been secured. This morphed into the "lockbox" notion that required an on-budget surplus. The lockbox then persisted as a politically powerful idea through most of President George W. Bush's first year in office, much though *Saturday Night Live* satirists had delighted in mocking Vice President Gore's wooden invocations of it. As of the late summer of 2001, many observers believed Bush was headed for political trouble because his tax cuts had endangered the on-budget surplus, thus inviting the critique that he had brought about the improper diversion of Social Security taxes.

We all know what happened next. On September 11, 2001, when the Twin Towers fell, so did any political pressure on our leadership to avoid running up enormous budget deficits. This was surely paradoxical, if one is naïve enough to expect a lot of logic in public political debate. It was admittedly true that fear of deficits could not reasonably be invoked to forestall the taking of needed national security measures. It was also true that the economic recession into which the terror attacks had helped plunge us might make immediate tax increases and spending cuts unwise. But the terror attacks indicated, if anything, that *more* fiscal restraint was needed in other respects than people had previously thought, not less. They suggested that we now would be bearing immense military and security expenses of a sort that had seemed unnecessary in the halcyon years just after the end of the Cold War. The money for this, under the no-free-lunch principle, would have to come from somewhere.

The lockbox seems, in retrospect, to have offered merely a soft taboo against any politician's being the first to breach its intangible barrier. Once al Qaeda plus recession had brought about the conditions for a breach without domestic political fault, it was as if the lockbox had never even existed. Huge tax cuts, hundreds of billions of dollars for Iraq, an unfunded new $18.2 trillion Medicare benefit – all could simultaneously be provided without any hint of where the money might come from. And immense, unending budget deficits, while embarrassing, were now so completely part of the political order of things that neither President Bush nor Senator Kerry, during the 2004 presidential campaign, thought it necessary to suggest that the deficit could be cut by more than 50 percent over the next four years, with big deficit increases likely to occur just past the four-year window.

## But (Why) Does Long-Term Budgeting Matter?

Writing *Do Deficits Matter?* at a time when lesser fiscal problems than those we face today were generating far more responsible political behavior from both parties, I felt comfortable with tut-tutting at some of the sillier aspects of the then-contemporary debate. I noted that much of the deficit issue's salience was purely symbolic, reflecting the public's association of deficits with "the inefficient and wasteful public expenditure produced by a bureaucratic and insensitive 'big government'" (Savage 1988, 195). Ross Perot, who at the time remained a prominent political figure, liked to boast that his business expertise would enable him to eliminate the budget deficit "without breaking a sweat" (Robinson 1992, 11). This association of deficits with unbusinesslike behavior had no bearing on whether deficits as such, or some improved version of the measure, would actually have bad consequences at any time.

Other leading reasons for popular concern about deficits tended to be off the mark as well. Some complained, for example, about "the inexorable sale of America to foreign interests" (Tsongas 1991, 5). This overlooked the fact that, so long as we are running a budget deficit, we should be glad if foreigners are willing to help finance it. The crunch will come when bondholders, including foreigners, finally lose their patience and faith in our creditworthiness. Even the need to pay foreigners principal plus interest in the future might not be a huge concern if the borrowed funds were being invested productively.

Moreover, at the heart of some expressions of deficit aversion I discerned a misguided analogy between the debt of a private household and that of a government that presides over a large economy, levying taxes and issuing its own currency. Charles Dickens buffs may recall the famous words of Mr. Micawber in *David Copperfield*: "Annual income twenty pounds, annual expenditure nineteen nineteen and six, result happiness. Annual income twenty pounds, annual expenditure twenty pounds ought and six, result misery." A government in these straits, however, would simply tax someone sixpence. To be in the same position, Micawber would have had to succeed in persuading his creditors that something commensurate with his "talents" really was about to "turn up." No government should fail to satisfy the credit markets because of Micawber's sixpence, or even the equivalent portion of an $11 trillion economy. Failure would more likely be based on big and politically ineluctable disparities between revenue and expenditure that investors make the judgment cannot and will not be reversed unless the plug is pulled.

There is a saying that just because you are paranoid does not mean people aren't plotting against you. In the same spirit, just because deficit aversion has involved some foolish or naïve ideas, it does not follow that all of the underlying concerns are spurious, even if people are mistaken in attaching any or all of them to this particular measure. In *Do Deficits Matter?* I identified four main concerns commonly associated with budget deficits.

## 1) Generational Policy

People have long objected to budget deficits on the distributional ground that they burden future generations, which presumably will have to repay the resulting national debt. As far back as 1820, a prominent member of Congress, appalled by the emergence of a budget deficit for the year that eventually reached $380,000 (!), demanded spending cuts, stating: "To me, there has always been something highly objectionable, if not immoral, in the idea of burdening our posterity, for the support of our extravagances" (Savage 1988, 101–102, 288). This concern has "echoed through American history" (102), as in President Eisenhower's repeated warnings, as he prepared to leave office, about the "burden of debt on our grandchildren" (Stein 1996, 350). To this day, the Concord Coalition website (http://www. concordcoalition.org) offers numerous references to deficits' unfair effect on future generations.

## 2) Macroeconomic Issues

Deficits and surpluses may affect allocation by helping or harming the performance of the economy in various ways. In times of recession, the most prominent concern is Keynesian fiscal stimulus,[1] which can take either of two forms. Automatic stimulus results, without any legislative action, from reduced income and payroll tax revenues and higher benefit payments, such as for unemployment insurance, simply through the operation of the laws on the books when employment levels and economic production decline. Discretionary stimulus involves the enactment of tax cuts or spending increases so that people will have more money in their pockets and, it is hoped, use this money to rev up the economy. The flip side of either type of stimulus is increasing taxes or cutting spending, whether automatically or through new enactments, when the economy is overheating and we therefore face a threat of inflation. Keynesian fiscal policy is countercyclical, in the sense that it tries to ease the natural swings of the business cycle by flattening both the peaks (hopefully in terms of inflation rather than real production) and the valleys.

Budget deficits also raise various macroeconomic concerns apart from their use in relation to the business cycle. A key concern is that, by requiring the government to sell more bonds, they will lead to higher interest rates that will make future deficits more costly for the government to finance, and that also may discourage business investment by increasing the "hurdle rate" that a project must exceed to offer a positive return. And they may reduce national saving relative to the case where the budget is balanced. If they are eliminated through tax increases, the idea is to reduce consumer spending, thus causing more to be saved in the absence of Keynesian effects on national income and investment. If they are eliminated by reducing government outlays, the idea is that the stricken items probably would have funded current consumption by voters (or else would have involved waste) rather than constituting productive long-term investment.

## 3) Size of Government

Conservatives for decades voiced frequent support for budgetary balance, on the premise that it would restrain government spending, which was equated as usual with the size of government. The idea was that spending programs would be easier to enact if they were debt-financed. The Nobel economist James Buchanan, for example, argued that "fiscal illusion" among voters caused debt financing to have a lower perceived (though not actual) cost than current tax financing, as a result of which deficits played a vital role in undesirable government expansion (see Buchanan and Wagner 1977). Conservatives have therefore urged the enactment of a balanced budget amendment to the U.S. Constitution.

Buchanan and Wagner were hardly alone in this, and balanced budget amendment proposals became, for a while, a regular feature of American politics, appealing predominantly, although not exclusively, to conservatives. Enacting a balanced budget amendment was one of the ten planks in the Republicans' 1994 "Contract with America." In 1995, a balanced budget amendment actually came within one Senate vote of being approved by the U.S. Congress and sent to the states for ratification.

Things obviously have changed since I wrote *Do Deficits Matter?* However misguidedly, tax cutting has replaced budget balancing as the anti–big government tool of choice. In President Bush's second term, however, deficit reduction has reemerged as at least a rhetorical conservative Republican aim, subject to the requirement that it be pursued through spending cuts and not through tax increases.

## 4) Policy Sustainability

The final issue associated with deficits, affecting both distribution and allocation, is what I call policy sustainability. The term may sound turgid and abstract. But you are raising it in your own mind if you wonder whether Social Security and Medicare benefits will be there for you when you retire.

The 1815 British version of this concern might have gone something like this: "We can't keep on waging costly wars, as we have for the last few decades, without radically raising taxes, which we do not want to do and perhaps could not do, politically or economically. Thus, unless a long-lasting peace is truly at hand, something will have to give – either reasonable taxes, or our national credit, or our vital interests in the continental European balance of power. Indeed, some combination of reasonable taxes, our Navy, and our credit may have to be sacrificed even if peace is truly at hand."

Suppose Great Britain had actually faced the expected fiscal crisis after 1815, rather than being rescued by a century of relative peace plus the Industrial Revolution. Two types of bad things might have happened, one concerning the new steady state and the other concerning the transition to it. First, the set of taxing and spending policies that dominant political actors preferred would have been unsustainable together. Parliament would have found it necessary, on a going-forward basis, to impose some combination of higher taxes and lower spending than were considered desirable. Second, at the transition, there might have been a shock from the change in policy. For example, bondholders who had relied on the English government's credit might have faced severe disappointment from an actual default or even an implicit one (had the English government repaid its debts by printing money and thus devaluing the currency). Ripple effects might have included not only a long-term loss of the British government's ability to borrow at low interest rates, but also a possible credit collapse that could have triggered a lasting recession, along with hyperinflation had the government staved off explicit default by printing money.

When we turn to the United States today, an important difference is that people are counting on the government to do a lot more than just maintaining national defense, paying off bondholders, and sparing taxpayers enormous increases. Whole industries and professions have grown up around the U.S. government's various interventions in the economy. Above all, we have  Social Security and Medicare on the books, promising people substantial retirement benefits. These are implicit obligations even if not legally enforceable. People expect them, and can bring a lot of political clout to demanding that they be honored.

Although the issues have thus multiplied, the basic problems remain the same. First, as to the steady state, the set of policies that we have come to expect and that a large majority evidently prefer, with substantial military and domestic spending, generous retirement programs, and non-stratospheric tax rates, will not be simultaneously sustainable if outlays sufficiently outpace inflows and new government borrowing cannot keep making up the difference. So unsustainability would require existing policy to change substantially. Second, as to the transition, if our policies cease to be sustainable, the course correction might end up involving such evils as hyperinflation, a credit collapse, and sustained recession. Not only bondholders but also implicit claimants such as seniors would suffer from the loss of government payouts on which they had been counting, and this might add to the ripple effects on the macroeconomy and thus on all Americans.

## How Important Are the Issues Raised by Long-Term Budgeting?

### Generational Policy

Does generational policy even matter, given the ubiquity of transfers between parents and children in any multigenerational household? The economist Robert Barro has prominently argued that it does not, because households will adjust their gifts and bequests to get the overall division of resources that they want in any event. The basic argument was neatly made nearly two centuries ago by David Ricardo, who did not, however, believe it.

Suppose, Ricardo said, someone who was planning to leave his children a bequest could either pay a tax of 1,000 pounds or leave it, through debt financing, to be paid with interest by the children. "Where is the difference, whether somebody leaves to his son 20,000 pounds with the tax still [to be paid], or 19,000 pounds without it?" (Ricardo, 1951 ed., 4:187). Ricardo "concluded there was no difference – as long as the taxpayer understood the tax burden and could not hope it would be shifted to other households" (Shaviro 1997, 31) – conditions that he did not think held (Ricardo 1996 ed., 172–173).

This irrelevance result (known in the literature as Ricardian equivalence) could result from adjusting cash flows from children to parents, as well as from adjusting those from parents to children. Suppose that, in the absence of Social Security and Medicare, working adults with retired parents would pay exactly the same amounts to support their parents as the payroll taxes that they actually pay to this effect. Then the massive transfers to seniors that we observe through Social Security and Medicare would not in fact be changing anything in terms of overall generational distribution, at least so far as these households were concerned.

Though often admired as an elegant theory, Ricardian equivalence "has received very little empirical support in the economics literature," and thus is thought "unlikely in practice" to offset government borrowing (Gruber 2004, 111). Moreover, even if you take the caricatured economist's view that it need not work in practice so long as it works in theory, Ricardianism has serious defects. Its requiring one to accept a strong version of the standard assumption in neoclassical economics that farsighted individuals consistently optimize, given their preferences, is only the starting point. Even with that assumption, it loses force if bequests are not altruistically motivated based on some consistent weighing of the parent's lifetime welfare against the child's. For example, what James Andreoni calls "impure altruism," motivated by the "warm glow" produced by giving rather than by an overall household utility calculation, would defeat Ricardian equivalence (Andreoni 1989, 447) by causing the parent to care only about the size of her gross bequest, as opposed to the net bequest taking into account the child's share of outstanding public debt. Strategic withholding of the purse until death in order to purchase care and attention from one's children would likewise suggest caring only about the gross bequest.

It seems clear, therefore, that the government's generational policy does matter, in the sense that it really does affect intergenerational distribution. Under present fiscal policy, moreover, it is clear that very large amounts are at stake, even allowing for some degree of Ricardian offset. For example, as we saw in Chapter 2, it has been suggested that, even before the recent tax cuts and Medicare prescription drug benefit were enacted, future generations might potentially face double the lifetime net tax rates of anyone now living. Moreover, as to the new Medicare benefit, one estimate suggested that it would result in an average lifetime transfer of $10,000 per person to people fifty-six or older at the time of enactment (Antos and Gokhale 2003), even if fully financed through contemporaneous tax increases. Since it was enacted without any financing, the actual transfer presumably was even greater.

Such estimates suggest that the politically realistic range of possible distributional outcomes as between generations is very broad indeed. And the issues of generational equity, as to which the stakes appear to be so high, are themselves complex and difficult. Ideas of duty toward one's elders and descendants are deeply engrained in human psychology. Moreover, future generations may live in a very different world than we do, adding to the difficulty of resolving how we should balance their interests against ours. They are not around today to tell us what they want, or to influence our decisions that will greatly affect them. Thus, conceivably we are improperly inclined to undervalue their interests relative to ours. On the other hand, if economic trends of the last few centuries in the Western world continue, it is possible that they will be a lot richer and better off than we are, perhaps to a degree that, if we could imagine it, would suggest that we are not being generous enough to ourselves. The equity tradeoffs are quite difficult, offering all the more reason for us to want good measurement tools for generational policy.

## Macroeconomic Issues

Any doubt about the importance of countercyclical policy was resolved by the Great Depression. However, the political demand for discretionary stimulus, through the enactment of tax and spending changes, has fluctuated over time. In the 1980s and 1990s, its undesirability was widely accepted. This was a matter less of macroeconomics than of political economy concerns about how, as a practical matter, discretionary policy was likely to be implemented. The main concerns were twofold. First, given the difficulty of short-term economic forecasting and the often glacial pace of the legislative process, stimulus would tend to come too late, at a point when the economy was already recovering and was therefore prone to "overheat," resulting in inflation. It could therefore be compared to a thermostat with a six-month lag, which detects cold weather in January but does not succeed in turning on the heat until July (Shaviro 1997, 207–209). Second was the concern that politicians would disingenuously misuse discretion as a one-way ratchet that could justify increasing deficits but never reducing them.

This rejection of discretionary stimulus, while never discredited, has in recent years been deliberately forgotten. As Alan Auerbach (2003, 109) notes, "[n]o politician wishes to be cast in the title role of *It's the Economy, Stupid.*" President Clinton paved the way by proposing a "stimulus plan" in 1993, but Congress declined to enact it. Still, few leading politicians have failed to observe the lesson, learned the hard way by the first President Bush, that a down business cycle, or even just the appearance of inattention, can be dangerous for incumbents.

In 2001, the second President Bush more or less stumbled into a one-time solution to the lag problem. Massive tax cuts, which Bush was planning in any event, were fortuitously enacted at just about the right time. Then, in 2002, things went a step further. Congress, "remind[ing] us that policy makers may go where economists fear to tread" (Auerbach 2003, 109), passed a conventional stimulus bill, with incentives for new investment and extension of unemployment benefits.

Finally, in 2003, the Bush Administration took the logical next step: portraying tax cuts as stimulative even if they had been designed to serve very different objectives. Dead set as ever on tax cuts but having lost the rationale from 2001 that they were justified by budget surpluses, the Administration now claimed that more stimulus was needed, since the economy was still stumbling. It evidently was untroubled by the fact that its main tax proposal, eliminating the double tax on corporate income, had been designed to meet very different objectives, such as creating a more level economic playing field over the long run. Leveling the economic playing field is a worthy and important goal, but entirely distinct from short-term stimulus. Had stimulus been the goal, the 2003 tax cuts would have had to be directed to individuals with high marginal propensities to consume an extra dollar, or else to new capital investment by businesses.

To fair-minded observers, the take-away lesson from 2003 was that the prior wisdom had been exactly right. Once discretionary stimulus is back on the table, the political system is just as prone to misuse it as had been feared. Public concern about recession or unemployment levels empowers a president to make whatever tax cut proposal he likes, labeling it a "stimulus" and holding over his foes the threat of blaming them for any and all problems in the economy if it does not pass. So the prior consensus against discretionary countercyclical fiscal policy, having been forgotten without being refuted, has now been confirmed without being restored.

## Size of Government

Deficits have never been a proposed measure of the size of government, which people typically equate with the nominal level of government spending. Rather, deficits have often been considered a variable the might affect political outcomes, relating to the size of the government, in practice. Clearly, the size of government is an important issue, given the range of views in our society concerning the relative virtues of private market and political outcomes. However, since in recent years so many conservatives have abandoned deficit reduction as a tool to fight government growth, plighting their troth instead to tax cuts, it is worth asking why the change occurred, as well as whether the size-of-government view associated with deficits has merit and/or is likely to recur.

As with discretionary stimulus, the prevailing view seems to have changed despite recent historical evidence, rather than because of it. The shift in norm is based on the view that tax cuts are a better tool than deficit reduction for reducing government spending (equated with the size of government). Events of the last two decades strongly support the contrary view. Repeatedly during this period, tax *increases* and spending constraint have been the trends that travel together, as joint products of a taste for fiscal responsibility. Likewise, tax cuts and spending increases travel together when the taste for responsibility weakens (Gale and Orszag 2004b).

This history has evidently been lost, however, on leading conservative thinkers. Milton Friedman, for example, started out favoring a balanced budget amendment, on the ground that deficits encourage political irresponsibility and higher spending (Friedman 1984). By 2003, however, he had decided that deficit reduction is a chimera, because, for reasons that remain unspecified, the politically tolerable deficit is fixed, beyond the very short run. "Raise taxes by enough to eliminate the existing deficit and spending will go up to restore the politically tolerable deficit. Tax cuts may initially raise the deficit above the politically tolerable deficit, but their longer term effect will be to restrain spending" (Friedman 2003).

How exactly Friedman persuaded himself that the politically tolerable deficit is fixed, notwithstanding the huge contrast between the politics of 1984 and 2003, is unclear. Perhaps a key factor was that, in 1984, Democrats controlled the House of Representatives and had substantial influence in the Senate, whereas in 2003 the Republicans controlled both. "Deficit reduction for them, tax cuts for us" can be a clever strategy, but it is not an especially candid one.

It is easy to guess that, as soon as the Democrats regain some measure of political control in Washington, conservative interest in deficit reduction will reemerge. So the prior view about deficits and the growth of government is merely dormant, not dead, and remains worth evaluating.

## Policy Sustainability

Perhaps the trickiest issue to evaluate is policy sustainability. On its face, a finding that current policy is unsustainable is merely a statement about statements. It shows that, so far as we now can tell, the currently announced or inferred policies do not add up, and thus cannot all happen. So the real set of policies that are followed in the future apparently will have to differ from the currently announced set.

Without more, a natural reaction to this is to ask: so what? Puffery and worse go on all the time. If Congress wants to say that it plans to impose a given set of rules over time, and we know that it cannot because the numbers are too far out of balance, where is the harm beyond that associated with telling tall tales generally? Why lose sleep about the prospect, amid all the uncertainties we face in life in any event, that Congress's current set of statements will at some point require revision? The magnitude of the "statement about statements" problem might still be worth knowing, because it might indicate to what degree change is likely, but it would merely be interesting, rather than downright alarming.

The question of whether we face more than a "statement about statements" problem has no general answer of a sort that would apply equally in all situations. Indeed, one could look at two countries with the same size economies, falling equally short of sustainability under currently announced policy, and conclude that one faced serious hazards down the road while the other did not. It all depends on such factors as the types of currently projected rules that give rise to the shortfall, the menu of plausible rule revisions, the broader world economic setting, and – perhaps most importantly – the functioning of the political system that is going to have to decide on the change in course.

One soft variable, critical but hard to measure, concerns the strength of the pre-commitment that a current statement about future policy actually represents (Auerbach 2004, 28–29). To what degree is it entrenched, or at least favored in its future prospects by reason of its being on the books? Just by the potential stalemate that would have to be overcome by a legislative majority in order for the rule to change? If so, then how likely, or hard to overcome, is such a stalemate? Do any additional political forces promote entrenchment of the current rules? An example would be the difficulty of "cutting benefits" in the Social Security and Medicare programs once their currently intended path has been announced. Or, for an even stronger pre-commitment, consider full-faith-and-credit debt obligations. If current statements about future policy are easy to change, then their unsustainability may not concern us very much. But the greater their political entrenchment, the more it matters.

Three main concerns may arise if the current statements are hard to change and yet must change. The first two matter to a degree, but the third is the really important one.

## Difficulty of Planning for the Future

Most of the time, we all prefer certainty in planning for the future. Thus, whatever one's Social Security and Medicare benefits will ultimately be, finding it out now would make retirement planning easier.

Symmetric uncertainty, where one is making the best guess possible under available information, is bad enough. The problem is even worse, however, if people systematically err in a given direction. For example, suppose that people planning for retirement were to assume that current-law benefits are just as likely to go up as down, notwithstanding the fiscal gap. This would tend to encourage entering retirement with too little saving, given that cuts are in fact more likely.

Whether this is actually happening today is hard to say. On the one hand, there is evidence that younger Americans are actually too pessimistic on average about their likely benefits, rather than too optimistic. According to a recent public opinion survey, 45 percent of Americans between the ages of twenty-two and sixty-one expect Social Security benefits to be cut, and a further 32 percent expect to receive no benefits at all (Farkas et al. 1997). The latter view is almost certainly too pessimistic. Current Social Security projections suggest that, even if absolutely nothing were done to forestall exhaustion of the Social Security Trust Fund, today's young people would still receive about two-thirds of the benefits promised by the law on the books. These amounts would indeed be significantly greater, adjusted for inflation, than Social Security benefits today, although they would be smaller relative to the size of the economy and retirees' pre-retirement wage levels.

On the other hand, while many of the respondents expressed undue pessimism, they do not appear to be acting on it. In the very same survey, nearly half of the respondents had less than $10,000 of retirement savings, and huge majorities (ranging from 68 to 80 percent) endorsed the propositions that they should save more and that they had enough disposable income to save more, and yet were unwilling to curtail their current consumption to this end.

One interpretation would be that these people need the mandatory retirement saving of Social Security and Medicare, and that the problem is their myopia rather than uncertainty as such. But a second interpretation would place some blame on the uncertainty after all. If people tend to base complex decisions on what they see others doing, then they may need an unambiguous shock before they reexamine the savings strategy that has worked well enough in the past.

## Loss of Policy Options over Time

A second problem caused by unsustainability is that the options available to address it diminish over time. The years in which nothing is done vanish, one at a time, from the overall set of years in which something could still be done. In illustration, suppose you were saving inadequately for your retirement, despite understanding the need for belt tightening at some point, because you were reluctant to get started. The longer you waited, the more severe the belt tightening would have to be once it finally did start. Delay would require much deeper cuts in your manner of living than far-sighted planning.

Medicare offers a concrete example. The longer we wait to start reducing the rate of its expenditure growth, the greater the cutbacks will have to be when they finally commence. If cutbacks involve rationing or denying the least important medical procedures first, then the longer we wait, the more we will end up applying the hard line to procedures that offer significant medical benefits. No rational person, planning for her own health care, would opt for a period of no restrictions followed by one of strict ones, rather than for a more even allocation of the cutbacks across time.[2]

While potentially important, this problem is easily misunderstood. An example arose in early 2005, when President Bush argued that delaying adoption of his Social Security plan by "just one year adds $600 billion to the cost of fixing Social Security" (Krugman 2005b). The basis for this claim was that the infinite-horizon Social Security fiscal gap was projected to rise by that amount in a year, due mainly to the increased present value of future projected Social Security cash flows that were now a year closer.

But would it really have cost $600 billion to wait a year before adopting Bush's plan? One problem is that his plan would not actually have reduced the Social Security fiscal gap, even if adopted immediately. But even if the benefit cuts the Administration suggested had been large enough to eliminate the gap, delay would have cost nothing, because they weren't scheduled to take effect for ten years anyway.

President Bush's argument that delay would "cost" $600 billion was therefore equivalent to the following. Suppose that you will have to pay someone $1 million ten years from today. At a 5 percent discount rate, this liability has a present value of about $614,000. Along comes George W. Bush, proposing that you start saving in five years to make sure that you will have the money on the due date. "You'd better not wait to adopt my plan," he says. "Wait just a year, and the cost of the fix will have increased by more than $30,000" (the one-year increase in present value of a $614,000 liability at a 5 percent interest rate).

Bush would be literally correct. At a 5 percent rate, the liability would indeed rise in present value by more than $30,000 in the course of a year. Yet you would not have lost anything by waiting to adopt his plan, or indeed any other plan that did not involve starting to save immediately. One way of putting it is that the value of the proposed fix would have increased as well, and by exactly the right amount to ensure that you would still have a million dollars on the due date. Another way of putting it is that the delay would have no effect on your ability to do exactly what Bush was counseling. More generally, the loss of policy options over time depends on when changes are implemented, not on when they are announced.

## Hard Landing versus Soft Landing

By far the most serious potential problem with unsustainability concerns how the necessary adjustments will end up being made. There are many possible scenarios, ranging from smooth readjustment to Weimar Germany–style economic chaos. Economists raise a similar question when they ask whether the U.S. trade deficit, which cannot stay at its current high level indefinitely, will change course via a "soft landing" or an economically disruptive "hard landing." In both cases, a lot depends on how the U.S. political system operates and on how investors in world capital markets perceive it as operating.

Devising a soft-landing scenario is not exactly rocket science, at least if you don't worry too much about the collateral damage. All one would have to do is raise taxes while cutting the growth rate of various outlays, such as the entitlements. The political difficulties lie in two areas: needing to impose losses on someone (or everyone), and needing to resolve ideological disputes regarding what course is least odious.

Given these difficulties, suppose that Congress keeps cutting taxes, raising current outlays, and expanding the entitlements. At some point, things would start to get ugly. As the Congressional Budget Office (CBO) recently explained (CBO 2003, 14), an initial result would be substantial crowding out of private investment, as a result of which "the growth of workers' productivity would gradually slow, real wages would begin to stagnate, and economic growth would tend to taper off." This would be only the start, however. At some point, investor confidence in the United States government as a borrower would collapse, resulting in a severe economic crisis:

> Foreign investors could stop investing in U.S. securities, the exchange value of the dollar could plunge, interest rates could climb, consumer prices could shoot up, or the economy could contract sharply. Amid the anticipation of declining profits and rising inflation and interest rates, stock markets could collapse and consumers might suddenly reduce their consumption. Moreover, economic problems in the United States could spill over to the rest of the world and seriously weaken the economies of U.S trading partners. (CBO 2003, 15)

Making things worse, these adverse economic developments tend to feed on each other, creating a downward spiral. In particular, "increased interest rates and diminished economic activity may further worsen the fiscal imbalance, which can then cause a further loss of confidence and potentially spark another round of negative feedback effects" (Rubin, Orszag, and Sinai 2004, 13).

At some point, the government, unable to sell enough bonds to keep its unsustainable policies going, would face the strong temptation to start printing money, thus triggering inflation. The Federal Reserve Board, while independent under present law, might not be able to resist these pressures forever, or might have its independence curtailed if it tried to hold the line. Before long, however, printing money would simply make things worse. As the CBO further explains:

> A policy of high inflation could reduce the real value of the government's debt, but inflation is not a feasible long-term strategy for dealing with persistent budget deficits. To be sure, unexpected increases in inflation would enable the government to repay its debts in cheaper dollars and make borrowers better off at the expense of creditors. But financial markets would not be fooled forever; investors would eventually demand higher interest rates. If the government continued to print money to finance the deficit, the situation would eventually lead to hyperinflation (as happened in Germany in the 1920s, Hungary in the 1940s, Argentina in the 1980s, and Yugoslavia in the 1990s). Moreover, interest rates could remain high for some time even after inflation was brought back under control. Once a government has lost its credibility in financial markets, regaining it can be difficult. (CBO 2003, 15)

The government need not succumb to a money-printing frenzy, however, for the hard landing to start. All this would take is a collapse in investor confidence. The history of financial markets suggests that shifts in investor confidence can be sudden, unpredictable, and triggered by seemingly trivial events (Ball and Mankiw 1995, 114–115).

It is too early to tell whether our political system will be able to avoid a hard landing through timely and credible adjustments to current policy. But also worth considering are the chances for a lucky escape, as favorable external shocks eliminate the sustainability problem without requiring hard choices. This has happened before – in England after 1815, for example, and in the United States after 1865. Might it happen again?

## Can We Outgrow the Sustainability Problem?

The most benign scenario would involve our simply outgrowing the fiscal shortfall, as happened after 1815 and 1865. Unfortunately, however, this time around the growth scenario is more complicated, even if we enjoy an productivity leap like that during the Industrial Revolution.

On the tax side, revenues are indeed roughly pegged to the size of the economy. If national income rises, so do income tax and payroll tax revenues. This is what permitted the Napoleonic and Civil War debts to be outgrown. The problem, however, is that various outlays are likewise pegged to the size of the economy. In effect, various claimants hold growth-indexed government obligations that make them, rather than taxpayers, the fiscal beneficiaries of growth.

This is clearest under Social Security and Medicare. Under the official Social Security benefit formula, retirees' starting pensions are pegged to the national wage growth that occurred during their working years. Medicare rises with health care expenditure, which historically has been growing faster than the economy as a whole. Economic growth could actually increase the fiscal gap if it caused sufficient extra growth in the health care sector.

Other expenditure programs, from military spending to everything else that is appropriated annually, are not formally linked to the size of the economy. However, there is a natural political tendency for them to grow as it grows. Moreover, even if fiscal pressures induce them to decline at least in relative terms, we should keep in mind forecasts suggesting that even reducing *all* government spending to zero, other than that for Social Security and Medicare, would not suffice to eliminate the long-term shortfall (Gokhale and Smetters 2003, 36).

In sum, while forecasts suggest that higher rates of economic growth might ease the sustainability problem, the effect is significantly muted by benefit design, which causes government outlays as well as inflows to rise in real terms with the economy. Given the partly growth-proof character of the problem, our current fiscal policy can be analogized to a hypothetical alimony agreement of the following kind (Shaviro 2002). Suppose that, in a divorce between a high-earning corporate executive and his nonworking spouse, the parties agree that each year he will pay her 30 percent of his salary, and she will get 50 percent of his salary. People can write these words on a piece of paper if they like. We know, however, that fulfillment of these terms is impossible. No matter what the husband earns, the 30 percent of his salary that he is supposed to pay can never equal the 50 percent that the wife is supposed to get.

Of course, economic growth remains appealing despite this problem. Even looking just at Social Security and Medicare benefits, seniors might actually get more if the government partially reneged under the high-growth scenario than if it fulfilled its obligations to the penny under the low-growth scenario. The threat of default, however, could prevent the high-growth scenario from occurring.

## Health Care

The biggest cause of the long-term shortfall is the continuing growth of health care expenditure relative to the size of the economy. Here, a change in current trends really could make a difference. Moreover, it is "not a law of nature that advances in healthcare technology must increase healthcare costs. Innovations may be cost-saving, not just more powerful, and improved medications or techniques for early diagnosis may help to forestall costly illness" (Shaviro 2004, 31). Thus, conceivably health care costs will adjust to a sustainable course of growth without requiring a federal policy intervention.

Perhaps it is possible. People and societies sometimes get lucky. But important incentive factors are pushing against it. Under Medicare, Medicaid, and employer-provided health care insurance, the overuse of which is encouraged by tax preferences, health care consumers have only limited cost-consciousness. Doctors often are not cost-conscious either, and indeed may benefit from providing costlier care. Insurance companies may want to cut costs, but face strong legal and regulatory obstacles to doing so. And by the time the insurance company is on the scene wanting to cut costs in a given case, it may be too late. The entire development of the health care field is driven by medical research and development firms, which "have operated with the understanding that they could more easily make money by increasing quality than by reducing cost" (Shaviro 2004, 32).

The United States now finds itself spending 150 to 200 percent or more of the amount spent by other leading nations on health care, whether this is measured per capita or relative to GDP (Reinhardt 2000, 73). Yet we seemingly have little or nothing to show for the extra spending in terms of better health care outcomes (World Health Organization Staff 2000, Annex Table 5). The implication seems to be that, in principle, we could spend a lot less on health care, thus greatly reducing the long-term fiscal problem, without adversely affecting health care results. This really would be like finding free money. Yet health care experts do not agree about how (or if) we could cut health care costs dramatically without affecting quality. And even if they did agree, those who benefit from the current system might stand in the way.

## Other Possible Cures

If life expectancy growth were to slow, the fiscal gap would likely shrink. This is considered unlikely, however (which is just as well for those of us in middle age or beyond). Another fix that some have suggested is immigration. Current taxpayers would gain if we attracted lots of young high earners from other countries, whose income and payroll taxes could help finance benefits for current residents. A recent study shows, however, that "the impact of immigration on fiscal balance is extremely small relative to the size of the overall imbalance itself" (Auerbach and Oreopoulos 1999, 180).

The upshot is that the sustainability problem appears to be here to stay, pending either major policy shifts, or fundamental demographic and technological changes of a sort that are unforeseeable today. Fiscal sustainability is therefore one of the biggest threats and challenges that the United States faces today.

## Summary

Four main issues underlie concern about budget deficits. The first is aversion to burdening future generations. The second is macroeconomic policy, ranging from Keynesian stimulus to effects on national saving. The third is the view, now in abeyance among conservatives but subject to revival, that deficit tolerance aids undue government growth. The fourth is concern about policy sustainability, whether to ensure that favored policies can continue, or to enhance certainty and limit the prospect of unpleasant surprise, or to forestall an economically disruptive hard landing through the collapse of national creditworthiness.

All of these issues are important, albeit in varying degree, and thus all call for measures that would help us in assessing budgetary policies. The next chapter therefore assesses alternative measures.

# 5

## Long-Term Measures in Lieu of the Budget Deficit

*He had bought a large map representing the sea,*
*Without the least vestige of land:*
*And the crew were much pleased when they found it to be*
*A map they could all understand.*
*"What's the good of Mercator's North Poles and Equators,*
*Tropics, Zones, and Meridian Lines?"*
*So the Bellman would cry: and the crew would reply*
*"They are merely conventional signs!*
*"Other maps are such shapes, with their islands and capes!*
*But we've got our brave Captain to thank"*
*(So the crew would protest) "that he's bought us the best -*
*A perfect and absolute blank!"*

         – Lewis Carroll, *The Hunting of the Snark*

In Lewis Carroll's poem, the Bellman and his crew eventually find a Snark despite their scorn for "conventional signs." But a political system cannot count on being so lucky. If long-term budgeting issues are important but deficits fail to illuminate them meaningfully, then alternative measures are needed.

This chapter therefore examines other possible measures for the four main issues raised by long-term budgeting. In making this inquiry, one should keep in mind the distinction between political salience and analytical merit. Some measures are easy to grasp but lack context and nuance. Others convey more information but could never inspire a newspaper headline. Both types are needed, although it is important not to confuse them.

The political and analytical realms differ not only in what sorts of measures are best, but also in how many can be used. Two or three measures is probably the limit for political purposes, given the public's limited appetite for long-term budgeting issues. Analysts have the luxury of using more measures.

## Measuring the Generational Effects of Long-Term Budgetary Policy

Distributional measures are familiar fare in tax and spending debates. Measuring generational distribution, as generational accounting (GA) tries to do, takes the distributional inquiry in a new direction – across time, rather than between groups at the same time – but is not otherwise a novel or startling enterprise.

As noted in Chapter 2, tax distribution tables are the standard tool for looking across groups at the same time. The tables are not very informative, however, if they fail to include all significant components of the fiscal system and offer only one-year snapshots. GA avoids these flaws by measuring net tax liabilities (gross taxes minus transfers), and by offering a long-term rather than an annual measure.

The president's annual budget briefly included GA estimates, but it ceased doing so during the Clinton Administration. Reportedly, senior officials found the estimates too embarrassing given the Clinton Administration's celebratory tone concerning budget surpluses. GA's proponents initially took up the slack by preparing and releasing their own estimates, but have not done so since 2001.

The political system's apparent rejection of GA is not a huge surprise. Bad news often prompts the impulse to shoot the messenger. GA has also, however, failed to win general acceptance among economists and budget experts. A key reason for its cool reception was that its chief proponent, Laurence Kotlikoff, vehemently argued that it should replace the budget deficit for all purposes. This claim aroused concern about all of the other deficit-related issues that GA does not even purport to measure, and about the political implications of using it. In particular, GA has been criticized for "offer[ing] opponents of government activism . . . [a] powerful trump card" by suggesting that programs such as Social Security and Medicare must be affordable not only today, but also into the indefinite future (Buchanan 2005, 282). This indeed was exactly the implication that Kotlikoff emphasized.

Analytically, the ideas of jointly considering taxes and transfers, and of looking at the long-term picture rather than just at one-year blocks, should be uncontroversial. Thus, even if one rejects GA as structured by its proponents, something sharing these features ought to be accepted as an informative distributional measure. This leaves considerable room to revisit GA's main design choices, including those that have undermined its acceptance.[1]

Several of the key design choices are as follows:

## Treatment of the Fiscal Gap

Suppose one is trying to measure the import of current policy if it continues indefinitely, rather than to predict what will actually happen. This is the most common use of distributional measures, since they typically are tools of policy analysis rather than, say, of personal financial planning. When projected outlays exceed projected inflows under current policy, estimators who are trying to project the policy forward into the indefinite future face a dilemma. If they ignore the shortfall, they may give an unrealistically rosy picture, in effect assuming that there is a free lunch to be had in the form of government outlays that no one has to pay for. If instead they try to predict how the shortfall will be addressed, they have then switched from measuring current policy to predicting how it will change.

Lacking a better solution, GA estimators typically use the concededly unrealistic assumption that the entire burden of eliminating the fiscal gap will fall on future generations, defined as people not yet born. This is not meant as a forecast, and would be questionable if it were. However, so long as one is trying to measure the distributional effects of current policy, rather than to predict actual future policy, it is hard to see what else one could logically do. It would be anomalous to credit Congress with politically painful decisions, as yet unmade, to burden current voters. Moreover, delay in addressing the shortfall does indeed tend to leave it to future generations.

While the usual GA treatment of the fiscal shortfall therefore makes sense compared to the alternatives, it unfortunately has proved confusing. The problem is that it effectively creates a shotgun marriage, within GA estimates, between (1) simply projecting cash flows under current policy and (2) seeming to assume a change in policy that looks, to the untutored eye, like a prediction. GA's prospects for general political acceptance have been seriously compromised by the apparent inconsistency, although analytically there should be no problem so long as users understand the convention and its rationale.

## Use of an Infinite Time Horizon

The assumption that the fiscal gap under current policy must be eliminated is not logically necessary unless one uses an infinite time horizon. For any finite time period, the government can use loans that remain outstanding at the end of the period. Thus, if one used a finite period in making GA estimates, there would be no need to assume that someone must be assigned the burdens that current policy leaves unaddressed.

The use of an infinite time horizon for *any* estimating purpose is controversial, and I discuss it later in this chapter in connection with measures of policy sustainability. With respect to GA, it is enough to note that the rationale for using an infinite time horizon depends on *whose* net taxes and lifetime net tax rates one is trying to measure. If one is interested in a measure that applies to all future generations (suggesting that one has already accepted infinite-horizon thinking), then its use is logically unavoidable. By contrast, if one is interested only in age cohorts up to a given cutoff point, assignment of the fiscal gap to any of them can be avoided. Thus, for example, to make GA estimates for present generations plus future ones born no later than, say, the year 2020, one can simply project the current rules forward and assume that the fiscal gap will be eliminated later still.

This would simplify the GA presentation, in the sense that one would no longer seem to be assuming future policies that are not actually specified in current policy. On the other hand, it would risk being misleading in a different way. Even short of adopting an infinite time horizon, an unaddressed fiscal shortfall surely is relevant, and affects the probable direction of policy change even for the near-term age cohorts one is considering.

## Examining One Set of Policies versus Comparing Two Sets

The GA methodology can be used, not only to provide distributional information about a single set of policies, but also to compare two different sets. Joseph Antos and Jagadeesh Gokhale (2003) offered a comparative measure of this kind during the Medicare prescription drug debate. They found that, if the proposed new benefit were fully and contemporaneously tax-financed through a payroll tax increase, it would impose a loss averaging $7,000 per person on those born after 1964 (with the youngest losing the most), while transferring on average more than $10,000 per person to people over age fifty-six.

The main dilemma in devising such a measure, underlying Antos and Gokhale's counterfactual assumption that the drug benefit was being financed, is how to deal with changes the fiscal gap. Under the usual GA convention of assigning the entire fiscal gap to future generations, those now living will always appear to win on balance when the fiscal gap increases, and to lose when it declines. While this is accurate enough as a description of the law now on the books, it could be criticized on either of two grounds, both of which relate to political as distinct from analytical uses of the measure.

First, if you want to discourage burden shifting to future gener-ations, treating increases in the fiscal gap as a benefit to all current voters points in the wrong direction. It also is potentially misleading if one does not explain the offsetting loss. Second, if a comparative measure aims to illuminate how people are likely to be affected by the underlying choice – as distinct from the "where are we headed?" question that might be central when we look just at one set of policies – then assuming that future generations will bear the whole cost might be misleadingly optimistic from the standpoint of current voters. Younger people in particular might be likely to pay for at least some portion of reversing the new enactment's effect on the fiscal gap.

While one does not want to foster the false impression that a free lunch is available, the Antos–Gokhale solution is not entirely satisfying either. People might reasonably ask why the computation treats them as paying higher taxes immediately, when in fact they are not being asked to do so.

The problem has no perfect solution, given the difficulty of predicting how future policy is likely to change by reason of a current enactment that changes the fiscal gap. My own suggestion is to emphasize two measures in public policy discussion. The first would state the per-person effect, in dollar terms, on members of future generations under the usual GA convention of assigning them the entire fiscal gap. This might help to make more salient the effect that an unaddressed fiscal gap can have on future generations. The second measure would assume deferred enactment of the unstated financing, in the manner of Antos and Gokhale but with, say, a five-year time lag.

## Lifetime versus Going-Forward Measure

GA-style estimates, whether of one set of policies or comparing two sets, need not take account of people's entire lives. The use of any shorter period is technically feasible. One reason for using a lifetime measure is that the use of a shorter period can be misleading. Thus, suppose that, on a lifetime basis, my Social Security payroll taxes greatly exceeded the value of my Social Security retirement benefits. If we measured the system's impact on me from age sixty-five on, we might be misled into thinking that I was a big winner. However, when we are comparing two sets of policies, such as present law versus a proposed change, a purely going-forward measure may focus on what many people really want to know, which is how they would be affected from now on.

## Dollar versus Percentage-of-Income Measure

As already noted, GA can be used to provide either lifetime net taxes or lifetime net tax rates for the average member of a particular group. The former is expressed in dollars, and the latter in percentage terms. While either form can be used, the percentage form provides greater context and thus is generally more meaningful. For example, a $3 million lifetime net tax payment may sound higher than it really is if I pay it out of $10 million in lifetime income.

On the other hand, for purposes of comparing two sets of policies, a statement in dollar terms may be more politically salient. Thus, recall the Antos–Gokhale finding that the package of changes they estimated would cost people born after 1964 an average of $7,000 each. Putting the measure in percentage-of-income terms might have made it harder to grasp. For this purpose, the fixed-dollar measure of going-forward effects may provide enough context, since people can judge it against what they know about their resources.

## Conclusions Regarding Generational Measures

For those who are willing to brave infinite-horizon estimates, two measures of the generational effects of long-term budgeting seem best. First, to provide analytically useful information, GA under existing practice, computed on a lifetime basis in percentage-of-income terms and with the fiscal gap assigned to future generations, seems best.

Second, to inform public debate concerning proposed enactments that would have major generational effects, a going-forward measure stated in dollar terms might be best. For unfinanced proposals, this might include a per-person cost estimate for future generations if they end up paying the entire thing, plus estimates for current generations under one or more plausible deferred-financing scenarios. As a further detail, such estimates might be offered for a few different living groups with specified age cutoffs. Just as an example, they might be offered for children up to age eighteen, young adults through age thirty-five, middle-aged adults through age sixty-five, and seniors above age sixty-five.[2]

## Macroeconomic Effects of Budgetary Policy

Keynesian countercyclical policy is premised on the idea that consumers are myopic or else liquidity-constrained, and thus tend to spend more when the government hands them extra cash even if a rational long-term planner would anticipate repaying the cash with interest in the future. This premise makes the short-term focus of the deficit more justifiable here than in other settings. However, the best time horizon to use is not necessarily a single year, but rather depends on the time frame being used by the people whose behavior one is trying to affect or predict. Suppose, for example, that we think the average consumer looks only at current-year cash flows, but that borrowers and lenders look five or ten years down the road. This would suggest using a current-year deficit measure in gauging consumer demand–side stimulative effects, and a five- or ten-year deficit measure in projecting effects on interest rates.

Public attention to a current or even a five- to ten-year deficit measure has two disadvantages, however. The first is that it can encourage misguided attempts to engage in discretionary stimulus. The second is that keeping deficits at center stage, without sufficient public understanding of how different purposes may call for different measures, invites submerging all of the other issues, such as generational distribution and policy sustainability, whenever our national economic output arguably lies below the attainable low-inflation optimum.

## Measures That Might be Useful in Restraining the Growth of Government

For conservatives who believe that strong political forces tend to produce undesirable government growth, the challenge of restraining this tendency may bring to mind squeezing a gob of Jello. Push it in over here, and it may simply start to bulge out over there. Thus, if you limit the growth of programs that rely on direct cash outlays, possibly all you will accomplish is shifting the center of action to the regulatory realm. Still, the approach of restraining one route at a time may potentially pay off. After all, if Route A is politically the easiest way to expand the government's reach, then blocking it may help even if there is a shift to Route B.

This line of thought may explain the view among small-government conservatives, from the 1970s through the late 1990s, that deficit reduction could restrain the growth of government. It presumably underlies as well the more recent "starve the beast" philosophy of cutting taxes without regard to deficits. As we saw in Chapter 2, the "starve the beast" idea reflects a basic naïvete about the relationship between fiscal language and underlying realities. By defining "tax cuts" as good and "spending increases" as bad, based purely on form, it confuses labels with substance. In addition, by supporting current tax cuts in exchange for future tax increases and benefit cuts, it can lead to increased redistribution and economic distortion.

Deficit reduction has neither of these flaws. For example, it treats a $10 billion net revenue loss the same way whether labeled as a "tax cut" or as a "spending increase." It also potentially moves in the direction of reducing transfers from future to current generations. The problem with using deficit reduction as a proxy for shrinking the size of government lies in its other flaws – in particular, its short-term focus and susceptibility to labeling with respect to the definition of "debt principal." Thus, the "starve the beast" idea should be replaced, not by a return to deficit aversion as such, but instead by using GA to measure generational transfers, along with the sustainability measures that I discuss next.

## Measuring Policy Sustainability

When we ask whether current budgetary policy is sustainable, we may have a number of different questions in mind. Is there currently a long-term fiscal shortfall? How big is it? Is it likely to become a serious political or economic problem? If so, when? How painful might the fixes be? How important is it to address the shortfall sooner rather than later?

This plethora of possible questions suggests that no single measure will be best for all purposes. And some of the questions, such as those concerning the seriousness of the long-term political problem and the painfulness of the fix, are qualitative rather than susceptible to precise measurement.

Perhaps the most straightforward of these questions concerns the size of the shortfall under current policy. Chapter 2 defined the fiscal gap as "current federal debt held by the public plus the present value of all projected federal non-interest spending, minus [the present value of] all projected federal receipts" (Gokhale and Smetters 2003, 2). While I kept it simple at that point, the design of a measure quantifying the shortfall requires making a number of choices.

## 1) Stock versus Flow

In present budgetary practice, the national debt is a "stock" measure, like the amount one owes on a mortgage. The deficit is a "flow" measure, like annual mortgage payments. A fiscal gap stated as a number, such as $68 trillion, is a stock measure, stating a present value in today's dollars for the sum of the current national debt plus all future net non-interest outlays by the government.[3] One can also state the fiscal gap as a flow measure, however.

Alan Auerbach (1994) proposed a flow measure that would instead provide the constant share of gross domestic product (GDP) by which the government's net inflows would have to increase immediately in order to make our fiscal policy sustainable.[4] Thus, in 2002, under certain assumptions about future policy, the estimated U.S. fiscal gap stood at 11.07 percent of GDP (Auerbach, Gale, and Orszag 2002, Table 4). Given that GDP at the time was $10.45 trillion, this suggested that the "flow" fiscal gap, stated in dollars, was $1.16 trillion per year, indexed to GDP and thus growing at the same rate.

Analytically, the choice between stock and flow measures is less important than that between absolute and scaled measures (discussed next). However, the stock measure has the political-salience advantage of being different enough from the budget deficit to require less comparative explanation. It also provides an attention-grabbing huge number. "Fiscal Gap Now $85 Trillion" is not an unimaginable newspaper headline.

## 2) Absolute versus Scaled

Both stock and flow measures can be stated either in absolute dollar terms or as a percentage of gross domestic product (GDP). Thus, the Auerbach measure, while I restated it in dollars, is actually set forth as a percentage of GDP. The stock fiscal gap can likewise be stated as a percentage of the present value of all expected future GDP. For example, if it is $65.9 trillion and the present value of GDP is $790.7 trillion (Gokhale and Smetters 2005), it can be restated as 8.6 percent of GDP.

A measure that is scaled to GDP is better analytically for two reasons. First, it offers more meaningful information, just as we would know more about an individual's debt burden if we knew her expected earning stream. A million-dollar debt might be crippling to one person and easily affordable by another. The same holds for a $5 trillion as opposed to a $50 trillion economy. Second, scaling reduces the measure's volatility in the face of changing assumptions about the discount rate or the growth rate of GDP, by causing effects on both numerator and denominator in the debt-over-GDP equation.

From the standpoint of political salience, however, absolute measures have a huge advantage. Percentages are too abstract to attract comparable public attention. "Fiscal Gap Now 11.07 Percent of GDP" is not easily imaginable as a newspaper headline. So absolute dollar amounts, whether stated as stocks or flows, are clearly more useful politically than scaled measures, albeit less meaningful analytically. This suggests that absolute and scaled measures should both be used, each in the domain where it is best.

## 3) Infinite Horizon versus Bounded Period

One of the biggest concerns people have about an infinite-horizon fiscal gap measure is that it requires express assumptions about the distant future. How can we possibly say, for example, what will be going on in the year 2095, or for that matter in the year 39,614? And why do we even care, given how little we can know today about periods that lie so far in the future?

This line of argument fails to address an important point. Since we discount future cash flows to their present value anyway, it makes little difference what we assume today will be happening in the year 39,614. Even the year 2095 does not matter much in present-value terms. The main point of infinite-horizon forecasting is simply to avoid the arbitrariness of establishing a specific cutoff that serves to limit the future periods that we take into account. Thus, under the seventy-five-year cutoff that the Social Security trustees typically use, there is a sudden jump as between the treatment of year seventy-five and year seventy-six, because the former is merely discounted to present value while the latter is completely ignored. This can result in the oxymoronic phenomenon that I call "predictable shocks." These are dramatic declines of our apparent long-term fiscal position that occur, even in the absence of any material new information, simply because future years that previously were outside the budget window have now moved inside.

Predictable shocks are perverse because they reflect a failure to make use of available information. In comparing any future year X to year X + 1, it is hard to see why we would ever care, or expect to know, absolutely more about the former than the latter. A constant discount rate, without arbitrary truncation, does justice to this point.

The main reason for the current controversiality of an infinite-horizon method is political. When the out years have a definite expected character that is large enough, people whose policy views are set back by calling the long-term fiscal problem large, rather than small, inevitably object. Nor does it help that people who prefer the infinite horizon in settings where it suits their interests drop it like a hot potato as soon as it points the other way.

A good illustration came during the debate in early 2005 concerning President Bush's Social Security reform plan. The Bush Administration insisted on using the infinite-horizon Social Security fiscal gap, which exceeded $10 trillion, rather than the conventional seventy-five-year horizon, under which it was only about $4 trillion. Foes of the Bush plan objected, arguing that it was ridiculous to look more than seventy-five years out.

As soon as the Administration was looking at tax reform rather than Social Security reform, things changed. The President's Tax Reform Panel, instructed to devise revenue-neutral plans, followed Treasury Department practice by looking only ten years down the road. The two plans that the panel issued, while complying with the president's directive within the ten-year window, included a number of proposals with highly back-loaded costs, suggesting that the plans would lose trillions of dollars over the infinite horizon (Shaviro 2005, 828). While the Bush Administration backed away from the plans due to their lack of political appeal, we can be confident both that it would not have been put off by the long-term revenue loss, and that its opponents would suddenly have discovered an interest in looking further down the road.

In a saner and less partisan world, perhaps the parties would be able to agree on a single time frame to be used consistently whether it benefited one side or the other. They might even agree to look both at the infinite horizon and at some shorter period of at least several decades.

## 4) How Should We Project Future Economic and Demographic Trends?

Under current long-term budgetary practice, such as the reports of the Social Security and Medicare trustees, informed experts make economic and demographic projections, fortunately without significant political interference.[5]

Inevitably, projections are speculative, but this does not make them entirely fanciful. Consider life expectancy, which has been rising in the United States for decades, reflecting improvements in medical technology and in people's diet, exercise, and smoking habits. For similar reasons, life expectancy has been rising in affluent countries around the world, and in many countries (such as Japan) it is notably higher than it is in the United States. Thus, there is good reason to predict a continuing increase. On the other hand, perhaps adverse factors are pushing against longer life expectancies, such as rising levels of obesity and environmental degradation. Demographic experts can examine all of this information and make projections that we may reasonably regard as having predictive value despite the remaining radical uncertainty.

Even though such projections are inevitably highly uncertain, they provide a reasonable midpoint estimate if the uncertainty is symmetric – that is, if a projection appears equally likely to err in one direction as in the other. Indeed, an estimate that is uncertain by reason of what appears to be symmetric risk should not be discounted relative to one that is 100 percent certain to be exactly correct. Thus, suppose the fiscal gap was estimated at \$60 trillion, but actually was certain to be either \$120 trillion or zero, with equal probability. If we are risk-averse, as people generally are, the double-or-nothing uncertainty should make us *more* concerned than if we knew the estimate was spot-on – not less concerned (Auerbach and Hassett 2002).

## 5) How Should We Project Future Policy?

Projections of future policy, for purposes of fiscal gap estimates, differ significantly from projections of future economic and demographic trends. Here, the aim often is not actually to predict future policy, but to say what current policy would imply doing in the future. This makes the law on the books an obvious starting point.

An immediate problem arises, however. Congress sets the law on the books, whereas it has generally avoided telling the economic and demographic experts what to assume. The power to have the law on the books for future years state rules that are not actually intended or expected to take effect thus offers an easy route to game playing. The recent tax cuts' scheduled sunsets, which congressional leaders loudly insisted would never be allowed to take effect, is a good illustration.

Alan Auerbach (2004, 3) notes another recent example of this problem, less crass but also in a sense less excusable, as it arose in an ostensibly nonpartisan setting:

> In January 1997, Social Security's quadrennial advisory council issued a report... laying out three options for achieving solvency. One of these proposals... would have closed part of the 75-year gap using an increase in the payroll tax of 1.6 percentage points, starting in *2045*!

Clearly, this was not a policy to be taken seriously, as it specified a tax increase beginning only 50 years hence. . . .

More generally, deferred adverse changes (such as spending cuts and tax increases) to applicable current-year law inherently have credibility problems. They invite manipulation, and do not seem likely to err as symmetrically as one would expect of good faith economic and demographic estimates.

In response to this concern, Auerbach (2004) examines how credibility problems might affect the "optimal budget window" for official use in congressional budgeting. He suggests extra discounting of future expected cash flows, beyond that reflecting the interest rate, to "reflect[] two factors: that policies announced for the future are not certain to take effect and, if they do, that their impact will be felt more by those [i.e., future generations] whom budget rules are intended to protect."

This does not distinguish between future changes specified in present law that are (1) adverse as opposed to favorable, or (2) discontinuous as opposed to continuous. Both distinctions can be illustrated by contrasting the supposed payroll tax increase that the advisory council suggested for 2045 with the rule, under existing Social Security law, that new retirees' initial benefit levels must be indexed to wage growth during their working years. The latter change is continuous rather than discontinuous, since it is supposed to be made regularly rather than once in the distant future. And it is favorable rather than unfavorable, because it increases benefits rather than taxes.

Given these differences, wage indexing of retirement benefits is more credible, as a statement of currently intended policy, than a 2045 tax increase. This is not to say whether we believe wage indexing will actually be affordable down the road. The point, rather, is that getting rid of it would be a genuine policy change, whereas deciding not to raise the tax in 2045 might not be. Accordingly, instead of applying extra discounting to future years as Auerbach suggests, one might instead disregard adverse discontinuous changes for purposes of official estimates.

## Different Purposes to be Served
## by Sustainability Measures

With this background, we can turn to the issue of what different questions a long-term sustainability measure might be designed to answer. At least three possible questions seem worth addressing. The first is the size of the fiscal gap. I suggested earlier that the stock fiscal gap, stated in dollars, provides the most politically salient measure of the shortfall, while its statement as a percentage of all future GDP offers the most analytically meaningful measure.

A second question is what degree of risk of default or other severe disruption we actually face, along with when the risk would be greatest. This cannot easily be measured, since it depends on what Congress does, and on what investors expect it to do, as the gap between receipts and outlays keeps increasing. One way of trying to get a rough handle on it is to estimate the fiscal gap by program (such as Social Security, Medicare, and defense spending), based on the assumption that each will keep its current share of general revenues. In terms of the likely timing of a crisis, it may be useful to project the expected course of the explicit debt-to-annual-GDP ratio over time. The faster this rises, the sooner a problem is likely to emerge if investors are myopic (or expect others to be).

A third issue worth examining is to what degree we are losing policy options over time by delaying any course correction. The social welfare costs of delay, while ultimately of greatest interest, are bound to be difficult to quantify, although econometric modelers could give it a try. There are also, however, two proxy measures that can be used to quantify something about the significance of delay. Both were first suggested, albeit solely with regard to Social Security, by David Kamin and Richard Kogan (2004).

To illustrate the first measure suggested by Kamin and Kogan, which I call the *percentage cost of delay*, one can start by thinking of the "GDP base" on which taxes can be increased and/or benefits cut, consisting of current-year and all expected future GDP. At any given moment, the GDP base has a measurable present value if one applies assumed growth and discount rates. Thus, in 2004, when GDP was

$11.735 trillion, the estimated present value of the GDP base was $762.9 trillion (Gokhale and Smetters 2005). Comparing the first of these numbers to the second, GDP in 2004 equaled 1.5 percent of the value of the GDP base.

The year 2004 went by without Congress's taking any steps to reduce the fiscal gap. One could view this inaction as tantamount to exempting 2004 GDP from being burdened by the corrective measures that would ultimately be necessary. This is similar to a case where, within a single year, Congress exempts 1.5 percent of the potential tax base from being burdened by legislation that has to meet a given net revenue target. The result, in both cases, is that higher taxes are necessary on the rest of the base because a portion has been exempted.[6]

Again, the percentage cost of delay is simply current year GDP divided by the GDP base. Unfortunately, the statement one makes by saying that the percentage cost of delay for 2004 was 1.5 percent may be hard to grasp intuitively. One way of making it a bit clearer is the following. Suppose that, as of mid-2004, a scaled measure of the fiscal gap had placed it at 10 percent of the GDP base. Then the passage of a year with no corrective action and no new information would have raised it to 10.15 percent of the GDP base. One can then continue to project forward how the scaled fiscal gap would continue to increase over time in the absence of congressional action.

In applying this measure, what matters is not when corrective policy changes are announced (even if they are credible), but when they take effect. Thus, suppose that Congress, on January 1, 2006, had completely eliminated the fiscal gap, through credible and genuine tax increases and benefit cuts that would take effect starting on January 1, 2007. Apart from providing greater notice, this would have been no different than waiting until 2007 to enact as well as implement the changes. Either way, 2006 activities would not be directly burdened (although people might try to shift economic activity forward to that year). What is more, these changes would have to raise a net amount equal to 10.15 percent of the GDP base from 2007 on, whereas the burden could have been kept at 10 percent had 2006 activities been included.

From the standpoint of political salience, this measure faces the usual objection of not being stated in absolute-dollar terms. Kamin and Kogan (2005) therefore suggest multiplying the percentage cost of delay by the amount of the GDP base. Thus, failing to act in 2006 would "cost" 0.15 percent of a GDP base worth $762.9 trillion, or $1.14 trillion. This amount, which I call the *notional dollar cost of delay*, requires careful explanation as well. Even under the assumed facts, $1.14 trillion has not actually been lost. Rather, the burden on GDP for 2007 and all subsequent years has increased by $1.14 trillion relative to the case where all post-2005 GDP shared equally in the burden, possibly leading to an as-yet-unmeasured (but possibly much smaller) efficiency cost.

The confusion that can result from misusing these concepts was well illustrated by President Bush's suggestion, during the 2005 Social Security debate, that failing to adopt his plan immediately would "cost" $600 billion. Bush was right that the Social Security fiscal gap, as estimated by the Social Security trustees over the infinite horizon, was expected to increase by that amount during the year. However, giving that no adverse benefit changes would take effect any time soon, the true cost of delay in adopting his plan, effects on uncertainty aside, was zero. Given this type of problem, perhaps both measures relating to the cost of delay are best reserved for analytical use.

## Summary of Measures

This chapter has reviewed a number of possible measures relating to the issues associated with concern about budget deficits. For political purposes, the main long-term measures worth using are:

1) the stock fiscal gap, stated in dollar terms, and
2) the generational transfer measure of proposed new enactments, with unfunded proposals being handled through estimates of the effect on
   a) future generations if no further financing is provided, and

b) children, young adults, the middle-aged, and the old if financing by some plausible method is introduced within a few years.

For analytical purposes, the list is as follows:

1) generational accounting;
2) budget deficits over a ten-year period, for purposes of evaluating possible macroeconomic effects;
3) the stock fiscal gap, stated as a percentage of infinite-horizon GDP;
4) the expected ratio of explicit public debt to current-year GDP over the next few decades; and
5) the percentage cost of delay.

# 6

## Fiscal Gap Politics

*Buzz: We're going to have us some real kicks. Little chickie-run. You been on chickie-runs before?*
*Jim: Sure – that's all I ever do.*
                                    – From *Rebel Without a Cause*

*Less! Bread! More! Taxes!*
                        – Crowd in Lewis Carroll, *Sylvie and Bruno*

*Mr. President, I'm not saying we wouldn't get our hair mussed. But I do say . . . no more than ten to twenty million killed, tops. Uh . . . depending on the breaks.*
                    – General Turgidson, in Stanley Kubrick's *Doctor Strangelove*

There can be no serious doubt that our current budgetary policy path places us at needless risk of a major fiscal meltdown. It remains unclear, however, whether such a "hard landing" is more likely or less likely than a scenario in which revenues and outlays adjust sooner and more gradually. This is in large part a question about our political system and its capacity to yield  mature and responsible policy decisions.

To understand the politics of narrowing the fiscal gap, a lot more is needed than just denunciation of the last few years of federal budgetary policy. I see the needed analysis as having five stages. First, what were the politics of creating the fiscal gap? Second, what led to the political consensus from 1982 through 2000 that favored deficit reduction and thus – however imperfectly, given the flaws in the measure – a narrowing of the fiscal gap? Third, why did that consensus collapse? Fourth, what must happen to permit the adoption of policies narrowing the fiscal gap? Finally, if the political preconditions for narrowing the fiscal gap were back in place, what sorts of budget rules could help keep Congress going in the right direction?

## The Politics of Creating a Large Fiscal Gap

### Fiscal Illusion and "Democracy in Deficit"?

In the 1970s and 1980s, budget deficits received enough attention to ensure that political scientists and others would spend a lot of time thinking about their causes. The first main theory to emerge, associated with the Nobel Prize–winning economist James Buchanan and others in the "Virginia school" of political economy (Shaviro 1997, 87–103), stressed fiscal illusion, or the view that debt financing dupes voters by lowering the perceived cost of government spending. Voters would continually approve even wasteful government spending that was not currently tax-financed, the theory posited, because they would see the immediate benefits of the spending but would not see the deferred cost of repaying the debt. Hence we were said to face endemic "democracy in deficit" (Buchanan and Wagner 1977), and the same gloomy prospects for hyperinflation and fiscal collapse that I have been warning about in this book.

As Buchanan and his colleagues saw things, fiscal illusion was so powerful a force in promoting deficit financing that the great mystery was why the United States and other leading democracies had not yet neared fiscal collapse, and indeed had consistently avoided significant budget deficits except in times of war or severe recession. The best explanation they could offer was that an unexplained moral sentiment of deficit aversion had kept the consequences of fiscal illusion in check until the sentiment was destroyed by Lord Keynes and his followers, with their advocacy of deficits not just to ease recessions but to manage consumer demand and the business cycle on a continuous basis. Hence, the rise of Keynesianism had paved the way for fiscal collapse, which would now be hard to avoid without constitutional barriers such as a balanced budget amendment.

The theory that fiscal illusion makes a preference for debt financing inevitable took a hit in the late 1990s with the disappearance of U.S. budget deficits. Even well before that time, however, the theory was seemingly begging the question of why so many politicians in both parties were willing to take action, often bipartisan, to lower deficits, leading not just to spending restraint but to the adoption of significant tax increases in 1982, 1983, 1984, 1990, and 1993.

This is not to deny the importance of fiscal illusion in budgetary politics. Any doubters should try to explain why presidential candidates almost invariably propose new spending programs in excess of the new taxes that they are willing to advocate. But fiscal illusion cannot be blamed for very much of the current U.S. fiscal gap, or for the even larger fiscal gaps in many other industrialized nations. The United States could probably afford a long run of budget deficits that equaled a couple of percent of GDP. What makes the long-term picture so dire is the projected growth of Medicare, Social Security, and Medicaid, even without any new enactments from Congress liberalizing them. But if future benefits are the main problem, this cannot be blamed on fiscal illusion, which emphasizes the perceptual difference between current benefits and deferred costs. So fiscal illusion has a convincing defense against the charge of prime responsibility for our current straits. The victim has the wrong fingerprints.

## Interest Groups and the Diffusion of Political Power

An associated theory from the earlier era of budget deficits emphasizes the role of interest groups in a highly pluralistic society. As Mancur Olson (1965) famously showed, interest groups thrive, capturing concentrated benefits for themselves in exchange for imposing diffuse costs on everyone else, because they are better situated than the general public to overcome the costs of information and organization that pose barriers to collective action. For example, the oil industry is much more assiduous in seeking tax benefits for itself than the rest of the public is in resisting these special benefits, even though other taxpayers have to make up for the lost revenues. The "few" accordingly oppress the "many," although, if all of us are occasionally among the few, then the real cost to the society is that of the transfers' frequent inefficiency, along with the inducement to seek them in lieu of engaging in genuinely productive activity.

Interest group politics is believed by many to become even more problematic when a political system, like that in the United States, fails to centralize power in the manner of a two-party parliamentary system. The same party may not control the White House and both houses of Congress. Moreover, the power of the congressional leadership fluctuates over time. When it is weak, as was generally the case between the early 1970s and the early 1990s, interest groups may benefit from the need for extensive logrolling to assemble majority coalitions. Each free-agent legislator who ends up joining the coalition may exact as his price a couple of favors for groups of his choice. Weak political parties, such as we have often had in the United States, may also lead to stronger interest groups. Strong parties may operate as cartels that exercise enough leverage to keep any one wayward interest group in line, even if they depend on interest group coalitions to hold political power.

The link between this problem and budget deficits is that debt financing for current payouts to interest groups offers one way to create diffuse costs in exchange for concentrated benefits. The unannounced future taxes that debt financing implies are almost inevitably diffuse in their discernible incidence, since until they are announced just about anyone could end up bearing them. For this reason, it has been argued that strengthening the political parties and/or the congressional leadership's control of the legislative process would be an important step toward making fiscal restraint possible (see Shaviro 1997, 300–301).

Again, the theory has some force but has been poorly served by recent events. If interest group politics in a pluralistic society were the big fiscal problem, we would expect death by a thousand small cuts, such as pork barrel projects and special industry handouts, rather than mainly through the long-term impact of Medicare, Social Security, and Medicaid. Moreover, the fiscal policies of George W. Bush have been adopted in about as quasi-parliamentary a fashion as one could imagine. The White House secured huge tax cuts and spending increases through party discipline enforced by the congressional leadership. The main effect of such limited member-level discretion as there was in Congress went in the direction of *reducing* the adverse fiscal impact. For example, a handful of moderate Senate Republicans succeeded in reducing the size of the  tax cuts in 2003. Thus, the main villain was not diffuse interest group politics but highly centralized leadership – inherently a black box, rather than a force necessarily pushing for greater restraint, until we specify or learn what the leaders want.

## Political Competition and Budget Deficits

A small but interesting political economy literature explores how political competition between parties or groups can lead to the creation of large budget deficits even if all actors view deficits as undesirable and thus would avoid imposing them if permanently and unilaterally in control of budgetary policy. Among the main results in the literature, reflecting a combination of theoretical modeling and empirical testing across countries and subnational units such as the American states, are the following:

1) "[I]n the presence of disagreement between current and future policymakers, public debt is used strategically by each government to influence the choice of its successors" (Alesina and Tabellini 1990, 404). Thus, if one party prefers military spending while the other prefers entitlement spending, each has reason to debt-finance its preferred choice while temporarily in power, so that the other party will be too bound up in paying off the previous period's debt to do as much of its own new spending. Alesina and Tabellini find that the use of this strategy should be increased by: (1) greater political polarization, which raises the stakes; (2) an increase in the likelihood that the current government will lose power soon, before the bills come due; and (3) greater downward rigidity of public spending programs (i.e., greater difficulty in curtailing them once set in motion).

2) Relatedly, "we should observe sustained budget deficits whenever a government with extreme preferences relative to the historic average wins the temporary support of a majority of the voters"

(Tabellini and Alesina 1990, 47). The idea here is that you have more reason to try to bind your successors if history suggests that their preferences are likely to differ sharply from your own.

3) Where there are liberal and conservative parties, distinguished by the liberal party's preference for larger and not merely differently allocated spending on public programs, the more conservative party may incur deficits in order to force its liberal successor to spend less (Persson and Svensson 1989). In effect, this is the "starve the beast" idea, coupled with the usual (and questionable) association between government spending and the allocative size of government. By contrast, the liberal party may be inclined to leave behind a budget surplus so that future spending constraints will be relaxed instead of being made more stringent. This claim seems startlingly prescient today in light of the post-publication budgetary history of the Clinton and George W. Bush Administrations.

4) When an enduring shock disrupts the federal budget, leading to persistent deficits until the course of fiscal policy is changed, a "war of attrition" between rival parties or other groups may delay the adoption of any new, deficit-correcting course (Alesina and Drazen 1991). Dispute over how the cost of the adjustment should be allocated may encourage groups whose consent is needed to hold out, in the hope that rival groups, recognizing that the adjustment gets costlier for everyone the longer it is delayed, will give in first.

Another term for Alesina and Drazen's war of attrition, familiar to game theory aficionados and movie fans, would be a "chicken game." Formally speaking, a chicken game is a strategic interaction between two parties in which each does best by "defecting" while the other "cooperates," but both do worst if both defect (Baird, Gertner, and Picker 1994, 303–304). Perhaps the best-known example of a chicken game occurs in the movie *Rebel without a Cause,* when Jim, the James Dean character, is challenged by tough guy Buzz to see which of them can act more fearlessly in driving a stolen car off a cliff. Whoever jumps out last, as they both send their cars over the cliff, is the winner. Hence, each driver does best if he "defects" from pursuing their mutual interest in staying alive by waiting for the other driver to jump out first, so long as the other party "cooperates" by jumping out early. But they both do worst of all if they both defect. As it happens in the movie, Jim waits until almost the last second to jump out of his car. Buzz goes over the cliff and dies when his door handle catches.

While each of these four explanations has a lot to offer, they do not, at least without further elaboration, explain as much of the current U.S. fiscal situation as one might like. First, even looking just at effects on the current budget deficit, which is the explanations' main focus, they leave one wondering why both of the major U.S. political parties have sometimes changed their stripes between periods. Second, the explanations need to be supplemented by a fuller sense of intraparty dynamics, reflecting the fact that both major parties typically have both anti-deficit and pro-deficit factions. Third and perhaps most importantly, the explanations once again have the wrong fingerprints, given the central role that the entitlement programs, with their projected future rather than current operating deficits, have played in creating the worrisome long-term fiscal situation that we now face.

## "Greedy Geezers?"

This leaves us with the "greedy geezers" explanation, emphasizing the rise of the elderly as a single-issue voting bloc focused on the entitlement programs. Here, the suspect's fingerprints are indeed all over the crime scene, given the role of Medicare and Social Security in creating a huge fiscal gap. Yet the story is more nuanced than this may seem to suggest. Until enactment of the unfunded Medicare prescription drug benefit in 2003, the main adverse influence of seniors as an interest group has merely been in blocking needed reform – not in creating the problem, which has a more innocent provenance.

To see this, let's return to 1935 and 1965, when Social Security and Medicare respectively were enacted. On both occasions, liberal Democratic presidents with overwhelming public support and huge congressional majorities were determined to create huge new programs that would provide benefits to then-current seniors. This, by the way, was a far more justifiable goal back then, when seniors were not nearly so affluent relative to younger Americans as they are today.

In 1935, the Great Depression had left many retirees with inadequate retirement resources. In 1965, the dramatic growth of the health care sector (only twenty years past the general spread of antibiotics) had caught many seniors by surprise, leaving them unprepared for their retirement health care needs.

But Franklin Roosevelt in 1935 and Lyndon Johnson in 1965 were determined to do more than just provide benefits to seniors. They wanted to create programs that would become lasting fixtures on the American political and economic landscape, and they understood that this required credible financing.

The solution adopted by both administrations was pay-as-you-go financing, through the use of dedicated new tax revenues to pay for Social Security and Part A of Medicare.[1] This handed then-current seniors a free benefit, since they were already retired and workers were the ones paying the taxes. But it was not unreasonable, either in 1935 or in 1965, to think that the financing was indefinitely sustainable, or even that it would be actuarially fair once the gift to the earliest participants was off the books.

Paul Samuelson (1958) famously explained the logic of Social Security's pay-as-you-go financing, which seemed to violate the no-free-lunch principle by giving the first group of retirees free benefits and then treating everyone else fairly. Why was this not inherently subject to collapse, like a Ponzi scheme? As I have noted elsewhere:

> Samuelson's basic idea can be explained as follows. Suppose initially, for simplicity, that each age cohort consists of the same number of individuals. Everyone lives for two equal periods: a work period and a retirement period. The society's demographics are therefore fixed: neither birth levels nor life expectancies ever change. . . .
>
> Under these circumstances, Samuelson pointed out, the workers of all generations might benefit from the adoption of the following program. The members of Generation 1 (retirees when the program is adopted) are supported at retirement by the proceeds of a permanently fixed, flat-rate payroll tax that first applies to the members of Generation 2. Those individuals, in turn, are supported at retirement by the proceeds from levying this tax on the members of Generation 3, and so on going forward indefinitely. So long as workers' earnings (which

make up the tax base) continually grow, each taxpaying generation ends up getting back more than it put in. Since workers are paid for the value of what they produce, these earnings increase over time at the rate of productivity growth (Shaviro 2004, 80–81).

Samuelson emphasized that such a scheme was feasible not only mathematically, leaving only the very last working generation to lose, but also politically. Reneging, through the refusal of a given generation of workers to support retirees, would not be a problem because each generation "would realize . . . that, if they reneged, the next generation would not pay them, whereas if they met their obligation then the next generation would face the same choice that they now did" (81).

Vital to Samuelson's conclusion of perpetual sustainability was his conviction that the ratio of workers to retirees – eternally fixed in his model by express assumption – would in fact rise, owing to population growth, if it changed at all. A rising worker-to-retiree ratio means that seniors can get even more without increasing the burden on each worker. He failed to consider, however, that rising life expectancies would cause worker-to-retiree ratios to get smaller, rather than larger, despite population growth. In the world of the Samuelson model, everyone lives for one work period and one retirement period. But in the real world, seniors who live longer collect more years of Social Security benefits. And while we surely should be glad that they are living longer, this is "bad news" fiscally, eventually requiring tax increases or benefit cuts. This resurrects the political sustainability problem that Samuelson thought had been solved. "Deciding how to respond to these [demographic] shocks is considerably more discretionary than just going along with a fixed program in place. As soon as demographic risk requires or invites tinkering with the system's parameters, the self-interest problem is back in full force" (Shaviro 2004, 85).

Medicare is the same story in spades, with the added factor of technological risk related to health care expenditure levels. Since seniors get a defined benefit, the cost of which depends on prevailing treatment options and norms, financing on Samuelson's model in effect places a bet that health care expenditures on seniors will not grow at a faster rate than the economy (or, more specifically, the wage base of the payroll tax). Given the healthcare sector's rate of growth, Medicare would have gotten into fiscal trouble even without the "bad luck" of increasing life expectancies.

We have, therefore, the outlines of a kind of tragedy without villains. It seems almost inevitable, in retrospect, that modern economies would have discovered retirement benefits as a natural area for government intervention. Retirees often do not save enough, and once they get there it is too late to ask them to help themselves. The decision to use pay-as-you-go financing also seems close to inevitable, given its political convenience and (at the time) seeming prudence. Building up advance funding, in the manner of a prudent private-sector pension plan, would have required unrealistic faith both in voters (to wait that long for the benefits), and in politicians (to keep their hands off the accumulating funds). Even the fact that benefits were regularly increased in Social Security, from the 1950s through the early 1970s, is relatively understandable given how well the system was doing in short-term cash-flow terms, along with the lack at the time of fiscal-language tools for taking a more long-term perspective.

But having taken these seemingly quite logical steps, it should be no surprise that numerous systems around the world failed to respond appropriately to the life expectancy and health care trends that followed. So the United States, like many other countries, backed into today's bad state of affairs as a result of demographic and economic shocks to which our political system could not adequately respond.

## The Politics of Deficit Reduction

Before examining why the Republican leadership, during the George W. Bush Administration, lost interest in fiscal responsibility, we need to start with what is arguably the bigger puzzle: the preceding period of bipartisan consensus that deficits ought to be reduced. Why not, as a raw political matter, court voters with tax cuts and spending increases while merrily leaving the bills to be paid at some point in the future? Surely the Bush Administration did not contain the only political operatives savvy enough to figure this out.

Similarly, it is worth asking why administrations prior to that of the second President Bush did not more consistently pursue the strategy, described by Alesina and Tabellini (1990), of using debt financing to bind one's successors to following more of one's own preferred policies. Moreover, if conservative governments have reason to prefer debt financing in order to shackle their liberal successors, as Persson and Svensson (1989) suggest, then why did the Reagan Administration from 1982 onward, as well as the first Bush Administration, pursue deficit reduction?

Part of the answer is that, during these earlier periods, Republican and Democratic leaders alike seem actually to have believed in fiscal responsibility, whether based directly on a concern for good policy, or on the indirect political benefits of deficit reduction. Neither the Reagan Administration when it agreed to tax increases in 1982, 1983, and 1984, nor the George H.W. Bush Administration in 1990, nor the Clinton Administration in 1993 could have thought that raising taxes was politically popular as an end in itself. The political gain, if any, could arise only from aiding the economy and/or from being viewed by voters as responsible and effective. Reagan and the first President Bush, who cooperated with Democratic congressional leaders in bipartisan deficit reduction efforts, could also share with those leaders the political credit for avoiding political squabbling.

How can we understand these choices that are so different from those of the George W. Bush Administration? An initial point worth making is that political leaders often have genuine tactical choices to make, as opposed to just a series of forced moves. They must decide whether cooperation or confrontation is politically more fruitful (as well as more personally and ideologically congenial), in the face of good arguments for both courses. This, in turn, reflects the fact that politics is not entirely a zero-sum game between rival groups. Politically, both parties' leaders may benefit, relative to nonincumbents as well as incumbents who are relative outsiders, from showing that they can cooperate to get things done. Ideologically, cooperation may also pay off if the leaders' preferences, while different, are not directly opposite. For example, if policies A and B are not in direct conflict, and the Republicans like A more than they dislike B, while the Democrats like B more than they dislike A, a compromise can involve adopting both.

At the same time, politics clearly is in part a zero-sum game. Only one candidate can win an election; in a two-party system only one party at a time can control a legislature; and competing policy preferences often are directly in conflict. So there is a mix of zero-sum and positive-sum elements.

To be sure, even cooperating for mutual gain involves a zero-sum element, concerning how the gain is divided between the parties. The Alesina–Drazen scenario, in which rival parties delay the adoption of sustainability-restoring measures that are desirable for both on balance, is an example. If taxes must be raised to the Republicans' dismay, while entitlements must be cut to the Democrats' dismay, each party is understandably reluctant to offer concessions too fast. Chicken games are notorious for having no dominant strategy, defined as the one that is best no matter what the other party decides (Baird, Gertner, and Picker 1994, 306). The whole point is to bluff just enough but not too much, given the other party's state of mind. With imperfect information, however, the parties may miscalculate. Moreover, destroying a mutually beneficial deal may pay off down the road by giving one a credible reputation for obstinacy as a negotiator.

The tension between emphasizing tax increases versus entitlement cuts raises another tactical ambiguity. Democrats may gain political traction from demagoguing the Republicans on Social Security and Medicare, while the Republicans may gain traction from doing the same to the Democrats on taxes. Yet each party can easily observe whether the other party is demagoguing or not, and play tit for tat by following suit. If the political payoffs are unambiguous and the game is purely zero-sum, then the party that gains on balance from mutual demagoguery will pursue it, leaving the other party no choice but to cut its losses by reciprocating. But positive-sum elements or tactical ambiguity can make mutual forbearance a plausible outcome.

Tactical ambiguity gives politicians considerable discretion in deciding which approach to follow. Personal and ideological preferences may play a role in the choice, as may differing views about the political merits of alternative routes. Indeed, preferences often seem to influence probabilistic assessments, as in the case of left versus centrist Democrats, each arguing with apparent sincerity that their approach is the best way to regain power. However, even if individual politicians just follow their preferences, those who end up making the best political choices are the most likely to end up in control. So the equivalent of shrewd political calculation may emerge via an evolutionary process even to the extent that individual politicians do not calculate well.

From 1982 through 1990, Republican leaders, no less than Democrats, frequently chose to cooperate on budgetary policy. This approach manifested itself not only in the tax increases of 1982, 1983, 1984, and 1990, but also in a number of other major bipartisan enactments during this period. Prominent examples include the Gramm–Rudman–Hollings Act of 1985, establishing strict five-year deficit reduction targets backed by automatic sequester provisions; the Tax Reform Act of 1986, estimated as revenue-neutral but requiring bipartisan agreement; and the Medicare Catastrophic Coverage Act of 1988, creating new Medicare benefits for seniors that they were required to pay for, leading to its swift (and again bipartisan) repeal the following year after seniors protested. During this period, there certainly were Republicans who favored a more conservative and confrontational approach, but centrists such as James Baker, Richard Darman, and Bob Dole almost invariably got the upper hand.

Surely one important reason for this approach was that Presidents Reagan and George H. W. Bush never controlled both houses of Congress, so they could not easily enact anything unilaterally. Yet this is not a full explanation. Reagan, in particular, with his noted rhetorical and campaigning skills, could have declared an impasse and campaigned against the congressional Democrats, in the hope of getting his own way in the next session of Congress. And the first President Bush certainly was not averse to confronting Democratic leaders with harsh political rhetoric during the presidential campaign season.

A key motivation for the Republicans' cooperative strategy between 1982 and 1990 may have been the accepted wisdom about how to maximize one's public support and win elections. It has long been a truism that you run "right" in the primaries as a Republican, or "left" in the primaries as a Democrat, but then head to the center in

| Party A → | | | ← Party B | |
|---|---|---|---|---|
| 0 | 25 | 50 | 75 | 100 |

Figure 6.1. *Source*: Downs 1957, 117.

the general election and when governing. In the contemporary U.S. budgetary setting, the way to occupy the center is to embrace bipartisan compromise in lieu of playing chicken games too aggressively.

The reason why it long made sense to move to the center has been modeled in the economic and political science literature. Anthony Downs (1957), building on the work of Harold Hotelling (1929), laid the groundwork for what is called the spatial theory of political competition, explaining why a two-party electoral system might be prone to yielding competing candidates who, as George Wallace famously complained in the 1960s, had "not a dime's worth of difference" between them.

Hotelling began by imagining a set of people equally distributed across a horizontal scale from point 0 at the left side to point 100 at the right side, as shown in Figure 6.1. In one straightforward application of the model, these might be geographical locations containing people's homes; the question is where each of two shops should locate in order to get the most business, if consumers prefer to shop as close to home as possible. In the political application, left and right are interpreted ideologically, with voters supporting whichever party is closest to their position.

As Downs (1957, 117) explains, the logic of two-party political competition under these circumstances should induce the parties to "converge on the same location until practically all voters are indifferent between them." Here, if the median voter is at point 50 on the scale, with half "residing" on either side, then 50 is where the parties would be expected to converge. The mechanism, if the parties start out, say, at points 25 and 75, is that "each party knows that extremists at its end of the scale prefer it to the opposition, since it necessarily is closer to them than the opposition party is. Therefore, the best way for it to gain more support is to move toward the other

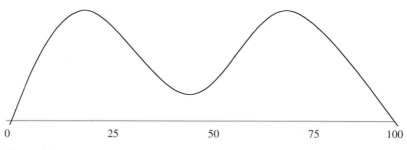

Figure 6.2.

extreme, so as to get more voters outside of it – i.e., to come between them and its opponent" (116). Only after convergence at the median would neither party be able to gain by shifting its position.

This example is perhaps unrealistic in assuming an equal distribution of political views across the political spectrum. One might instead expect to see bell curves in the distribution of political views. The distribution might involve a single peak, such as at 50 if the greatest number of voters are right at the middle. Or it might have multiple peaks. Suppose, for example, that centrist voters are rare and that there are two equal-sized groups, liberal and conservative, peaking respectively at 25 and 75. Then the distribution might be as depicted in Figure 6.2.

Different though the distribution in Figure 6.2 is from the uniform distribution in Figure 6.1, they both yield the same result – convergence of the two parties at 50, if that is where the median voter is found, and if the parties are only trying to win the general election, as opposed to converging around their own median voters at the candidate-selection stage. The underlying logic gives rise to the "median voter theorem," holding that, under the assumptions of the general Hotelling–Downs spatial model, the voters' median position on a single-dimensional issue will prevail under majority rule (Mueller 1989, 66).

If median voters in the political center are effectively calling the shots, we should not be surprised to observe bipartisan cooperation in U.S. budgetary policy, involving a mix of tax cuts and spending increases if voters sufficiently dislike deficits. So perhaps the politics of 1982 through 1990 are not so surprising after all. But then we have to ask the question: Why haven't the forces that underlie the median voter theorem produced similar political results more recently?

The contrast between 1982 to 1990, on the one hand, and the period since 1993, on the other, is quite stark. First, the tax increase of 1993 passed on a straight party line vote, without Republican cooperation, even though President Clinton labored to show balance between tax increases and spending cuts. There followed the Clinton health care fiasco, again in the face of united Republican opposition; the budget showdown of 1995, founded on Republican threats to shut down the government unless they got their way; the impasse preventing major tax or Social Security changes during Clinton's second term; and nearly everything in budgetary politics since 2001.

There have been a few bipartisan efforts during this period, such as the adoption of welfare reform, but these were generally limited. It was symptomatic of the period that, in the 1996 presidential election campaign, even so noted a centrist and tax-increasing compromiser (over the prior fourteen years) as Senator Dole embraced major tax cuts, at a time of continued budget deficits, as a centerpiece of his general election platform. And if one looks beyond budgetary issues to episodes such as the Clinton impeachment, the contrast with the preceding era looks even stronger. No matter what one thinks of this strange episode, no one could possibly view it as an effort by the Republicans to stake a claim to the political center. Even in this apparently unpopular effort, however, the Republicans did not end up paying the sort of political price borne by Barry Goldwater in 1964, and George McGovern in 1972, for departing from the political center. What could be the underlying political dynamic behind the Republicans' thus-far successful departure from centrism?

## What Happened?

The Republicans' departure since 1993 from seeking the political center, and thus their shift in budgetary policy from cooperating to defecting, has been no accident. To the contrary, it has been a centerpiece of a sustained political effort that, as Karl Rove has frequently emphasized, is designed to secure lasting political dominance. Republicans in recent years, while occasionally gesturing to the center, and while eager to portray the Democrats as far to the left, have in the main notoriously followed Rove's "energize the base" strategy of appealing to the party's right wing even in general elections. This strategy, while heavily concerned with symbolic "moral" issues such as abortion, the death penalty, and gay marriage, also includes a prominent budgetary component, calling for aggressive tax cutting without concern about deficits or concession to the Democrats.

Why would this be a successful strategy, when Democrats, such as Senator Kerry in 2004, have recognized that it invites them to try to seize the center? Republicans' superior resources and tactical skills in various recent elections may be part of the answer, but perhaps there has been more at work. Indeed, the spatial model of political competition supplies an important part of the answer.

To see this aspect, we need to trace the model's development a bit further. Arthur Smithies (1941) added an important refinement, developed in the political setting by Downs (1957), by positing that the proximity of a shop or party to the consumer or voter would affect demand. In Hotelling's initial model, consumers were assumed to have to shop somewhere, and voters to have to vote for someone. Hence, only relative proximity mattered. In Smithies's refinement, however, consumers would increasingly stay home, rather than shopping at any store, as the distance to the nearest store increased. Or, in the political application that Downs developed, voter turnout would decline as the distance between's one views and those of the nearest party increased.

Recall the example in Figure 6.2, where the distribution of voters is twin-peaked, with liberals peaking at 25 and conservatives at 75. As soon as we add the Smithies modification, the prospect of losing far-right or far-left voters as one moves to the political center checks the two parties' convergence. Their optimal electoral stances now depend on "how many extremists each loses by moving towards the center compared with how many moderates it gains thereby" (Downs 1957, 117).

With this model in hand, the Karl Rove "energize the base" approach begins to make sense politically as an alternative to moving toward the center. Suppose we posit a couple of very plausible details about current U.S. politics. The first is that a large group of voters now lies well to the right side of the political spectrum, reflecting the widely noted rise of the fundamentalist Christian right. Under the median-voter theorem, a shift further to the right by voters who already were to the right of the median would make no difference in the general election. Suppose, however, that right-wing fundamentalist voters are far more sensitive to ideological distance in deciding whether to vote than those in the middle of the spectrum. Now, depending on how the numbers play out, a strategy of tilting significantly to the right and paying much less attention to the median eligible voter may make sense politically.

Two distinct aspects of turnout increase the payoff to a Rovean "energize the base" strategy. The first is that the extremists, if they vote en masse, command a higher percentage of the voting population than of eligible voters. The second factor, perhaps more crucial, is that their high degree of turnout variability, based on the nearest candidate's ideological proximity to their position, gives them disproportionate influence at the stage where candidates are selecting strategies. Ideologically based turnout variability enhances any group's influence, extremist or not, but appears to be linked (at least on the right) with having off-center views.

Despite these considerations, it may make perfect sense that the Democrats have not comparably tilted to the left. Not only has any shift to the left by Democratic voters been much smaller (Hacker and Pierson 2005), but left-leaning Democrats may differ from fundamentalist conservatives and centrist voters in their sensitivity to the nearer candidate's distance from their position. Those who sufficiently dislike President Bush and the congressional Republicans to vote against them no matter what lose some of their ability to pressure Democratic leaders to stay close to their positions.

So the traditional median-voter approach may remain the Democrats' best strategy, even while "energize the base" works well for the Republicans. As is shown by the closely contested 2000 and 2004 presidential elections, as well as by the knife-edge (and Texas gerrymandering-enhanced) Republican majority in the House of

Representatives, the parties' support is close to even notwithstanding recent Republican predominance. Moreover, this close competition does not, as one might typically expect from spatial models of politics, promote convergence. So long as at least one party follows an "energize the base" strategy, close competition makes instead for a harsher partisan climate, given the ideological stakes attached to losing when the parties are far apart.

The end result is to make the Democrats, even if not inherently more drawn to fiscal responsibility, more willing in practice to consider the sorts of bipartisan deals that are necessary to make any headway. Bipartisanship, or at least a demonstrated willingness to engage in it, is a better fit with their general-election positioning and strategy than it is for the Republicans. It takes two to dance, however. Moreover, Republican aggressiveness may lessen what the Democrats need to do to persuade voters that they are the more fiscally responsible party. The Republicans' aggressive chicken-game strategy also may invite tit-for-tat responses by the Democrats. So having one party that is willing to compromise, but only at what it considers the right price, may in practice bear no more fruit than having neither party willing to compromise.

In the House of Representatives, a further factor weakens the impetus for compromise. Due to the increasing precision of computer-directed gerrymandering, members of the House increasingly have safe seats so far as the general election is concerned. Thus, a huge majority of House members have no reason to move to the center as a prudent reelection strategy. Instead, especially in the Republican Party, being too moderate is often the more dangerous course, in terms of both career advancement and avoiding the risk of a primary challenge from someone closer to the median primary voter.

Senate seats, of course, cannot similarly be gerrymandered. However, the rise of geographical sorting between Democratic "blue states" and Republican "red states," with fewer states regularly in play, makes senators as well safer in general elections than they once were. Senators as well, therefore, often are mainly concerned with primary challenges from the "base" of their party (Hacker and Pierson 2005). For presidential elections, this same geographical sorting may likewise weaken the impetus to drive to the center, since one can instead simply tailor one's efforts to winning the "battleground states" by focusing on issues of special importance to them.

The end result of all this has been the partisan politics and unsustainable fiscal policies of the last few years. This is not to say, however, that the policy course we have followed was inevitable. Obviously, the outcome of the closely contested 2000 presidential election and the events of September 11, 2001, had important domestic political repercussions.

In addition, the collective attitudes and procedures of the George W. Bush Administration may have encouraged fiscal irresponsibility. One enabling factor has been the Administration's lack of a coherent policy process, something noted most prominently by Secretary of the Treasury Paul O'Neill and domestic policy advisor John DiIulio after their unhappy departures. In contrast to all prior administrations since at least World War II, this one often did not have experts preparing studies under rival assumptions and scenarios that then received due internal consideration and debate. Instead, political operatives such as Karl Rove could impose their will without facing internal challenge and review (Suskind 2003).

More speculatively, the dominant temperaments in the Administration may have played a role. These were not people who liked to negotiate, to engage in give and take. Consider the Bush foreign policy, which has been based on the view that a dominant America could and should unilaterally impose its will on the world through military force, whether anyone else liked it or not. The domestic policy version of this seems to have been a decisive rejection of bipartisanship, compromise, and cooperation with others in the political community. Grover Norquist, a longtime close associate of Karl Rove, was perhaps the most forceful in expressing this view when he said: "We are trying to change the tones in the state capitals – and turn them toward bitter nastiness and partisanship" (Farrell 2003, A-1). "Bipartisanship is another name for date rape," he continued.

For many before the election of George W. Bush, both Norquist and Rove had been preaching the imminence of a long period of Republican dominance of all branches of government. Norquist had also several times predicted that decades of Democratic rather than Republican dominance might follow if the Democrats won the next election (Suellentrop 2003). So, just as one could not cooperate with the other party, but only rape or be raped, one also had to dominate the political process, election after election, or risk being dominated.

Adapt this bare-knuckled approach to the federal budget, and what you get is $40 trillion worth of added fiscal gap within three years. Defect or cooperate was not a hard choice, once translated to mean rape or be raped. The implication for budgetary policy was to take chicken games to a new level.

Unfortunately, chicken games can backfire, as happened in *Rebel without a Cause*. The single-mindedness with which Republicans can and evidently will attack Democrats who propose needed tax increases may simply be too great for the Democrats to accept the dupe's role. The spirit of trust and cooperation that is needed for each party to give up something and refrain from attacking the other may have been too greatly damaged for some years to come. Democrats' anger about Rovean tactics may also predispose them to pay back Republicans in the same coin.

A broader, if more amorphous, concern goes to the practice of politics in a well-functioning democracy. The parties are expected to compete, and to hunt for tactics that pay off electorally. But there have to be limits, based on mutual acceptance that lasting and unchallengeable dominance is a chimera in any healthy democracy. The acceptance of limits can be enforced by some combination of principle, the fear of tit-for-tat retaliation, and shared concern about mutual assured destruction. But rape or be raped is a contagious attitude, and a political system can only take so much of it.

## The Politics of Narrowing the Fiscal Gap

Technically, it is not hard to determine how the fiscal gap could reasonably be eliminated. While there is no one canonically right way to do it, the basic elements are clear. First, the rate of Medicare and Medicaid expenditure growth must somehow be greatly slowed. This might have to be linked to a broader trend of reining in the growth rate of health care spending, including that done through private insurance plans, which face grave sustainability issues of their own. Second, the rate of growth in Social Security outlays probably should be slowed – for example, by responding to rising life expectancies. Third, controls on wasteful discretionary spending, such as pork barrel spending, farm subsidies, and unneeded weapons systems and military bases, would be desirable. Fourth, significant tax increases are necessary. Here as well there are a number of reasonable alternatives, such as cutting back the big-ticket income tax preferences for home ownership and employer-provided health insurance, enacting a broad-based value-added tax (VAT), enacting a tax on carbon emissions, and increasing gasoline taxes. I am but one of many authors who have addressed various of these issues at length elsewhere.[2]

The hard part is not identifying a reasonable course of action, but getting Congress to adopt and stick to it. The sooner such measures are adopted, the less harsh they need to be, and the less we risk long-lasting harm to future seniors' retirement security and our national creditworthiness. It seems clear that this would require bipartisan agreement to call off the chicken games and propose painful medicine together, as was done in the 1983 Social Security package that won the joint support of President Reagan and House Speaker O'Neill. And it seems likely that budget rules would have to play an important role both in encouraging responsible changes and in countering ongoing pressures to pander to current voters by backsliding.

Neither a shift in the political atmosphere toward greater bipartisanship nor a better set of budget rules could do the job alone. Without bipartisan consensus about moving cooperatively toward restored sustainability, good budget rules, even if they somehow got adopted in the first place, would inevitably be overridden and ignored. Without effective budget rules, even the best intentions could end up leading to repeated iterations of one step forward, two steps back. So both aspects require serious attention.

## Back to Bipartisanship?

As of early 2006, the chances for a major bipartisan budget deal reducing the fiscal gap could hardly look worse. On the Republican side, the Bush Administration seems highly unlikely to change course so drastically. In Congress, 253 Republican members, or 91 percent of the total Republican membership, recently signed a "Taxpayer Protection Pledge" stating that they would oppose any income tax rate increase and any revenue-raising net elimination of tax deductions and credits (Gale and Kelly 2004, Table 3). The pledge appeared to commit all signers to supporting extension of the 2001 and 2003 tax cuts and preventing growth of the alternative minimum tax. The signers had overwhelmingly supported such recent big-spending Republican initiatives as the Medicare prescription drug benefit and the notoriously pork-laden 2004 highway bill (11, 13). On the Democratic side, even if a centrist general election strategy suggests a willingness to consider bipartisan deals under the right circumstances, it is hard to imagine any concessions being offered to the current Republican leadership. The level of distrust is simply too great.

Still, given the saying that in politics even just a week is a long time, the current impasse is not as significant as the underlying forces that have helped to create it. So the key question is when, and under what circumstances, Republicans might discard the energize-the-base strategy that has worked so well for them recently.

This question can be answered on a couple of different levels. An initial point concerns the salience of contemporary historical lessons. Just as the defeat of the first President Bush in 1992 appears to have taught Republicans the lesson (whether or not accurately) that bipartisan deals to raise taxes are politically costly, so there must be a lesson, or perhaps a series of lessons, suggesting that the energize-the-base strategy has run its course. The Republicans may need to lose several elections, both in Congress and at the presidential level, before the needed lesson sinks in. It would help the process still more, however, if the Democrats were to fall short of winning effective control. This would not only limit what they could do, but also give them reason to seek moderate Republican allies, who in turn might end up with something to show for bargaining and cooperating.

This hope, however, involves little more than trusting to chance. Since the main problem is the Republicans' shift from centrism to an energize-the-base strategy, the real key is structural changes that tilt political incentives back toward the centrist strategy. There are several forms that this could take. In elections to the House, impeding gerrymandering is important, so that members seeking reelection have more reason to appeal to independent voters and those in the other party. Unfortunately, since gerrymandering benefits incumbents of both parties, inside players have little reason to limit it.

A second important step would be to seek generally increased voter turnout, on the theory that this would reduce the expected electoral payoff to the energize-the-base strategy. If everyone voted more, the greater ideological turnout variability of people on the far right might be reduced. Turnout could be increased in a number of ways, such as by easing voter registration, rewarding voting or penalizing nonvoting, requiring that the polls be open for twenty-four hours or even as long as a week, and arranging easier absentee and even internet voting procedures.

Here at least there is a possible political mechanism for the change. Democrats may regard increased turnout as to their partisan advantage, on the theory that the eligible electorate is to the left of the voting electorate given lower turnout rates among poor voters. Thus, they have much more motivation to pursue increasing turnout than to try to impede gerrymandering. However, reducing ideological turnout variability should reduce the power of the far right whether or not increased turnout moves the median voter to the left.

A wholly different, albeit complementary, approach to restoring cooperation toward achieving fiscal responsibility is political, cultural, and intellectual. Partisanship and political anger have been notably intense in recent years, with Presidents Clinton and George W. Bush both evoking intense hatred from people in the other party. A lowering of partisan temperatures is clearly needed in order for a compromise solution to the fiscal gap to be politically feasible. Today's media environment pushes against anything so dull as the spread of calmer feelings. But individuals on both sides of the political divide can try to make a positive difference.

## Budget Rules

### A Capsule History

Even with an improved political climate for bipartisan progress toward fiscal responsibility, it would be important to have budget rules in place. The existence of a comprehensive budget process dates from the enactment of the Congressional Budget and Impoundment Control Act of 1974. Congress began setting annual revenue and expenditure targets and allocating specific levels of budget authority to the various congressional committees. While the hope was to restrain budget deficits, in practice Congress generally declined to follow its own rules, and budget deficits continued to increase (Shaviro 1997, 248–250).

By the mid-1980s, deficit concerns were leading to the pursuit of multiyear aggregate budgetary targets in legislation. The Tax Reform Act of 1986, for example, proceeded legislatively, from its 1984 inception onward, under the effectively binding assumption by proponents that it had to be revenue-neutral over a five-year period. This nearly led to a last-second derailment, during the House–Senate conference that was charged with producing a final version, when changing economic forecasts forced the conferees to find extra revenues (Birnbaum and Murray 1987, 274–276).

The biggest 1980s innovation, however, was the enactment of the Gramm–Rudman–Hollings law (GRH) in 1985. Passed out of bipartisan frustration with the seemingly intractable character of budget deficits in the ordinary course of politics, GRH set specific budgetary targets for the five-year period starting in 1987, over which the deficit was supposed to decline by 20 percent annually until it reached zero in 1991. While GRH did not specify how this was to be done, it provided that, if Congress fell short for a given year, the deficit target would be met through sequestration – automatic, across-the-board reductions in all government outlays other than those in a few categories (such as interest payments and entitlements). Congress therefore would have to act affirmatively, through superseding legislation, in order to prevent a target from being met, thereby shifting the burden of inertia.

Sequestration seemed such an arbitrary blunderbuss that contemporary observers called it "budgetary terrorism" and a "doomsday machine" (White and Wildavsky 1989, 431–432). For example, it could "interrupt important government services, require irregular employee furloughs, and lead to breaches of contracts with private individuals" (Shaviro 1997, 252). The hope was that the mere threat of its occurring, along with the embarrassment of simply calling it off, would be sufficient to force Congress to meet the guidelines voluntarily in advance. Sequestration nonetheless occurred five times in six years. This reflected, not just the difficulty of the task, but the shifting character of the budgetary targets when revenue forecasts changed for the worse, along with politicians' predilections to play chicken games with each other by waiting to see who would blink first by offering a concession. Moreover, in each case the budgetary target ended up being relaxed by Congress. GRH is nonetheless widely credited with having helped to bring about significant deficit reduction.[3]

By 1990, both sides in Washington were tired of having to deal with GRH, and they agreed to trade it in for a combination of one-time deficit reduction (including President George H. W. Bush's abandonment of his "no new taxes" pledge) and its replacement by the Budget Enforcement Act of 1990. This act had two main features: the creation of spending caps, except on entitlement, for the next five years, and pay-as-you-go (PAYGO) rules for taxes and entitlement spending. Under PAYGO, any tax cuts or entitlements spending increases had to be offset by tax increases or entitlement spending cuts, as determined both for the current year and for a five-year period that subsequently was extended to ten years. Sequestration would apply, absent congressional action to override it, if the spending caps or PAYGO rules were violated. Congress was less the hostage of macroeconomic changes than it had been under GRH, however, since only new enactments could lead to sequesters.

The PAYGO rules were reaffirmed in a 1997 budget deal between President Clinton and the congressional Republicans, but then were allowed to expire in 2002. Even before their expiration, however, their effectiveness and that of the Budget Enforcement Act's spending caps, while apparently significant through 1997, had sharply declined. Emboldened by budget surpluses in the late 1990s, Congress began exploiting a loophole permitting "emergency" spending to be exempted from the caps. As Rudolph G. Penner and C. Eugene Steuerle (2004, 550–551) recount:

> Between 1991 and 1998, Congress had used the emergency provision sparingly as emergency spending averaged only $5 billion per year outside the amounts required for Desert Storm. In 1999, emergency spending soared to $23 billion and then, in 2000, to $36 billion as even the census was declared to be an emergency. For fiscal 2001, the Congress simply raised the caps to whatever they wanted to spend and did not use the subterfuge of an emergency. PAYGO was not violated to the same extent, but it too frayed for fiscal 2000 and 2001. Laws violating the PAYGO limits decreed that the excess should be ignored and that no sequester should occur.

One important budgetary rule remains in force, however. This is the Byrd Rule in the Senate, named after maverick Democratic Senator Robert Byrd. Under the Byrd Rule, budget reconciliation legislation (often the vehicle of choice for important budgetary changes) is subject on the Senate floor to a point of order raised by any senator, with the consequence that it needs sixty votes to continue being considered, if, among other sources of objection, it would increase the deficit beyond the time horizon that was used by the underlying budget resolution. The Byrd Rule helped to prevent the 2001 and 2003 tax cuts from being made permanent, since sixty votes were unattainable given the closely divided Senate and bitterly partisan atmosphere. However, it would not prevent repeated piecemeal extensions of the tax cuts.

This brief history suggests that budget rules can potentially make a difference if the political preconditions for their effectiveness exist, in the form of widespread support for fiscal responsibility. Where there is a will, they can help provide a way. However, for budget rules to matter, waiving them must be politically costly, or else they must change the voting dynamics – for example, by requiring a super-majority. Within these parameters, there are many different forms that budget rules can take.

## Where Next with Budget Rules?

There has recently been talk of restoring PAYGO, and presumably restoring as well the informal convention, from its early years, of not simply waiving it each time that it would otherwise be violated. A more ambitious proposal to establish budgetary rules using long-term fiscal measures was the Honest Government Accounting Act of 2003, introduced by Senator Joseph Lieberman but promptly tabled by the Senate leadership. The main features of the Honest Government Accounting Act included the following:

a) Official budgetary forecasts would include both seventy-five-year and infinite-horizon estimates of the fiscal gap, along with subestimates for various components such as Social Security and Medicare.

b) Both the president and a newly created Commission on Long-Term Liabilities and Commitments would be instructed to submit plans for reducing the fiscal gap, as computed on both a seventy-five-year and an infinite-horizon basis, to no more than 1.25 percent of the present value of projected future payrolls in the economy.

c) Whenever the president submitted legislative proposals other than annual appropriations that, on either a seventy-five-year or an infinite-horizon basis, would increase the fiscal gap by more than 0.25 percent of the present value of projected future payrolls, he would be instructed to recomply with (b).

d) In both the House and the Senate, a Byrd Rule–style point of order would apply to legislation that, when considered in combination with prior legislation passed by that body during the same calendar year, would increase the fiscal gap by more than 1.25 percent of the present value of projected future payrolls, on either a seventy-five-year or an infinite-horizon basis.

e) PAYGO rules would be restored, requiring one-year, five-year, and ten-year budgetary balance from new proposals, with violations leading to a point of order as under the Byrd Rule, rather than to sequesters.

f) In making long-term estimates, the Congressional Budget Office would be instructed to disregard scheduled changes that purport to save money (such as tax increases and entitlement cuts) unless they take effect immediately, but to take account of scheduled changes that would cost money (such as tax cuts and entitlement increases) even if they are deferred. Thus, the scheduled 2011 sunset of the 20001 tax cuts would be disregarded, but the deferred Medicare prescription drug benefit would be included from the start despite its delayed implementation.

There plainly is no chance that anything like the Honest Government Accounting Act will be considered in Congress anytime soon. Perhaps a bond market crisis will be necessary before any such approach is politically feasible. On the other hand, if deficit concerns start to rise during the next few years, a plan like this might appeal to a politician with national ambitions who wanted to stand out from the field of presidential aspirants. Senator Lieberman may have thought so in 2003, however unpresciently, given that he introduced the act during the run-up to his own short-lived 2004 presidential campaign. But perhaps the time for such a measure will come, raising the question of how it might best be structured.

## Measures for What Purpose?

As discussed in Chapter 5, the fiscal gap is a measure of our sustainability problem under current policy. However, this is only one of the two biggest concerns about long-term budget policy that normally are associated with the deficit measure. The other goes to generational equity. People who are highly concerned about this issue may favor a budgetary rule that addresses it directly. Such a rule might target legislation that overly increased lifetime net taxes for future generations, although in practice this would overlap with addressing the fiscal gap.

## Requiring Specified Improvements in the Long-Term Forecast versus Discouraging Changes That Would Make Things Worse

A further issue in designing budget rules is whether, like GRH, they should require specified degrees of improvement in the measured disparities or whether they should instead, like PAYGO, merely impede making things worse. The fact that the long-term budgetary outlook currently is so bad gives strong appeal to the GRH approach, but this approach has been criticized by commentators who share its goals. Penner and Steuerle (2004, 548) question "any quantitative target" for movement toward budgetary balance, on the ground that "the balance usually is affected much more in any year by the vagaries of the economy and technical factors than it is by legislation. That is to say, [GRH] forced the Congress to aim at a rapidly moving target," and also to worsen the business cycle by raising taxes or cutting spending if a recession increased the budget deficit. The GRH approach can also be criticized on the ground that automatic sequesters, penalizing legislative inaction, are undesirably disruptive yet likely to take effect repeatedly, given politicians' incentives to play chicken games as the deadline approaches.

This critique may not apply as fully to long-term budget rules as to those based on annual deficits. Increasing the time span reduces the effect of business cycle fluctuations. In addition, mandatory corrections may not affect the business cycle as badly if they do not apply in full immediately.

As to whether budgetary rules should try to mandate annual improvement over a multiyear period, or instead simply impede making things worse, one should keep in mind how difficult it is to legislate major reductions in the fiscal gap. There may be little to be gained by trying, against the grain, to make them an ordinary part of the annual budget process. The model I would have in mind, therefore, is moments of big progress, followed by holding the line for a while, followed by trying for more big progress when the political will has revived. This is the approach of the  Honest Government Accounting Act, which tries to mandate a one-time improvement up front, followed by trying to hold the line (in the manner of PAYGO) thereafter.

## Consequences of Violating a Budget Rule

The other big choice in budget rule design concerns the consequences of a violation. Here, PAYGO lines up with GRH, since both provided for mandatory sequestration, while the Byrd Rule and the Honest Government Accounting Act instead require super-majorities for enactments in violation of the restraints.

The two types of rule may work best in tandem. Sequestration need not be overly disruptive if it is linked to new enactments, as under PAYGO. Without a super-majority rule, however, Congress could avoid sequestration whenever it liked by simply including a clause in any violative legislation to the effect that this time it did not apply. One last detail is that sequestration might be expanded to include automatic tax rate increases, thus loading the gun a bit more symmetrically.

## Summary

The U.S. fiscal gap has been expanding due mainly to life expectancy gains and the improvement of health care technology. These were great developments in human terms, as anyone who is past middle age or who has older relatives can attest. They were bad developments fiscally, however, because voters and politicians of all stripes had no interest in supporting timely and responsible adjustments to Social Security and Medicare.

Things got worse with the Republicans' march to the right and rejection of political centrism. This, in turn, responded to the emergence of a highly conservative Republican "base," the impact of which was magnified by gerrymandering and the "base" voters' high ideological turnout variability.

Movement toward restoring fiscal responsibility may have to await a serious fiscal crisis. With or without such a crisis, however, it will require restoration of the cooperative bipartisan process that predominated from 1982 through 1990. Structurally, increasing voter turnout and impeding gerrymandering might increase the chances for restored bipartisanship.

Budgetary rules are also a necessary part of achieving greater fiscal responsibility. While no substitute for a political willingness to do the right thing, they can vitally reinforce inclinations that lie in that direction. An effective set of rules might include the following:

1) The use of multiple time periods, such as one year, five years, ten years, and the infinite horizon.
2) A requirement that, for estimating purposes, scheduled changes that would reduce the fiscal gap be disregarded unless they take effect immediately or are being phased in at a constant rate.
3) The use of PAYGO-style rules to impede legislation that would make things worse, along with occasional bipartisan commissions (when the will is there) to propose changes that would actually make things better.
4) The use of both super-majority rules and mandatory sequestration plus tax increases where legislation has overly increased the fiscal gap.

# PART 3

# LABELS AND POLICIES ACROSS BUDGET CATEGORIES

*Bad though the long-term U.S. budget picture currently is, the looming danger of a default or hyperinflation will not always be with us. At some point, either the danger will recede or the bad things will happen. The longitudinal dimension, involving budget policy across categories rather than across time, may then regain preeminence. With or without a fiscal gap, "tax" and "spending" issues are always with us.*

*Part Three examines three of the principal such debates in which fiscal language issues have been important. The first involves Social Security and related entitlements. Second, I discuss tax expenditures, a term that has provoked frequent controversy centered on the meaning of "taxes" and "spending." Finally, I examine how the tax/spending distinction has shaped, and perhaps dramatically worsened, social safety net programs that provide aid to the poor.*

# 7

## Benign Fictions?
### Describing Social Security and Medicare

*[M]ight we contrive one of those opportune falsehoods . . . so as by one noble lie to persuade if possible the rulers themselves, but failing that the rest of the city?*

— Socrates, in Plato's *Republic*

*Those who think it permissible to tell white lies soon grow color-blind.*
— Austin O'Malley

If artful fiscal language had not already existed when Social Security was enacted in 1935, the program's proponents would have had to invent it. Social Security, along with its 1965 half-sibling Medicare, is a locus like few others for the carefully devised use of fiscal language to influence not just current voters but also future policy makers.

Until recently, the fiscal language history of Social Security and Medicare had two main aspects. One was the use of fiscal language to put the programs in as favorable a light as possible, helping them to become the widely noted twin "third rails" of American politics. The other was the creation of a set of fiscal language conventions to guide how the programs operate in practice, as a way of trying to keep them on their intended course.

These two parts of the story, while closely related, are in some ways quite distinct. The use of fiscal language to enhance the programs' political prospects comes close to the territory of the "noble lie." Operating conventions, by contrast, might actually become true behavioral constraints, like the requirement that everyone drive on the right side of the road.

President Bush's 2005 initiative to change Social Security gave rise to a new fiscal language episode. Open battle over the program's fiscal language broke out for the first time since its early decades. The Administration opened two fronts. The first involved challenging Social Security's previously accepted fiscal language, by arguing that its features are shams even when they are actually conventions. The second involved creating new terminology to describe the proposed changes. Here, the story changes to sledgehammer irony. Proponents of what became the Bush approach, having mislabeled it as "privatization" – a term with a positive valence in the world of conservative think tanks – learned too late that this label was political poison in the broader political world.

## Reasons for Building Pre-Commitment to Social Security and Medicare

There are times when having too much power paradoxically makes one weak. Thus, governments, by reason of their sovereign authority, may find it harder than private individuals to win trust from other parties by binding themselves to a course of action. Laws intended to generate reliance can always be changed. The claim that either a benefit, such as an amnesty for tax evaders, or a detriment, such as expropriating assets, is strictly a one-time proposition is hard to make credible. Even a government's debt obligations and other contracts may be hard to enforce against it, except through procedures that the government itself establishes and can change.

In some respects, the obstacles to government pre-commitment are unfortunate, as they impede arrangements from which everyone affected could benefit. Consider what economists call the time-consistency problem, epitomized by the difficulty that third world countries face in attracting outside investment if they cannot offer outsiders a credible guarantee against subsequent expropriation. This may prevent the host country and outside investors from making a deal that would be good for both.

Yet there also are reasons to be glad that governments cannot too easily bind themselves. One problem with too much government pre-commitment power goes to the issue of stable governments' indefinite life. Even if I can bind myself to keep some commitment for the rest of my life, we might be uneasy about allowing me to bind my descendants through the last (or even the next) generation. The government, however, potentially binds all descendants of today's voters and taxpayers if its commitments are irrevocable.

A second problem with government pre-commitment pertains to changes in political control. We may be reluctant to let the majority at any given time take too much power away from future majorities, by pre-committing the jurisdiction to a particular long-term policy course. The political economy explanations of budget deficits that I noted in Chapter 6 show some of the problems that can result from strategic efforts to increase pre-commitment. Even without such problems, however, democratic theory may not applaud permitting earlier majorities completely to disenfranchise later ones.

What should policy makers do, therefore, when they want to create some degree of pre-commitment, but either cannot or do not want to create anything as binding as a private contract? One approach is to create obligations that are procedurally difficult to renounce. Constitutions do this if they are hard to amend, as do super-majority rules for regular legislation. Indeed, all laws follow this approach to the extent that they are entrenched by the practical difficulties of changing them.

Fiscal language also can play a role. If the terms in which a program is described make it sound like a binding commitment, it may be stronger politically than an ordinary law, even without any of the procedural safeguards of a constitutional or super-majority rule. Proponents of what are intended to be long-term programs therefore have good reason to load the linguistic dice in the programs' favor.

## Labels and Policies across Budget Categories

Government retirement programs, such as Social Security and Medicare, are classic examples. One cannot have such programs without facing up to the credible commitment problem. Workers will have neither real nor apparent retirement security if the benefits' continuation is purely at the whim of future legislators.

This does not mean, however, that participants should be given ironclad debt obligations, backed by the same full faith and credit as Treasury bonds. Such a level of pre-commitment might unduly encourage self-interested voters to award themselves excessive benefits at the expense of future generations. The use of fiscal language to create an intermediate level of effective pre-commitment – above that for a purely discretionary decision but below that for a legal contract – therefore makes sense.

The pre-commitment problem alone would have weighed against choosing fiscal language for Social Security and Medicare that merely offered neutral description. Yet a more controversial consideration also seems to have influenced the enactors' fiscal language choices. From the start, proponents of the two big entitlements wanted to do two distinct things. The first was to create a social safety net for everyone, assuring all participants a minimum level of retirement resources even if they lost or spent everything. In addition, however, the retirement programs were considered tools for progressive redistribution that would be politically more effective if their character as such weren't too transparent. This suggested emphasizing the programs' "universality" while deemphasizing or even obscuring their distributional character.

One peculiar consequence of this use of Social Security and Medicare for hidden redistribution has been a frequent tendency for Democrats to favor making the programs less progressive, while Republicans favor making them more so, based on the jointly held view that overt progressivity would reduce the programs' level of political support. The problem with too much overt progressivity from the Democrats' standpoint, and its virtue to Republicans, was its tension with fiscal language terms that were crucial to the programs' political strength.

This pattern starts with the enactment of Social Security, funded by a payroll tax with a relatively low annual dollar ceiling, above which the tax rate was zero. President Franklin Roosevelt, in response to a complaint that the tax was too regressive, said:

> I guess you're right on the economics, but those taxes were never a problem of economics. They are politics all the way through. We put those payroll taxes there so as to give the contributors a legal, moral, and political right to collect their pensions. . . . With those taxes in there, no damn politician can ever scrap my social security program. (Schlesinger 1959, 308–309)

During the Medicare enactment process in 1965, Democrats again favored using the payroll tax. Republicans, more progressively, favored using general revenues. While the Democrats ended up adopting the Republican approach for Medicare's Part B outpatient benefits, the parties had unmistakably switched sides regarding tax progressivity, by reason of the mutually expected effect on program size.

This pattern has continued to the present day. Thus, Democrats usually oppose means testing for Social Security benefits, most recently in their rejection of Bush Administration suggestions, floated during the 2005 Social Security debate, that high earners' benefits be reduced. As Paul Krugman (2005) put it: "It's an adage that programs for the poor always turn into poor programs. That is, once a program is defined as welfare, it becomes a target for budget cuts." So the program had to stay less progressive, the better (it was thought) to preserve overall progressivity.

## Fiscal Language and Conceptual Tools for Building Pre-Commitment

### Social Security and Medicare as Promised to Current Seniors

The view that Social Security and Medicare benefits have been promised to current seniors, and thus cannot properly be scaled back for them, involves a claim of reliance. Retirement programs might be good or bad policy, under this view, but once you have neared retirement with a given set of benefits on the books, they are untouchable.

This makes permissible policy change for current seniors a one-way ratchet. Offering them new benefits for which they have not paid, such as Medicare prescription drugs, is fine, but existing benefits cannot be cut. The restriction on policy change is limited, however, by its reliance on the formal boundaries between distinct government programs. Thus, as we saw in Chapter 2, while President Clinton was harshly criticized for labeling increased income taxation of Social Security benefits as a "spending cut," he avoided being charged either with means testing or with breaking a sacred commitment to seniors via benefit cuts.

Reliance arguments when the laws change to one's detriment are not limited to entitlements. Thus, people would complain about repealing the home mortgage interest deduction in the tax code unless they received some form of transitional relief. Once again, however, reliance seems to be a one-way ratchet, permitting favorable but not adverse changes. Standing alone, therefore, the reliance argument might not be able to make Social Security and Medicare as unique politically as they in fact are.

## Social Security and Medicare as Having Been Paid for by Seniors

A second reason for viewing Social Security and Medicare as owed to seniors is that they ostensibly have paid for their benefits via payroll taxes. In part, this view is an application of earmarking, which I will discuss later. Given the fungibility of money and the fact that Social Security and Medicare are merely a subset of people's overall fiscal dealings with the government, one could argue that it makes little sense to treat one particular subset of tax payments as entitling people to one particular set of outlays, when the overall picture is what really matters. Should you bother to insist that I give you a dollar with my left hand if I am free to take back an extra dollar with my right hand?

Even if we accept the earmarking convention, however, it is not true that current seniors have paid in full for their benefits. Neither Social Security nor Medicare requires any sort of equivalence between taxes paid and benefits received. Older generations have notoriously gotten much more back from the programs than they put in, a result made less transparent by the lack of any direct link between taxes and benefits.

## Retirement Benefits as Owed to Seniors by a Decent Society

A third, very different ground on which Social Security and Medicare might be considered special is the view that every decent society should assure an adequate minimum standard of support to people who are too old to work. However appealing this view may be, it has the interesting feature, from a fiscal language standpoint, of presenting a *limitation* on people's freedom to do what they like with their lifetime resources in the guise of a *right* that they are said to have.

In illustration, suppose we say that I am entitled to retirement support that will be worth some given amount on the day I retire. This expected receipt is part of my anticipated lifetime income, net of taxes and transfers. Yet, if it is structured like Social Security or Medicare, I am not permitted to access it in advance.

Why not let me have and spend the present value of my retirement benefits whenever I like? If people always know what is best for themselves, this would make me better off without costing taxpayers anything extra. Two reasons might support limiting my freedom of choice. The first is paternalism, based on the concern that I will choose badly. The second is to protect others from the risk that, if I am permitted to fritter everything away, they will feel compelled to give me retirement support anyway. So the "right" to retirement support is really a means of protecting myself and others from the consequences of free choice. Obviously, calling it a limit rather than a right would risk reducing its appeal.

## Social Security as "Social Insurance"

Public support for Social Security (as well as Medicare) is also bound up with its being considered "social insurance." This concept is politically influential even though it may not be well known by name outside the Beltway, because it underlies the widely accepted view that Social

Security is fundamentally different from the progressive income tax or the welfare system.

The use of the term "social insurance" reflects the fact that Social Security is structured to look like private insurance. In particular, its dedicated payroll tax financing can be analogized to the payment of insurance premiums. The benefits it offers also strengthen the analogy to private insurance, as they are event-conditioned (triggered by one's reaching retirement age) and are not explicitly means tested.

This private insurance–style structuring was no accident. While Social Security proponents initially denied that the program was insurance, on the view that this would expose it to constitutional challenge (Derthick 1979, 224–225), they soon shifted gears. Indeed, "[a]s the link between tax payments and benefits grew more and more tenuous, the program became less and less like insurance, and the less like insurance it became, the more its executive leaders insisted that that was what it was" (224). Republican opponents responded in kind, reversing their initial arguments that the Social Security tax was "not a tax at all . . . but an enforced insurance premium for old-age annuities" to argue instead that "social insurance is not, in fact, insurance" (225).

If we look at the analogy more closely, it begins to weaken. Insurance is a device for spreading risk. Thus, your car insurance means that you will pay the same amount (leaving aside deductibles and copayments) whether you have an accident or not. Social insurance might logically be defined as relating to risks that private insurance markets are unable to handle. Establishing a minimum permissible level of retirement saving, out of paternalism and to limit the costs you impose on others, is quite a different proposition than supplementing the risk coverage that private markets can offer.

Oddly, the income tax and welfare systems, which almost no one calls "social insurance," are functionally more insurance-like than Social Security. They address income risk, or the risk that one's income will turn out to be low rather than high (Shaviro 2000a, 48–56). The less you earn, the less you have to pay for government services, and, if your earnings are low enough, the government may actually pay you. This genuinely insurance-like function, however, evidently matters less to people's habitual classifications than Social Security's formal use of insurance-like features.

## Baseline for Defining "Benefit Cuts"

As noted in Chapter 2, behavioral economics shows that people generally consider "losses" much worse than foregone "gains." This makes the adoption of "benefit cuts" a lot more painful politically than foregone "benefit increases." So the baseline for defining cuts and increases is all-important to the politics of Social Security or Medicare.

Both programs are structured in a manner that, under present economic and demographic circumstances, causes their benefits to grow faster than inflation, without Congress's having to do anything. In Social Security, the initial benefit level for each new age cohort of retirees is pegged to wage levels, rather than just to inflation. Over a sixty-year period, this is projected to cause annual real benefits almost to double (Munnell and Soto 2005, Table 1). Medicare outlays are effectively pegged to the size of the health care sector, which has been growing faster than the overall economy, with the consequence that the outlays are expected to more than triple as a percentage of GDP over the same sixty-year period (Boards of Trustees 2005, Table III.A.2).

One could reasonably dispute whether these are truly benefit "increases," given that the Social Security rule keeps benefits constant in replacement-rate terms (i.e., relative to pre-retirement wages), while the Medicare rule keeps coverage constant relative to the health care options available at any given time. The choice of a baseline is inevitably arbitrary, or at least subject to differing interpretations. By having the rules they do, however, Social Security and Medicare effectively end any such dispute and dictate the choice of a relatively generous baseline. The Bush Administration learned this the hard way during the 2005 Social Security debate, when it found few takers for its argument that eliminating wage indexing for high earners, and henceforth pegging their benefits just to the inflation rate, was not really a benefit cut, as it would keep current benefits constant in real terms.

Present law is not the only baseline people ever use in defining "cuts" versus "increases." Thus, Republicans in recent years have argued that allowing the recent tax cuts to expire, as scheduled under present law, would actually be a tax increase. But the scheduled growth of Social Security and Medicare benefits under present law clearly is important to the programs' prospects and to the likely near-term course of the fiscal gap.

## Operating Conventions for Social Security and Medicare

### Reasons for the Operating Conventions

The previous section noted the importance of dedicated payroll tax financing to creating stable political support for Social Security and Medicare. Such financing was critical both to creating the view that seniors were entitled to their benefits and to positioning the programs as social insurance rather than redistribution. Even the lack of dedicated financing for Medicare's Part B outpatient benefits may not have mattered given the halo effect of association with Medicare's Part A. Surely more people know that there is a Medicare payroll tax than that it covers only part of the program.

The decision to use dedicated financing had multiple implications for the programs' design. In particular, with dedicated revenues meant to equal outlays over the long term, operating conventions were needed to keep track over time of the relationship between the two. Without such conventions, the claim of using dedicated financing might not have been credible at the time Social Security and Medicare were enacted. The conventions also, however, offered a means of exerting continued influence on legislative decisions down the road.

### Earmarking

On its face, earmarking particular revenues to be used in a particular way may seem to be a policy with direct substance, rather than an operating convention. The complication is that, while earmarking actually does dictate how particular funds must be used, money is fungible. Thus, unless the amount of a given type of outlay actually depends on the existence and amount of dedicated financing, the fact that given dollars have been earmarked for a particular use makes no difference whatsoever.

Suppose, for example, that a governor wants to impose beer taxes in his state, and suppose he's looking to discomfit opponents of the proposal. What better way, perhaps, than to announce that the revenues will be dedicated to some worthy cause, such as buying textbooks for schoolchildren? The beer lobby might have to think twice about inviting the critique that they were opposing children just to aid beer drinkers. Whether the earmarking was purely formal or not, however, would depend on whether the amount collected through the tax actually determined the amount spent on the dedicated purpose.

To determine whether earmarking actually matters in this sense, one must ask a counterfactual question: What would the legislature have done in the absence of the earmarked funds? For Social Security and Medicare Part A, the level of dedicated revenues does indeed appear to matter. Earmarking may have encouraged unfunded Social Security benefit increases from the 1950s through the early 1970s, when the system was running annual cash flow surpluses. And it clearly motivated the benefit cuts and payroll tax increases of 1983.

One thing earmarking cannot do is discourage large-scale generational transfers through Social Security and Medicare. Thus, if the Medicare prescription drug benefit had been fully funded by an earmarked increase in the payroll tax, there still would have been a huge transfer from younger to older generations. Indeed, such earmarking might even have increased the eventual transfer to older current generations via the prescription drug benefit, by helping to entrench it politically. People might have thought: "We" are entitled to our prescription drug benefits because "we" have paid for them, even if the two "we's" were not the same.

## The Social Security (and Medicare Part A) Trust Funds

Once it has been determined that dedicated revenues must equal benefits only over the long run, accounting records are needed to keep track of the commitment. And once such records are being kept, what better name for them than "trust funds"? The term is familiar and sounds businesslike. It helps makes the promise of future benefits seem asset-backed.

The Social Security and Medicare Part A Trust Funds take the accounting-record concept a bit further. Rather than simply recording a net positive balance based on historical program operations to date, they actually are deemed to hold specific financial assets, in the form of U.S. Treasury bonds that are specially issued to them at the going interest rate. What to make of this convention, however, has prompted intense and at times emotional debate among politicians and policy experts.

The view that the whole thing is a sham was put most provocatively by President Bush, during a photo opportunity amid his 2005 Social Security campaign. In early April of that year, he "visited the office of the federal Bureau of Public Debt in Parkersburg, [West Virginia]. . . . and posed next to a file cabinet that holds the $1.7 trillion in Treasury securities that make up the Social Security trust fund. He tossed off a comment to the effect that the bonds were not 'real assets.' Later, in a speech at a nearby university, he said: 'There is no trust fund. Just I.O.U.'s that I saw firsthand.' " (*New York Times* Editorial 2005).

Many responded indignantly to Bush's photo-op debunking of the Social Security Trust Fund. The *New York Times* compared it to his hypothetically "visit[ing] the vault at the Bank of Japan, where that country's $712 billion in United States government bonds is stored, . . . . [and t]here, as the cameras roll, . . . announc[ing] that the bonds, backed by the full faith and credit of the United States, are, in fact, worthless I.O.U.'s." To similar effect, leading Democrats insisted that "[i]f the full faith and credit of the United States government is not an asset, I don't know what is" (quoted in Smetters 2003, 2), while liberal economists argued that "Treasury bonds held by the Social Security Trust Fund are every bit as 'real' as the Treasury bonds held by private investors" (Aaron et al. 2001, 11).

The Bush photo-op comment seems to have induced confusion on all sides concerning what can make financial claims valuable. Pieces of paper evidencing financial claims inherently have no value in and of themselves. What makes them valuable is that they evidence a claim on someone's resources. Despite the serious risk of a United States fiscal crisis, I personally would be delighted to hold $1.7 trillion worth of U.S. Treasury bonds, in a secure file cabinet or elsewhere. The fact that these are simply pieces of paper held in a file cabinet in no way discredits their value.

The more significant challenge to the "reality" of the Social Security Trust Fund assets rests on their being self-owed by the United States government. They give the government a claim on itself. Once Social Security begins experiencing annual cash flow deficits, the government's only options for financing current-year net benefits will be to (1) raise taxes, (2) reduce other outlays, (3) issue debt to third parties, or (4) print money. And under (3), it makes no difference whether the government purports to sell the bonds that were previously held by the trust fund, or issues new bonds with the same terms.

Does this mean that the U.S. government ought instead to hold third-party assets in the Social Security Trust Fund, as would have happened under President Clinton's suggestion that a portion of the trust fund be "invested" in stocks and other private sector securities? On the one hand, this would give the trust fund genuine third-party financial assets that the government could sell to help fund Social Security's operating deficits. But on the other hand, if the U.S. government had funded its purchase of the securities by issuing debt, rather than by raising taxes or reducing outlays, it would have increased third parties' claims on it, in addition to increasing its claims on third parties. The combined effect would net to zero except insofar as the government's "long" and "short" positions performed differently. That is, it would gain if the assets earned more than the liabilities paid out; it would lose if the assets earned less; and in the interim it would bear risk regarding the resolution of this uncertainty.

So the merits of the Clinton proposal depended on whether the government ought to be borrowing money to buy stock. Whether meritorious or not, however, Clinton's proposal seemingly would have affected President Bush's critique of the file cabinet in West Virginia. Had the Clinton plan been implemented, this cabinet would actually have contained valuable securities issued by third parties – indeed, even if the government had lost billions of dollars on the transaction (as it might have, had it issued debt to buy stock at the peak of the late-1990s stock market bubble). Clearly, then, the contents of the file cabinet, considered in isolation, were of little import one way or the other, so far as the government's future ability to pay Social Security benefits was concerned.

Where does all this leave the Social Security Trust Fund? It still matters, as a device for keeping track of earmarking, to the extent that earmarking matters. That is, its reported level may affect political decisions about changes to the payroll tax or to Social Security benefits. Whether anything else about it matters remains controversial.

The economist Kent Smetters (2003) helpfully poses the main controversy in terms of what he calls the "storage technology" claim. According to this claim, the trust fund induces genuine pre-funding of future Social Security benefit obligations, by causing Congress to disregard the system's operating surpluses when making annual tax and spending decisions. Rather than regarding the surpluses as available funds, the claim holds, Congress disregards them on the ground that they have been deposited in the trust fund. This ostensibly results in smaller budget deficits than if Congress viewed the operating surpluses as free money.

Smetters tests the storage technology claim empirically, by examining whether Social Security surpluses have been correlated, after suitably adjusting for independent variables, with larger on-budget deficits (or smaller on-budget surpluses). The absence of any such correlation would suggest that Congress actually does disregard the Social Security surplus when making its other decisions. Smetters finds, however, that an extra dollar in the trust fund tends to worsen the on-budget measures, and indeed by *more* than a dollar. Other studies find that a dollar of trust fund buildup tends to increase on-budget deficits by about a dollar, suggesting no net benefit.[1] Accordingly, at present the weight of empirical evidence fails to support the "storage technology" claim, suggesting that the trust fund structure has not induced Congress to view the Social Security operating surpluses as unavailable for other uses.

## Are Operating Surpluses Being "Diverted" to Fund Other Programs?

A further dispute about earmarking zeroes in, with unfortunate formalism, on the question of how Social Security's annual operating surpluses are being used. Under a popular Democratic view, associated with the Clintonian lockbox , improper "diversion" of Social Security occurs whenever there is an on-budget deficit. The idea here is that Social Security dollars are improperly being used to pay for something else if the government otherwise fails to fund all of its outlays through current revenues.

Concern about "misuse" of Social Security funds also comes in a Republican version, popular with advocates of individual accounts, under which the current-year Social Security surplus melts away, like ice cubes in a cup of hot coffee, unless the government immediately gives it away. In this view, dramatized by President Bush's West Virginia photo-op comment, past years' operating surpluses are gone, and there is nothing more we can do about it. However, current and future years' operating surpluses can still be "saved," by promptly getting them out of the government's hands and into people's individual accounts.

Neither the Democratic nor the Republican view makes a whole lot of sense on its face, but both can be interpreted as attempting to improve Social Security's  storage technology via the use of fiscal language. The Democratic view applies a naïvely short-term view of earmarking by objecting to this year's use of a Social Security dollar to pay for something else, even if Social Security taxes and benefits match over the long run. It does, however, try to increase overall fiscal responsibility (which could help in paying future Social Security benefits) by requiring an annual on-budget surplus.

The Republican view attempts to force Congress to ignore Social Security surpluses by actually distributing them, albeit into individual accounts rather than as free cash. But this hope could fail in either of two ways. First, suppose Congress concludes that, with its obligation to pay future Social Security benefits having been eased by funding the accounts, it can now more readily afford to run large deficits. Then it might act no differently than if the government were still directly holding the cash for people's retirements. Second, suppose that out of sight really does mean out of mind – that Congress really does ignore the money it sends to individual accounts. This may be even worse, if the accounts are provided on top of existing Social Security benefits. If Congress simply adds funding for the accounts to everything else it has already promised, the fiscal gap increases without any offset.

## "Privatizing" or "Personalizing" Social Security

### Genesis of the Idea

The drive to replace part or all of traditional Social Security with a system based on individual accounts seems to have started in the 1970s. Prior conservative opposition to Social Security had withered, at least so far as Washington politics was concerned, with the defeat of Barry Goldwater in 1964. It did not revive much before the late 1970s, by which time the individual accounts idea had spread far enough that George W. Bush, not known as a careful student of the fiscal scene, had become a fan (Birnbaum 2005b).

So far as the privatization movement in Washington is concerned, "the book that started it all," as the website for the Cato Institute online bookstore accurately says, was Peter J. Ferrara's *Social Security: The Inherent Contradiction,* published by Cato in 1980. Cato spent much of the 1980s pushing the individual accounts idea, which by the end of the decade had caught on with other conservative think tanks in Washington, such as the Heritage Foundation and the American Enterprise Institute. However, "the real boost came later – during the go-go years of the 1990s. . . . [as] the stock market boomed, creating an environment friendly to personal investing" (Birnbaum 2005b).

During this time, support for individual accounts showed signs of expanding ideologically beyond the core conservative constituency. Even such Democrats as President Clinton, Senator Daniel Patrick Moynihan, and Senator Robert Kerrey began expressing interest in it. Democrats, however, tended to prefer individual accounts on top of traditional Social Security rather than in lieu of it. In addition, some Democrats favored having the government invest in the stock market directly through the Social Security Trust Fund, rather than via individual accounts.

The broader appeal of individual accounts soon began to recede, however. For one thing, the stock market boom of the 1990s had made investment in stocks look almost like free money, guaranteed to keep on offering huge annual returns. This was the era of books like *Dow 36,000* and *Dow 100,000*. The stock market bust in 2001 showed everyone that this was not a realistic scenario.

In addition, one of the big reasons for favoring individual accounts – that it would deter Congress from dissipating the unified budget surplus that included Social Security – weakened with the disappearance of any surplus. Once Congress was tolerating annual deficits in the hundreds of billions of dollars, it became hard to argue that it would be cautious if we only could find a way to make the deficit look bigger still.

Accordingly, by 2005, the political appeal of individual accounts had largely disappeared outside of conservative circles. President Bush nonetheless made them his leading second-term domestic policy initiative. He tried to motivate the change by emphasizing Social Security's long-term funding "crisis." This might have been a hard sale politically in any event, since the danger appeared to lie many years in the future. It became even harder when the Administration conceded that individual accounts would do nothing to improve Social Security's financing.

While the Bush Administration never fully spelled out the details of its proposal, the main features were as follows: (1) cause a portion of people's Social Security payroll taxes to be deposited in their newly created accounts, rather than being held by the government; (2) give people some discretion in investing the money held in the accounts, although the choices might be limited to a set of reasonably diversified stock and bond funds; and (3) reduce current-law Social Security benefits, although only for people below age fifty-five and possibly only for high earners. The benefit cut would apparently have included allowing the government to recoup the diverted payroll taxes, plus 3 percent annual interest, through dollar-for-dollar reductions in people's old-law benefits.

## Why (Initially) Call the Package of Changes "Privatization"?

Until recently, "privatization," was the universally accepted word of choice for a plan of this kind. Yet this term arguably was something of a misnomer.

The overall effect of the Bush plan would have been to orchestrate the debt-financed purchase by individuals of government-approved securities funds. To be sure, people's purchases through their accounts would not have been formally or directly debt-financed. But if people repaid the government for the diverted payroll taxes through what was effectively a secured interest in their traditional benefits, then in effect they would be debtors and the government a secured creditor. Moreover, the government in the interim would have replaced the lost revenue by borrowing trillions of extra dollars on world capital markets. In effect, then, the government would be borrowing money for on-lending to the account holders. Mandating the debt-financed purchase by individuals of trillions of dollars worth of government-approved securities, with the government interposing itself between account holders and world capital markets as the borrower of record, is not the sort of thing one might expect to hear described as "privatization."

Why, then, was the term so consistently used for so many years? One implicit rationale may have been that people would now "own" their individual accounts, whereas they ostensibly do not own their expected future traditional Social Security benefits. Given all the likely regulatory limits, however, along with the possibility of ongoing legislative tinkering, this view is not enormously robust. Another rationale might be that trillions of dollars were being moved from the public to the private sector via the accounts. But again, this was just a loan, and the government's allocative role in the economy would not necessarily shrink. Indeed, the government might even have more allocative sway than previously, through its ability to dictate permissible account holdings.

Misnomer though "privatization" may have been, it seems to have been adopted in good faith. The motivation from the start, however confused, had been to eliminate the evils, ranging from reduced competition and choice to the effects on government power and personal freedom, that proponents attributed to Social Security's "nationalizing the purchase of annuities" (Friedman 1962). The system should not be allowed to "transfer a larger and larger fraction of the productive assets of a country into the hands of a government bureaucracy" (Friedman 1999). Social Security's pending insolvency supposedly was a result of its being government-run, as George W. Bush argued as early as 1978, and as Peter Ferrara emphasized in his influential 1980 book. Likewise, the fact that Social Security was government-run ostensibly accounted for the low rates of return that it offered participants.

This last claim, made frequently by President Bush, had resonance to skeptics about government because it invoked, however inaptly, analogies such as the inability of Soviet centralized production to create adequate consumer products. It was based, however, on a fundamentally mistaken comparison. Current Social Security could easily and affordably be restructured to offer much higher benefits, and thus a much higher implicit rate of return, if not for the fiscal burden of paying off past claims to people who are at or near retirement age.

Supporters of individual accounts generally agree that current seniors' claims should be paid off in any event. So the game they are playing, whether they realize it or not, is to include the cost of paying off past claims when discussing current Social Security, and yet to ignore the very same claims, which account holders would have to pay as taxpayers, when discussing individual accounts. The claim about higher returns from individual accounts was therefore comparable to a borrower's saying: "I will increase your return by $100 a month, if you will agree to pay me $100 a month."

Perhaps the main reason for the use of the term "privatization" was that this gave it a positive valence to its longstanding main audience of economists and conservative think-tankers. Then, however, came the political stage, when the audience for changing Social Security broadened beyond conservative think tanks to the general public. This swiftly changed the operative fiscal language considerations.

## The Fiscal Language War of 2005

Proponents' widespread use for many years of the term "privatization" is easy to document. The Cato Institute ran something called the Project on Social Security Privatization from 1995 through 2002, when Republican leaders asked them to change the name to the Project on Social Security Choice (Allen 2005). An academically influential book-length study, edited by Martin Feldstein and published by the National Bureau of Economic Research with the University of Chicago Press in 1998, bore the title *Privatizing Social Security*. The term has been used by Karl Rove, Stephen Moore, and Grover Norquist.[2] President Bush referred to "privatizing Social Security" as late as the 2004 presidential campaign (Suskind 2004b). Throughout this period, demanding a different term would have been like demanding a new word to replace "banana."

In 2002, however, Republican leaders began doing exactly this. Having learned that the term "privatization" polled badly, they began instructing congressional candidates not to use it. In what even a writer for the conservative *National Review* called a "piece of brazen historical revisionism" (Ponnuru 2002), campaign officials at the National Republican Congressional Committee sent a memo to Republican candidates stating: "'Privatization' is a false and misleading word insofar as it is being used by Democrats to describe Republican positions on Social Security. . . . It is very important that we not allow reporters to shill for Democrat demagoguery by inaccurately characterizing 'personal accounts' and 'privatization' as one in the same" (Noah 2002a).

By December 2004, the term "privatization" was verboten among Republicans, notwithstanding its use by President Bush during the presidential campaign. "Private accounts," however, remained acceptable. Bush himself used it at a December 2004 economic conference, although now insisting that "this is not privatization of Social Security."[3] Others at the conference frequently used the term as well.

In January 2005, "private accounts" joined "privatization" on the scrap heap. As House Ways and Means Committee Chairman Bill Thomas put it, "They're personal accounts, not private accounts. No one is advocating privatizing Social Security" (Allen 2005). Likewise,

John McLaughlin, a Republican pollster, criticized the AARP for claiming that Bush favored "private accounts." He called this a loaded term, being used deliberately by the AARP to bias their polling results (Lang 2005).

Creating "personal accounts" and bringing about the "personalization" of Social Security were now the terms of choice. As a Republican strategy memo explained: "Personalization suggests increased personal ownership and control. Privatization connotes the total corporate takeover of Social Security" (Martinez 2005). The stakes were high, as "[we] win if the issue is defined as personal accounts. We lose if it is defined as privatization" (Associated Press 2005). Hence, Republicans not only frequently claimed to favor "personal accounts" while opposing "privatization,"[4] but vigorously lobbied the press to reject all other terms as nefarious and biased Democratic spin. President Bush, for example, chided a Washington Post reporter for using the banished term "privatization" in an interview, saying that "[w]e don't want to be editorializing, at least in the questions" (Allen 2005).

Some reporters promptly fell in line and altered their usage as demanded by the Republicans (Lang 2005), and "privatization" became a primarily Democratic term, commonly identified as such when used by the press. However, "private accounts" hung around more stubbornly, and "personalization" took off like a lead balloon.

There are several explanations for the Republicans' incomplete success in compelling a fiscal language change. For one, while "personal accounts" was a plausible term, one could not easily argue that it was more apt than "private accounts." The term "Social Security personalization" sounded downright ludicrous, its desperate contrivance all too plain. Choosing among diversified stock and bond portfolios on a government-supplied list does not have the same "personal" feel for most of us as choosing, say, a car, a cologne, or a breakfast cereal. And it is hard to completely rewrite the history of a given term within so short a time while facing opponents as determined and well-organized as the Democrats were in the Social Security debate.

In George Orwell's *1984,* an early landmark in the study of political language manipulation, the residents of Oceania are prone to suddenly learning that they have always been at war with Eurasia and allied with

Eastasia. Or they suddenly learn that it has always been the other way around. They are not allowed to notice the switch. This is not, however, the world we live in. At least not yet.

## Summary

The earmarking convention, under which payroll tax revenues are treated as paying for benefits under Social Security and Part A of Medicare, is those two programs' most distinctive fiscal language feature. The use of this convention reflects the enactors' goal of creating significant political pre-commitment to the programs, without creating the same level of obligation as that associated with government bonds.

Earmarking is perhaps the biggest reason for the view that seniors have a right to their current-law Social Security and Medicare benefits. The prevalence of such a view is politically desirable up to a point, given the necessary element of pre-commitment in a credible retirement program, and given as well how the programs' political palatability might be affected if they were viewed more accurately as in the main paternalistically imposing limitations on how people can use their lifetime resources. The "rights" view can be politically harmful, however, if it makes benefits changes a one-way ratchet, with increases for current seniors being permissible, but not cuts.

Social Security and Medicare also benefit politically from being viewed as "social insurance" that is fundamentally distinct from redistribution under such little-loved systems as the income tax and welfare. In fact, however, Social Security and Medicare are less easily rationalized than those other fiscal systems as providing a type of insurance that markets are unable to offer. Their widely accepted social insurance label is largely a product of form, reflecting the fact that their earmarked revenues may be analogized to insurance company premiums, and that their benefits are not overtly income-conditioned within their formal program boundaries.

The earmarking convention, when not being followed annually, requires something like the Social Security and Medicare Part A Trust

Funds to keep track of the tax–benefit relationship over time. The trust funds matter insofar as they help in keeping track of an accepted convention. In practice, however, there is much confusion about their significance. They do not hold third-party assets that can be used to finance future benefits, and yet they are not shams or frauds for failing to do so.

The trust funds, in addition to implementing earmarking, could in principle aid genuine pre-funding of future benefits by influencing Congress to overlook the programs' accumulations when making other budgetary decisions. However, the evidence suggests that not even the Social Security Trust Fund, additions to which are excluded from the on-budget deficit, has had this effect.

The 2005 Bush Administration drive to replace part of Social Security with individual accounts brought fiscal language choices explicitly to center stage. Proponents of accounts learned to their dismay that just because one's term of choice is arguably a misnomer does not mean that one can banish it overnight. The aesthetics of language choice are offended by repeated hairpin turns, or at least those that so transparently serve a controversial agenda.

# Tax Expenditures

*What's in a name? That which we call a rose / By any other word would smell as sweet.*

— Juliet, in William Shakespeare's *Romeo and Juliet*

*[S]ometimes you need to conceal a fact with words.*

— Niccolo Machiavelli

## Names versus Structural Terms

The dispute over what to call the "privatization" or "personalization" of Social Security was simply about a name. While some names for rules or policies may be more accurate, or alternatively more misleading, than others – "Clear Skies," for example, is not an honest name for a proposal to allow more air pollution – in the end, names are a matter of convention, like words generally. Thus, consider the recent renaming of the "estate tax" as the "death tax." While the new name is less accurate than the old one, given that estates are the tax base and that death alone does not trigger the tax, still, if "death tax" becomes the accepted usage, then "death tax" it is, just as a dog is called a dog because, when you use that word, other people know what you mean.

For fiscal language that is associated with a specific empirical content, by contrast with the use of names, convention is not enough. Thus, as discussed in Chapter 2, once we define the "size of government" to reflect what people have in mind when they discuss it, the question of whether some set of policy changes will result in a smaller government is empirical. Likewise, if we are interested in distribution, and define "progressivity" as transferring resources from high earners to low earners, then a given set of changes either are or are not progressive, no matter what people call them.

Convention has no bearing on the proper use of fundamental economic concepts such as "distribution" and "allocation." Things are more complicated, however, for fiscal language terms such as "taxes" and "spending." These terms are treated as if they were meaningful, rather than as arbitrary names, yet in practice they are defined formally in terms of the direction of discrete cash flows.

Under one possible approach to the use of these terms, one could say that, since they are purely formal, a "tax rule" is any rule that is placed in the tax code or administered by the IRS. Perhaps we might add to this constraints from the folk definition of taxes, such as barring the trading or refundability of tax credits and deductions.

Either way, we are saying that anything goes. A good example of this approach, from the George H. W. Bush Administration, is the statement of Office of Management and Budget (OMB) Director Richard Darman that the "tax increases" Bush had foresworn during the 1988 presidential campaign were to be defined purely by public perceptions of the term:

> "I think that the President meant no new taxes as it would ordinarily be understood by ordinary Americans. I think a version of that is the duck test. . . . – 'if it looks like a duck, walks like a duck, and quacks like a duck, it's a duck.' That is the test that it seems to me is to be applied with respect to taxes. If ordinary people think that what we are talking about is a tax increase, it's a tax increase." (OMB 1989)

For purposes of interpreting a campaign promise, perhaps Darman's "duck test" was good enough. However, when common usage affirmatively misleads people, we need to do better. Thus, if people think that the government is smaller when taxes and spending are lower but we know that converting a particular "spending" rule into a "tax benefit" would do nothing to change its substance, we may want to counteract the confusion by modifying the prevailing fiscal language.

The aim of improving our terminology underlies the most long-standing fiscal language debate in U.S. budgetary politics. This is the debate about "tax expenditures," a term coined in 1967 by Stanley Surrey, the renowned Harvard Law School professor who at the time was nearing the end of an eight-year stint at the U.S. Treasury Department as assistant secretary for tax policy. Tax expenditures soon became (and have remained) an official budgetary category for estimating and reporting purposes, but are widely controversial.

## Origins and Reception of Tax Expenditure Analysis

Tax expenditure analysis seems to have been invented twice. In Germany as early as 1954, writers had noticed the "equivalence between special tax deductions, credits, and other allowances and government subsidies" (Shannon 1986, 203). This apparently was no criticism. Rather, "the German literature generally affirms that the tax system furnishes a useful instrument for implementing economic and social policy and acknowledges that it is often used for such 'nonfiscal' purposes" (204). By 1959, the German government had begun reporting on subsidies in the federal budget, including those supplied through the tax system, with an eye to improving budgetary control. The stated motivation was to place these "invisible" and indirect subsidies (measured by the foregone revenue) on a par with those that were provided more overtly through direct spending (204). By 1967, the German government was issuing budgetary reports that included measures of tax subsidies that it classified as indirect spending.

The actual term "tax expenditure" starts with Stanley Surrey, who had long been prominent as an advocate of applying progressive tax rates to a comprehensive income tax base. On November 15, 1967, in a widely noticed speech to a group called the Money Marketeers, Surrey called for a "tax expenditure budget" that would report the revenue cost of "deliberate departures from accepted concepts of net income . . . [through which] our tax system does operate to affect the private economy in ways that are usually accomplished by expenditures – in effect to produce an expenditure system described in tax language" (Surrey 1973, 3).

Surrey subsequently supplied a convenient creation myth for U.S. tax expenditure analysis. In September 1967, two months before the speech, while sitting in a hearing of the Ways and Means Committee of the House of Representatives, he ostensibly had experienced a sudden "illumination" (3). The hearing had been called to assess President Johnson's proposal that a 10 percent income tax surcharge be enacted to help pay for the Vietnam War. Many committee members, however, wanted to cut spending rather than just raising taxes. They spent several days examining how this could be done, and learning that it was harder than they had hoped. As Surrey later recalled:

> For the moment, the committee, in its desire to see expenditures controlled and thus make a tax increase more palatable if it must be voted, became an Appropriations Committee. But in its scrutiny of the expenditures listed in the budget, the committee had forgotten what it knew as a tax committee. Never once in its examination of the direct expenditures listed in the budget did the committee pause to consider the dollars involved in the tax incentives and tax subsidies contained in the Internal Revenue Code.
>
> It was not for lack of knowledge. The committee members were completely aware that through tax benefits the income tax law provided financial assistance to this or that business [as well as to state and local governments and to such groups as the aged, the sick, and the blind]. . . . But the committee kept the financial assistance furnished by these tax provisions completely separated and isolated in its mind from the task at hand. Indeed, the connection with that task simply did not occur to the members. (1–2)

The experience of sitting through this, Surrey tells us, "suddenly illuminated many questions." Could this gap in the members' understanding be addressed? What if he were to have the Treasury Department staff prepare a tax expenditure budget, parallel to the official budget listings for direct expenditures? This would aid the policy process, the next time spending cut issues arose, both by creating a ready list of special tax provisions that really were spending, and by giving policy makers the numbers that they would need to put these provisions on a par with direct spending in the budget process.

In actual fact, Surrey seems to have had this in mind as early as 1953, when he wrote a paper (apparently never published) criticizing "technical escape routes [from the income tax] for favored groups" that Congress had deliberately enacted, and quantifying the revenue lost due to these provisions (see Surrey 1953). Moreover, for a year previously, the U.S. Treasury Department had been devoting substantial resources to outlining the subsidy elements of the tax code. With Surrey's approval, Gabriel G. Rudney, a Treasury economist, had spent a year at the Brookings Institution working on the question of how a tax expenditure budget would be presented. Rudney had even produced a paper in August 1967 (Forman 1986, 538), a month before Surrey's sudden "illumination."

The reason for the creation myth is easy to discern. Surrey's stated motivation simply to improve the budget process (the same motivation as that in Germany), while undoubtedly sincere, was also somewhat bland. He had a more controversial motivation as well. Applying progressive tax rates to a comprehensive tax base had long been a personal cause of his. The tax expenditure budget thus served for him as a tool of tax policy, not just of budget policy. It offered a hit list, identifying preferential provisions that he thought should be removed from the tax code and disappear altogether unless they could be justified as direct spending.

Back at Harvard Law School, Surrey spelled out his arguments against tax preferences. They generally were "upside-down subsidies," unfairly aiding the rich more than the poor, because their value depended on one's marginal tax rate (Surrey 1973, 134–138). Moreover, "by dividing the consideration and administration of government programs, [they] confuse[d] and complicate[d] that consideration in the Congress, in administration, and in the budget process." (141)

From the start, therefore, tax expenditure analysis in the United States was both a purportedly objective descriptive tool and a weapon of political combat. Surrey avowedly made political calculations, such as keeping off the list certain items (including gifts and imputed rent) whose inclusion would unduly have "puzzled" the public because expert understanding that they really were income remained too "novel" (Surrey 1973, 18). The fact that he had a well-known political agenda – and, in a town like Washington, might have been assumed to have one even if he didn't – inevitably colored reception of the idea. From the start it attracted greater controversy in the United States than in Germany.

Under Surrey's direction, the Treasury Department published its first tax expenditure budget in 1968, although he was unable to get it included in the president's official budget. The Nixon Administration, being "cool to the tax expenditure concept" (Forman 1986, 541) but not completely opposed, continued to prepare estimates like those done under Surrey but to deny them official status. However, the Congressional Budget and Impoundment Act of 1974, a response both to deficit concerns and to turf wars between the Democrats in Congress and a Watergate-weakened President Nixon, made mandatory the inclusion of tax expenditure estimates both in the president's budget and in certain congressional reports (544–545).

Tax expenditures were officially defined as "those revenue losses attributable to provisions of the federal tax laws which allow a special exclusion, exemption, or deduction from gross income or which provide a special credit, a preferential rate of tax, or a deferral of tax liability."[1] As the twice-used word "special" helped to show, the key idea was one of departures from the normal or regular income tax structure. Accordingly, tax expenditure status did not extend to all departures from taxing economic or Haig–Simons income, conventionally defined as the market value of the taxpayer's consumption plus her change in net worth during the taxable year (Simons 1938, 50). For example, the failure to tax unrealized appreciation in the value of assets held by the taxpayer, or the imputed rental or use value enjoyed by the owners of durable consumer assets such as homes and cars, are not defined as tax expenditures. They are considered structural departures from taxing Haig–Simons income, rather than special concessions that could alternatively have taken the form of explicit government spending.

Official recognition of tax expenditure analysis did not eliminate the view in many quarters that it was a tendentious exercise in furthering Surrey's tax reform agenda. Its chances of broader intellectual acceptance suffered a particularly heavy blow in 1969 when Boris Bittker, one of the few tax law professors whose renown approached Surrey's, published a widely noted critique.

Bittker pounced in particular on Surrey's call for a "full accounting" of expenditure items in the income tax law. The accounting was far from full, Bittker noted, and the decisions regarding what to include and exclude were arbitrary. Worse still, many rules' status as tax expenditures or genuine tax rules simply could not be ascertained, due to the lack of an "agreed conceptual model" for the spending-free income tax (Bittker 1969, 258).

In fact, Bittker's article is more of a "yes, but" than a "no," because he agreed at the end that "a more limited accounting" could be useful, "provid[ing] information that would be helpful in applying our political, economic, and ethical criteria in making policy judgments about the income tax system" (260–261). However, it was a "yes, but" in which the "but" came first and accounted for almost seventeen of the article's eighteen pages. Bittker therefore played an important role in conveying the message that experts were split about the cogency of tax expenditure analysis and that the analysis was more a partisan weapon than an objective descriptive tool.

Another big objection to tax expenditure analysis that colored its acceptance was its supposed implication that "our money belongs to the government, and that the government is doing us a favor by not taxing it" (see Thuronyi 1988, 1178). This is not a valid criticism unless the "normative tax" that is being used to define "spending" applies at a 100 percent rate to all of our money. Tax expenditure analysis identifies *differences* in the tax treatment of different items, and assumes no taxation in excess of that which the government actually applies to *something* – although concededly it benchmarks the treatment of higher-taxed items and has not traditionally been used to measure instances of overtaxation or tax penalty.

Still, once one sheds spending illusion, or confusing the size of the nominal dollar flows between individuals and the government with the actual size of government, tax expenditure analysis can aid a small-government agenda. It helps to identify narrowly targeted government interventions in the economy that presumably make the government allocatively larger than if it raised the same overall revenue more neutrally.

Spending illusion offered only one reason for conservatives in particular to be hostile to tax expenditure analysis. They also responded to the liberal political agenda of many of its proponents. Surrey in particular, it was well known, "felt very strongly that the tax system should be sharply progressive, and he regarded 'all the Mickey Mouse stuff in the Code' as attenuating the progressivity of the rate structure" (Forman 1986, 538).

One last source of objection to tax expenditure analysis became ever more important in the decades after its official adoption. In the late 1960s and early 1970s, comprehensive income taxation was a dominant intellectual norm among economists and lawyers, as it had been for several decades. Starting in the mid-1970s, however, consumption taxation began to attract significant intellectual support. To consumption tax advocates, tax expenditure analysis as practiced gave undue aid and comfort to the income tax enemy, by labeling as "tax expenditures" rules that actually were correct from a consumption tax standpoint, such as exempting certain types of interest income.

The end result of all these cross-currents has been a state of affairs in which tax expenditure analysis lacks general acceptance even though it is officially enshrined. Its status as an objective descriptive tool is shaky even though the most powerful critique has not prominently been made. This is the point that, if taxes and spending are themselves arbitrary categories, then the claim that something is "really" spending rather than a tax is hard to credit.

## Rationales for Redescribing Actual Tax Rule A as Hypothetical Tax Rule B Plus Spending Rule C

### Choosing among the Infinite Possible Counterfactuals

Tax expenditure analysis rests on an equivalence. Tax Rule A, it suggests, is really a spending rule, and should thus be restated as hypothetical Tax Rule B plus Spending Rule C, which in combination are equivalent to it.

Thus, recall the example from Chapter 2 in which a hypothetical "weapons supplier tax credit" (WSTC) replaced $60 billion of weapons procurement "spending" with a $60 billion "tax reduction" that caused the very same people to end up with the very same cash in exchange for the very same weapons. In such a case, where the rule at issue seems wholly unrelated to tax system design, the redescription is simple and easily rationalized. Tax Rule B is simply the tax code minus the WSTC, and the provision's entire $60 billion cost is attributed to Spending Rule C.

In other cases, even if a given tax rule is "wrong," some sort of replacement rule is needed. Thus, consider accelerated depreciation for a particular type of machinery. Since some sort of cost recovery should be allowed if we are taxing net income, the process of redescription requires a bit more work. We must first work out the details of the correct hypothetical Tax Rule B before completing the exercise.

So long as hypothetical Rules B plus C sum to actual Tax Rule A, the exercise is tautologically correct. To have any significance, however, the restatement must have a credible motivation. After all, we could just as easily decompose Tax Rule A into the even more favorable Tax Rule D (say, triple WSTCs) plus Negative-Spending Rule E (requiring the taxpayer to refund two-thirds of the triple WSTCs). Actual Tax Rule A could then be described as a tax penalty relative to hypothetical Rule D, as measured by hypothetical Rule E. One thus needs to explain why a particular counterfactual should be chosen from among the infinite possibilities as capturing the "true" character of Tax Rule A.

In practice, the claim that actual Tax Rule A is really hypothetical Tax Rule B plus Spending Rule C rests on the further claim that, if the legislature had meant only to raise revenue under its general policy for doing so, B is what it would have enacted. This claim is easy enough to credit when A is the WSTC and B is its absence. Even for cases as easy as that, however, it needs to be spelled out more carefully.

## Defining Tax Expenditures Relative to a "Tax System" That Serves Distributional Purposes

Why do we tax income? If the aim were just to raise revenue, this could be done in any number of ways – through a uniform head tax, for example. The idea behind using an income tax is to distribute burdens equitably based on a particular measure of ability to pay. More broadly, adding transfers to the mix, the idea is to "put into practice a conception of economic or distributive justice" (Murphy and Nagel 2002, 3).

In addition to offering a measure of ability to pay, an income tax discourages people from earning income. This allocative effect, however, presumably is not the aim. Rather, it is an unavoidable by-product of using a distributional measure that people can influence through the decisions they make. So the idea of levying an income tax remains purely distributional, not allocative, although its effects inevitably lie in both realms.

Many people dislike the income tax and believe that we should switch to a consumption tax. Indeed, I have advocated this myself, conditioned on the system's remaining sufficiently progressive (Shaviro 2004c). This would change both our distributional measure and its allocative by-products. A consumption tax, no less than an income tax, discourages work and market consumption, but it avoids discouraging saving. Just as under an income tax, however, the allocative effects are viewed by most people as collateral damage, rather than as desirable and intended.

Income and consumption taxation, therefore, are both best viewed as tools of the government's distribution branch. This branch would "want" to measure income or consumption accurately, subject to issues of administrative burden. It might also "want" to treat various other types of information as distributionally relevant – for example, health care needs or family size. But it would not consider adopting the WSTC. That provision, if included in a set of rules called the income tax, would have to reflect the input of the allocation branch.

This suggests that taxes versus spending is not really the distinction that proponents of tax expenditure analysis have (or ought to have) in mind. As we have seen repeatedly, the direction of a particular cash flow, within a larger series of cash flows, is not meaningful. Rather, the idea that reasonably could lie behind recasting Tax Rule A as "really" Tax Rule B plus Spending Rule C is one of addressing confusion between provisions attributable to the distribution branch and those attributable to the allocation branch.

Labeling primarily allocative rules within the income tax as "tax expenditures" does not require endorsing Stanley Surrey's view that all such rules should be purged. The existing federal income tax might well, in some set of cases, be the best available instrument for pursuing particular allocative goals (see Weisbach and Nussim 2004). The point is simply to improve public understanding of what is going on.

The motivation for doing this should be clear. Tax expenditure analysis, as redefined to address the economically coherent distinction between allocation and distribution rather than the empty one between "taxes" and "spending," helps to counter the undue political advantage, in some settings, of pursuing allocative policy through the tax code. Surrey's story about sitting in the Ways and Means hearing describes only a trivial (because easily corrected) manifestation of the problem, in the form of political actors not recognizing the practical interchangeability of tax and appropriations rules.

The deeper problem, especially after thirty years of tax expenditure analysis, is not that policy makers fail to recognize the practical interchangeability of tax and spending rules. Nor is it that they fail to give tax rules significant scrutiny. Tax changes are almost always on the political agenda. The problem, rather, lies in people's differing intuitive responses to "tax" and "spending" rules, even when the two are identical beneath their outer attire. Relabeling a tax provision as a "tax expenditure," on the view that it is the type of thing the allocation branch would typically do through "spending," may improve public understanding of the provision's rationale.

To show how tax expenditure analysis, thus reconceptualized, might work, several leading examples from the long-standing debate merit discussion.

### Medical Deductions

Deductions for medical expenses have been included from the start in official tax expenditure lists. Almost from the start, however, this has been controversial. William Andrews (1972) argued that medical deductions are not really tax expenditures, but rather are appropriate adjustments in measuring ability to pay. Thus, suppose that Jones and Smith both earn $50,000, but Jones stays healthy while Smith gets injured and has to pay $10,000 for restorative surgery. Even if Smith fully recovers, we might think of him as $10,000 worse off than Jones, since he had to pay that amount just to get back to the same place.

Many tax policy writers disagree with Andrews. They argue, for example, that receiving health care is no less a form of consumption than eating food. Moreover, they note that medical deductions are effectively a kind of health insurance, since outlays are effectively reimbursed (via reduced income tax liability) at the taxpayer's marginal rate. Why should low-bracket taxpayers get lower reimbursement rates than high-bracket taxpayers?

Whichever way one comes out in this debate, it clearly is a live issue in the distribution realm about which people reasonably disagree. Surrey's way of handling the dispute, which was to insist on treating his view as correct, is unsatisfying as well as impolitic. It would be far more reasonable to classify this as a disputed case – one that is neither a clearly appropriate deduction from the ability-to-pay standpoint, like the cost of earning gross income, nor something clearly different, like the WSTC.

### Adjustments for Household Characteristics

The principal adjustments for household characteristics that are included in the United States income tax include

1) distinct filing statuses for married individuals, single individuals, and unmarried heads of households (with implications for such features as the width of rate brackets);
2) deductions for each qualifying member of the household, called "personal exemptions"; and
3) the allowance of child tax credits.

As it happens, only the last of these is officially treated as a tax expenditure. This presumably reflects the optics of offering a credit, since deductions at least may look like inputs to measuring "income."

Household characteristics plainly are relevant to distributional policy. For example, in assessing a given individual's ability to pay, all household resources, not just those that he or she personally owns, may matter. Mrs. Bill Gates is unlikely to need public assistance even if she earns nothing. Moreover, it certainly is plausible that, as between two households with the same resources, we might want to treat the one with twelve children more generously than the one with none. Thus, classifying any household adjustment as a "tax expenditure" seems questionable.

### Double Taxation of Corporate Earnings

Many countries, including the United States, impose two taxes on corporate earnings: first at the corporate level, and then again at the shareholder level when the earnings are distributed. Is double corporate taxation properly attributed to the distribution branch? That depends on how one interprets the question.

On the one hand, only individuals can bear tax burdens. A disparity between the tax burdens placed on the owners of corporate and noncorporate investment is on a par, from a distributional standpoint, with disparately taxing wages depending on one's profession. From this perspective, double corporate taxation clearly is a negative tax expenditure or tax penalty.

On the other hand, the double tax may reflect voters' genuine though mistaken belief that corporations, like flesh-and-blood individuals, actually can bear tax burdens. It also may reflect some policy makers' belief that double corporate taxation is a politically convenient way of increasing progressivity. And it may reflect administrative considerations in operating the distribution branch. Finally, if we ask whether the double tax reflects conscious allocative policy of the sort typically left to appropriations committees, the answer is probably no. From these perspectives, double corporate taxation is not a negative tax expenditure or tax penalty.

Given the conflicting perspectives, the answer to how double corporate taxation should be classified depends on the question. I address this dilemma later by suggesting a separate category for "structural" rules, which depart from pure Haig–Simons income taxation but appear more administratively motivated than straight appropriations substitutes.

### Realization Requirement and the Lack of an Inflation Adjustment

A tax on economic income would reach unrealized fluctuations in asset value. It also would adjust comprehensively for price-level changes, so that nominal inflationary gain would not be taxed. An income tax that makes neither adjustment arguably includes a tax expenditure for unrealized gain, along with tax penalties for unrealized loss and the inclusion of nominal inflationary gains.

Leaning against a tax expenditure classification, these two features of most actual income taxes reflect administrative considerations of the distribution branch. And it is hard to imagine Surrey's tax committees, if they adopted a purer income tax, handing off to the appropriations committees the question of whether or not to replicate the incentives created by a realization-based system without inflation adjustments. Thus, the classification problem resembles that for double corporate taxation, and ought to be similarly handled.

### Municipal Bond Interest versus Other Interest Income

Under U.S. tax law, interest on the bonds issued by state and local governments generally is tax-exempt, whereas other interest income generally is taxable. One cannot say which of these two approaches to taxing interest income is correct, from the standpoint of the distribution branch, unless one is prepared to wade into the decades-old debate between income and consumption tax advocates.

It is clear, however, that the contrast between the tax treatment of the two types of interest income makes no sense in purely distributional terms. A dollar of interest income is a dollar of interest income, so the disparity could be defended only on allocative grounds, such as the aim of aiding state and local governments when they borrow. Thus, tax expenditure analysis ought to apply here somehow, but requires more than just distinguishing between allocation and distribution.

In response to this issue, Stanley Surrey successfully argued early on that official measures should reflect only the income tax perspective. He presented this argument (Surrey 1972, 21) in ostensibly neutral terms, and wholly without reference to his own well-known support for income taxation:

> Each tax has its own appropriate structure and each has its advantages and disadvantages. But the scope of each such tax in its actual application must be tested by *its* concepts, which concepts led to its choice in the first instance. The structure of a normative income tax is not to be tested by the values or concepts used by those who prefer that a consumption tax be chosen instead, and vice versa. A tax expenditure budget for an income tax, to be useful in seeing what objectives that tax has been asked to carry in addition to taxing net income, is to be framed by using a normative definition of "income."

In other words, we actually have an income tax — that is what we have enacted — so income tax principles must be used in the tax expenditure budget whether they are right or wrong, until such time as a consumption tax is officially enacted. Never mind that, according to most tax experts, what we really have is best described as a hybrid income/consumption tax including numerous features of each.[2] "Income tax" is the official name, so an income tax is what it is.

Surrey's failure to win general acceptance of his solution is no surprise. Consumption tax advocates could reasonably interpret his arguments as amounting to the following: "Please forget for the moment that I am an income tax advocate. I want you to accept as 'normative' the type of tax that we officially have, which I know you do not like, because we have it, and even though in fact we do not have it. I will of course do the same for you, either in comparatively trivial settings such as state sales taxes, or if you win outright at the federal level, which we both know is highly unlikely. Please do not be swayed by the fact that, by accepting the income tax as normative for these purposes, you may help me in our ongoing disputes concerning tax reform."

This is an offer that one definitely *can* refuse. The suspicion that tax expenditure analysis served unacknowledged and controversial political agendas may further have been heightened by several other features. One is its one-way ratchet in measuring tax expenditures but not tax penalties. Another is its treating double corporate taxation as the norm, on the ground that it is a merely structural feature of the U.S. system. This meant that any relief from double taxation, even if it brought the system closer to Haig–Simons, would be treated as a tax expenditure.

In the meantime, Surrey had left himself open to such critiques as the following: "[H]aving abandoned the purity of Haig-Simons, [he] is adrift in a sea of value judgments and his is no better than any other expert's. Thus, it is presumptuous for him to label his definition (i.e., the Treasury's) as the one correct definition, any deviations from which will be labeled tax expenditures" (Bartlett 2001, 415). Such critiques could not be fully rebutted by arguing that, say, the realization requirement really is a "structural" feature of the income tax in the sense of serving administrative aims and not being readily transmutable into a direct spending program. Nor would it have helped to point out that similar approaches to tax expenditure analysis are followed in other countries without arousing as much controversy. The setting was simply too politically loaded for a creature as unlovely (and unloved) as the "normal income tax structure" to win requisite acceptance as the one and only baseline for measuring deviations.

In short, Surrey overreached by making tax expenditure analysis, while well designed to advance his policy aims, unduly controversial. Not sufficiently respected as an objective descriptive tool, it could not function effectively as a political weapon. By keeping basic distributional issues too far from center stage, based on the dubious claim that they have been wholly resolved for purposes of the particular tax at issue, Surrey invited the lack of acceptance that has continued to plague the tax expenditure concept.

## Design in Light of the Purposes of Tax Expenditure Analysis

Tax expenditure analysis is too inherently flexible a tool to have only one or a single set of narrowly defined purposes. Restating actual Tax Rule A as hypothetical Tax Rule B plus Spending Rule C need only be interesting and informative in order to be justified, since it is tautologically correct if C is defined as the positive or negative outlay that is needed to reconcile A with B.

One reason for valuing such a measure is budgetary. As in Surrey's creation myth and the actual German history of tax expenditure analysis, one might mainly be interested in provisions that, as a matter of presumed intent and/or convenient design, could alternatively be done through "spending." For example, if one is trying to reduce budget deficits, placing narrowly crafted special tax benefits on a par with appropriations would make sense, whereas the gap between realized income and economic income might not be of as much immediate interest.

If we are interested in distributional policy as well as budgetary control, then all arguable or clear departures from some version or other of an ideal system may be of interest, whether or not they could be converted into direct spending. Thus, one might want to compare the existing U.S. "income" tax to a pure Haig–Simons income tax, and also to a broad-based consumption tax. From such a perspective, moreover, the aim of offering more information, rather than less, would be advanced by making reasonable distinctions in the accounts. For example, even if one includes medical deductions on the ground that they arguably are a tax expenditure, one might want to distinguish them from provisions that (after the fashion of the WSTC) are unambiguously allocative. Likewise, one might want to distinguish between structural provisions (such as the realization requirement) and those resembling the WSTC. So the main difference between the budgetary and tax policy perspectives is simply that, under the latter, more information is potentially interesting.

Arguing for more varied and informative tax expenditure analysis might approach banality (who wants to argue for *less* information?) if the United States history of the analysis were different. Indeed, various countries provide alternative benchmarks and distinguish structural provisions, or those whose classification as "spending" is relatively ambiguous (OECD 1996, 10). In the U.S. income tax setting, however, the analysis has been sufficiently waylaid by the aftershocks of Surrey's bold play that such a proposed revision verges on the radical. Proponents of Surrey-style income tax reform are reluctant to surrender the income tax's pride of place. And some opponents of the Surrey view are simply too hostile to the analysis in all forms. Nonetheless, the development of fuller and better information is worth exploring.

## Suggestions for Modifying Tax Expenditure Analysis

Currently, official tax expenditure estimates are organized by budgetary function, such as "transportation" and "community and regional development." In addition, they are generally quite lengthy, due to their including a host of relatively small items (such as numerous separate listings for different uses of tax-exempt municipal bonds). This structure is better suited for the use of tax expenditure analysis as a tool of budgetary policy than of tax policy.

In the future, the budgetary and tax policy reporting functions could be separated. For budgetary reporting purposes, the analysis could largely keep its present form, apart from clearly identifying items that (1) are not tax expenditures from a consumption tax baseline, such as the exclusion of municipal bond interest, and (2) arguably are not tax expenditures even from an income tax baseline, such as the allowance of medical deductions.

For tax policy reporting purposes, items such as all municipal bonds could be aggregated, and the organization should generally be in terms of tax policy status, rather than budgetary area. Moreover, negative tax expenditures (tax penalties) could be folded into the various categories. While there is no single right way of organizing the tax policy version of tax expenditure analysis, one possibility, which I offer here in the hope of stimulating further discussion, is the following:

1) Comprehensive Income Tax Baseline
   a) *Structural departures from the baseline*: Items listed here, as positive or negative adjustments depending on the circumstances, might include homeowners' imputed rental income, the double corporate tax, the realization requirement, and the lack of inflation adjustments.
   b) *Other clear departures from the baseline*: The exemption for municipal bond interest is an example of an item that would go here, as would the WSTC if enacted.
   c) *Arguable departures, depending on how one defines the baseline*: Items listed here might include medical deductions and exclusions for employer-provided health insurance, charitable deductions, individuals' state and local tax deductions, and the exclusion of gifts received.[3]
2) Comprehensive Consumption Tax Baseline
   a) *Structural departures from the baseline*: Just as under the income tax baseline, items such as imputed rent, the double corporate tax, and the lack of inflation adjustments could go here. The nontaxation of unrealized gain would not be included, as it is consistent with consumption tax treatment.
   b) *Clear departures from the baseline*: Items akin to the WSTC would go here, as would income tax–style rules such as taxing most types of interest income.
   c) *Arguable departures, depending on how one defines the baseline*: As they are under the comprehensive income tax baseline, items such as charitable, medical, and state and local tax deductions would go here.

## Summary

Tax expenditure analysis is too potentially useful to be rejected on the ground that no single conceptual model for a tax system has won universal acceptance. Nor need the emptiness of the distinction between "taxes" and "spending" prevent it from improving information and reducing the tendentiousness of our fiscal language. At least in the United States, efforts to make tax expenditure analysis do too much — by shaping it to serve as an instrument for one particular vision of tax reform — have unnecessarily undermined its acceptance. By adapting it to use more flexible and varied measures that clarify its relationship to underlying distributional aims and that take account of reasonable disagreements as to those aims, we can hope to improve both its informational content and its general background influence on budgetary and tax policy debate.

# 9

## Welfare, Cash Grants, and Marginal Rates

*"Contrariwise," continued Tweedledee, "if it was so, it might be; and if it were so, it would be; but as it isn't, it ain't. That's logic."*
— Lewis Carroll, *Through the Looking Glass*

### Taxes, Spending, and Marginal Rates

The tax expenditure concept offers a constructive, albeit imperfect, response to the problems for allocation policy that result from mistakenly treating "taxes" and "spending" as meaningful categories. But distribution policy has been badly waylaid as well. In particular, while lifetime net tax rates (treating transfers as negative taxes) have begun to receive some attention in discussions of long-term budget policy, discussions of aid to the poor remain mired in the old terminology, leading to important policy failures.

The point that transfers are simply negative taxes dates back at least to Richard Musgrave (1959). Many economists and lawyers understand it. Yet it has so little penetrated public discourse that, even among experts, few seem to keep it in mind when discussing such basic questions as what the marginal tax rate structure in our country either actually is or ought to be.

Consider two truisms – or actually, falsisms – that are so conventional as to seem almost banal. Both concern the degree of graduation of marginal rates, or the extent to which they increase with income. The first holds that graduated marginal rates are the defining attribute of a progressive system. Thus, the renowned and still frequently cited study by Walter Blum and Harry Kalven (1953), *The Uneasy Case for Progressive Taxation,* takes as its subject the justifiability of the graduated marginal rate structure of the income tax. Blum and Kalven decline, on grounds of unfeasibility, to examine progressivity in terms of the relationship between taxes and benefits. The second widely accepted truism holds that the United States actually has graduated marginal rates at present, in that poor people pay the lowest marginal rates.

Neither of these two truisms is actually true. First, graduated marginal rates are not necessary for progressivity, defined more meaningfully in terms of the fiscal system's overall treatment of the poor and the rich. Indeed, having low marginal rates in lower income ranges may not be a good idea even if one favors significant progressivity. Second, marginal rates often are highest for poor people, to a degree that might widely be considered shocking if it were better understood. Indeed, the marginal rates for some poor and near-poor individuals are so high, approaching or even exceeding 100 percent, that they create harsh "poverty traps" that frustrate people's efforts to better their circumstances through work. The fact that marginal rates need not be as low as is commonly thought near the bottom of the income distribution does not mean that they should be anywhere near 100 percent.

The poverty traps result from the rapid phasing out of transfers, such as Temporary Aid to Needy Families (TANF), food stamps, Medicaid, the earned income tax credit (EITC), and housing subsidies. The rapidity of the phase-outs reflects the common view that only poor and near-poor people should get these transfers. As you leave poverty, therefore, you may rapidly lose many thousands of dollars worth of benefits, on top of also paying various positive taxes on your earnings.

Why hasn't a view of transfers as negative taxes, and of phase-outs as part of the overall tax rate, caught on more generally? The problem is one of fiscal language. Transfers are "spending" rather than anything having to do with taxes. In addition, it is hard to dissuade people from treating as significant the formally designated boundaries of particular distinct programs, even though the whole is what really matters.

Thus, it seems abhorrent for anyone who is not poor to get "welfare," regardless of how she does overall.

It is not as if supporters of significant aid to the poor want it to come at the price of creating poverty traps. Fiscal language simply makes this ugly trade-off seem necessary, reflecting not just prevailing conventions but underlying psychological heuristics. One such heuristic is the endowment effect, which encourages unduly distinguishing between a dollar paid out by the Treasury and a dollar that never is paid in. Another is the inclination to create multiple distinct "mental accounts through which losses and gains, including losses and gains in simple monetary terms, are not fungible with each other" (Sunstein 2000, 6). This way of thinking encourages evaluating formally distinct programs separately, as an intuitive preference rather than simply because the broader picture requires more information.

## Welfare versus Cash Grants: Is the Distinction Purely Semantic?

### Welfare for Bill Gates?

I would not want to be the brave politician who proposed a welfare program under which Bill Gates got benefits. The awkwardness of making such a proposal is one reason why George McGovern was so widely mocked and condemned, during the 1972 presidential campaign, when he proposed a $1,000 per person "demogrant." It did not help McGovern, in trying to fend off accusations of far-left quackery, that his idea had features in common with a "Family Assistance Plan" that President Nixon had been promoting within the past year. Nor did it help that demogrants or similar benefits had been endorsed, not only by the liberal economist James Tobin, but also by such conservative icons as Friedrich Hayek (1944, 133), George Stigler (1946, 365), and Milton Friedman (1962, 191). Part of the problem was that the McGovern campaign had not thought through the plan very well before unveiling it. Another problem, to which I return shortly, is that the idea of a universal guarantee raised concern about rewarding and encouraging idleness, and ran afoul of the widely held belief that people who decline to work do not deserve support.

It nonetheless is worth asking the full question on the merits: Should Bill Gates get welfare benefits?

"Obviously not," one might be inclined to answer. But the correct answer is that, if we care about the fiscal system's effects as a whole rather than about the functioning of particular formally designated parts it does not matter. What is more, the question of whether Gates *should* get the benefits is hard to make sense of, when even the question of whether he actually *does* get them can be answered only formalistically.

Starting with the point that it does not matter, suppose we have two choices. The first is to deny Gates welfare benefits while keeping his current tax liability constant. The second is to give him $5,000 of welfare benefits, but simultaneously to increase his taxes by $6,000. Does anyone really think that the second alternative unfairly benefits him relative to the first, given that it leaves him $1,000 worse off? And, if one is concerned about "cutting [him] that completely unneeded check" (Block 2001, 86) – although why this should matter, in today's world of electronic transactions, is unclear – would it help if the welfare benefits were simply credited against his income tax liability? Then he would be directly "getting" the benefits in one sense, since there would be a line on his tax return crediting them, but not in another, since he would never actually receive a $5,000 check.

In what sense does Bill Gates currently not get welfare benefits, however? We may be certain that he does not go to see a caseworker at the Department of Social and Health Services in the state of Washington, requesting TANF cash benefits, and that if he did go his prospects of establishing eligibility would be slim. In a formal or literal sense, therefore, he indeed does not get welfare benefits.

Gates does, however, lose out on various benefits because his income and assets are too high. After all, he presumably would be eligible for welfare benefits if he and his wife, along with their three young children, had nothing at all. This means-related loss of benefits could alternatively be accomplished, without changing either gross or net cash flows, by restructuring his income tax return so that he both

(1) got a tax credit for the full benefit that he would have received with zero income and assets, and (2) was subject to a "welfare phase-out tax," collected via the income tax return although using the welfare system's measure of means, and equaling the full amount of the credit.

To make this look a bit more like existing welfare, we might add one further administrative detail that would make no substantive difference. We could have the state of Washington provide that anyone who does not go to see a Department of Social and Health Services caseworker is nonetheless allowed the welfare tax credit, but is conclusively presumed to owe a welfare phase-out tax that equals the full credit. Moreover, we could provide that those who did come in to see a caseworker not only would avoid this presumption, but also could elect to get a check for any net cash that was due, rather than having to claim a refundable credit from the income tax authorities.

If the means test for welfare benefits were conformed to the federal definition of taxable income so that the same computation governed both systems, it would be even simpler to redescribe Bill Gates as a recipient of welfare benefits. Now the tax credit for welfare benefits at zero income could simply be offset by higher marginal rates in the lower-income echelons, without requiring a distinct "welfare phase-out tax" based on a different income measure. So the only observable instruments would be the income tax with its restated rates, the refundable welfare tax credit, and the rule permitting application to a caseworker for direct payment.

Under this system, Bill Gates would apparently be getting welfare benefits as under the McGovern demogrant, rather than not getting them as under present law. Yet nothing about his overall treatment by the fiscal system would actually have changed.

## What to Call Cash Grants

The idea that Friedrich Hayek, George Stigler, Milton Friedman, James Tobin, Richard Nixon, George McGovern, and Daniel Patrick Moynihan (the principal architect of Nixon's Family Assistance Plan) all advocated goes by a number of different names. The leading terms, some of which describe only particular variants, include not only "demogrant" but also "basic income," "guaranteed income," and "negative income tax." As Tobin and his colleagues (1967, 2) explained:

> These proposals can be described and compared in terms of two identifying features: the *basic allowance* which an eligible individual or family may claim from the government, and the *offsetting tax* which every recipient of the basic allowance must pay on his other income. The *net benefit* to the recipient is the basic allowance less the offsetting tax.

In lieu of any of these terms, I will use the admittedly imperfect term "cash grant," for several reasons. The terms "demogrant," "basic income," and "guaranteed income" have negative political connotations, in part because of the McGovern episode but also because they seem to imply that everyone should get the grant. This runs afoul of the view that, as critics of the Family Assistance Plan argued, we should not use cash grants "to show able-bodied people how they can avoid going to work" (Moynihan 1973, 485). "Income support" is better, except that it fails to signal the distinction from traditional welfare.

Identifying the cash grant idea with universality is not just politically inconvenient but also misleading. Fiscal language games are not likely to permit one to dodge public aversion to giving out universal grants if that in fact is what one is doing. However, the question of whether cash grants should be universal is no different from the question of whether welfare benefits should be universal. Either one can be provided to everyone, or alternatively just to qualified individuals.

The only distinction between cash grants and welfare benefits, as I will use the terms, is that welfare benefits are expressly means tested, while cash grants are not. In the case of the cash grant, any income or asset testing takes place only outside the formal boundaries of the program, although the overall results could be exactly the same as under welfare. In short, speaking of cash grants rather than of welfare is purely a fiscal language change, not necessarily associated with any overall policy difference. As we will see, however, there is a reason for it.

The term "negative income tax" arguably has greater descriptive merit than the other customary terms, including "cash grant."

In addition to not implying the universality that might or might not be a program feature, the term "negative income tax" has the descriptive virtue of emphasizing the symmetry between paying a net tax and getting a net benefit (Tobin et al 1967, 2). But it not only shares in the unfortunate history of the term "demogrant," it is further removed than "cash grant" from what arguably is a better term than either: "non-income-conditioned cash grant." Such a term seems unacceptably turgid, however. "Cash grant" as simply a shorthand version of it.

One further problem with the term "cash grant" – shared, however, by "negative income tax" if we think of "taxes" as necessarily involving cash – is that certain benefits for the poor are provided in kind, or else through the use of vouchers that can be used only for specified purposes. Prominent examples include food stamps, Medicaid, and housing subsidies. The issues raised by providing such benefits in lieu of cash (see Bradford and Shaviro 2000) are distinct from the fiscal language point being considered here. To give Bill Gates food stamps clearly would matter administratively, even if he remained in the same position overall due to paying extra offsetting taxes and keeping his overall food expenditures constant. For Medicaid, which is not simply a voucher for the purchase of $X worth of medical services, the differences are more than just administrative. Again, however, the choice between cash and in-kind benefits is distinct from the fiscal language choice between "welfare" and "cash grant."[1]

What "cash grant" really is shorthand for, then, is "non-income-conditioned cash or in-kind grant." I trust readers will forgive me for not using the longer term.

## The Cash Grant Description versus the Welfare Description of a Given Policy

To further show how formal descriptions do and don't matter, a simplified example of aid to the poor may help. Suppose that the poverty line in a given jurisdiction is defined as $20,000 annually. Initially, there is only a 30 percent income tax, from which the poor are exempted. That is, everyone gets a $20,000 exemption, creating a zero tax rate on income up to that amount. Any income over that amount is taxed at 30 percent.

The legislature then decides that no one residing in the jurisdiction should be forced to live on less than $15,000 annually, or three-quarters of the poverty line. This amount will therefore be given to people with zero income. The amount that people get will be reduced as income rises, and at some point they will once again be paying a net tax. In addition, tax rates will have to go up somewhere in order to finance the new benefit.

Suppose initially that the designers think of the program as conventional welfare. Only the poor should get it, they therefore conclude. In particular, no one who is earning more than $20,000 should get it. They might provide that, for every extra dollar a poor person earns, the benefit is reduced by seventy-five cents. That way, the constraints of paying $15,000 to someone who earns zero and nothing to someone who earns $20,000 are satisfied on a straight-line basis.

Suppose further that, in order to fund the benefit, the positive tax rate must be raised from 30 percent to 35 percent. Effectively, there are now two tax brackets, with marginal rates of 75 percent on income up to $20,000 and 35 percent above that amount. However, the 75 percent bracket was not chosen through an evaluation of proper rate structures. Rather, it was forced on the designers by their decision to eliminate the benefit by the time one reaches the poverty line.

Now suppose instead that the designers opt for a $15,000 universal cash grant, to be funded by eliminating the zero tax bracket and making such other rate increases as may be necessary. The designers might start with a 35 percent rate that now applies without any exemption amount. Unfortunately, this will not raise enough revenue given the numbers in the first example, where the break-even tax brackets were 75 percent and 35 percent. The designers must increase the marginal tax rate somewhere in the income range.

One possibility would be to adopt a 75 percent marginal tax rate on everyone's first $20,000 of income. If the designers do this (and we already know from the first example that it raises the right amount of revenue), then the two systems are identical. In both cases, everyone pays (a) 75 percent of the first $20,000 of income, plus (b) 35 percent of all additional income, minus (c) $15,000, with any excess of (c) over [(a) plus (b)] being refundable by the government.

The big procedural difference is that the designers in the second case have given themselves more freedom in setting the marginal rate structure. Rather than boxing themselves in at the start by stipulating the maximum benefit and the point at which it must be gone, they have allowed themselves to think in terms of which marginal rate structure is best, and thus to adopt either the very same scheme or a different one.

This greater freedom could make all the difference in the world. Suppose that a 75 percent marginal rate is simply too high given its incentive effects. Only the second methodology eliminates the risk of imposing excessive marginal rates by mistake.[2]

There is a kind of sledgehammer irony to our having combined the view that marginal rates should be progressively graduated with a convention in describing welfare that invites ignoring the marginal rate effects of phasing out aid to the poor. After excluding as a matter of principle the idea that marginal rates might reasonably be higher in the low-income brackets, we end up not even looking at what those rates actually are. This has resulted not only in nongraduated rates, but also in some that are affirmatively confiscatory and in sharp conflict with making work pay.

## Cash Grants versus Welfare in Relation to Work Incentives

Both welfare and cash grant–style proposals, such as President Nixon's Family Assistance Plan, have been criticized at times for blunting work incentives. This issue played an important role in the welfare reform legislation enacted in 1996. Welfare reform, among other changes, set strict work requirements and imposed a five-year lifetime limit on eligibility for benefits.

Before evaluating the significance of work incentives, we must start by clarifying what they are. When economists discuss the effects of fiscal rules on work incentives, they generally have in mind the rules' impact on the net payoff from working. Hence, the higher the marginal tax rate, the more one's incentive to work is blunted. Within this terminology, handing someone a ten-million-dollar check would not be regarded as affecting her incentive to work, except indirectly if it brought about a change in her marginal rate bracket. Those using this terminology recognize, of course, that someone who had an irksome and low-paying job would almost certainly quit if she got a ten-million-dollar check. This, however, is classified as an income or wealth effect that alters her choice under a constant set of preferences.

In popular usage, by contrast, the notion of work incentives includes income effects. While imposing, say, a 95 percent marginal tax rate on poor people would certainly be understood to dampen their incentive to work, the term also would extend to giving able-bodied individuals, who could have found jobs if sufficiently motivated, enough resources to meet their basic needs without working. Hence, a cash grant, and certainly a universal demogrant, would be criticized in common usage for dampening poor people's work incentives even if their marginal rates were reduced.

Work incentives in the economist's sense matter for reasons of efficiency. If Smith would be willing to pay Jones up to ten dollars to perform a given task and Jones would be willing to do it so long as he got at least seven dollars, the deal between them would create three dollars of surplus (the excess of the value to Smith of having the task done over the disvalue to Jones of doing it). If the deal was subject to a 40 percent tax, it presumably would not get done. The tax would have prevented the realization of this social surplus, without anyone's benefiting (since the government gets no revenue from a deal that fails to happen).

This analysis does not, however, apply to work incentives in the popular sense. If Jones is given enough money to meet his basic needs and decides that he does not want to do the task even for ten dollars, then evidently his disvalue (given his new circumstances) now exceeds the value to Smith. From this standpoint, withholding aid from able-bodied poor people, on the ground that they will not work if their basic needs are already met, would make no more sense than telling millionaire professional athletes that they cannot retire just because they are already rich.

This is to say, not that popular concern about "work incentives" is wrong, but rather that it must rest on some other ground. The claim could be that poor people make cognitive errors when deciding whether to work. For example, they might undervalue the benefits to them of learning to function in the workplace, or of increasing their earning capacity for the future. Or their work might have positive externalities, such as reducing crime levels, setting better behavioral models for children, or simply relieving taxpayers of the need to provide support.

Cash grants clearly affect work incentives in the popular sense. Just as under the welfare definition, however, policy makers who consider this undesirable can respond in a number of different ways. One approach would be to limit eligibility on some basis other than income. Thus, cash grants could be limited to a subclass of the population that is not expected to work, such as seniors and the disabled.

Another possible limit is work requirements such as those under TANF. This makes the marginal rate analysis more complicated. A work requirement may in effect impose a minimum income requirement for the grant, resulting in a wage subsidy (a negative tax rate on earnings) in the range where one increases one's net transfer by working. Time limits on eligibility, which amount to disqualification for subsequent cash grants if one's income for each of the requisite number of years is sufficiently low, have similar effects.

The difficulty of drawing a clean line between income conditioning and other types of limits on grant eligibility should not, however, obscure the two central advantages of the cash grant description of benefits to the poor. Again, the first of these is its focusing attention on overall marginal rates, rather than just on those associated with particular instruments within the fiscal system. And the second is its making the entire marginal rate structure a matter of deliberate choice, without requiring extremely high rates in lower income ranges simply as a consequence of an arbitrary constraint holding that particular distinct benefits must be limited to the poor.

## Cash Grants versus Welfare in Evaluating "Program Cost" and "Targeting" of Benefits

Welfare experts have long recognized the issue of work incentives in the economist's sense. However, the language of "spending" can affect the apparent nature of the trade-offs in policy design, potentially encouraging worse policy outcomes.

If welfare is a distinct "spending" program, then slowing down a benefit phase-out appears to increase the cost of the program. Thus, recall the earlier example in which a decision has been made to offer $15,000 to eligible individuals with zero income, phasing down to zero when income reaches $20,000. Such a program would have a measurable direct budgetary impact, equaling the cash disbursed by the program plus the costs of administration.[3] Suppose initially that changing the size of the basic cash grant is not an option. Slowing down the phase-out, by reducing the marginal rate in the benefit reduction range from 75 percent to 50 percent, and thus changing the phase-out point to $30,000, would substantially raise the program's direct budgetary cost.

Under a cash grant description, "program cost" would not in this sense be an issue. We would simply be changing net taxes and net grants for people in various income groups. In particular, people earning zero to $20,000 would gain financially and have their marginal rates reduced, while those earning from $20,000 to $30,000 would gain financially but have their marginal rates increased. Those earning more than $30,000, if their taxes were increased to pay for the change, would lose financially and might also have their marginal rates increased. This is an important set of changes, but calling it a "spending increase" encourages a false analogy to, say, increasing highway spending, which directly changes the mix of the assets in the society rather than simply shifting dollars and marginal rates around between groups.

If the only available choice lies between a 75 percent phase-out and a 50 percent phase-out of a fixed $15,000 grant, few advocates of aid to the poor are likely to have any objection to shifting from the former to the latter. After all, reducing the phase-out rate to 50 percent is a win–win proposition so far as the poor and near-poor are concerned.

Suppose instead, however, that the size of the cash grant is also in play. Under this scenario, shifting to the slower phase-out would imply making the cash grant smaller if the "program size" (i.e., the maximum feasible financial impact on higher-income taxpayers) is fixed. It would thus favor the near-poor over the poor, worsening the "targeting" of aid to the poorest individuals. While the trade-off is clear, and generally rightly understood even under prevailing fiscal language, it might be easier to avoid politically if the choice were framed as involving distribution among all groups rather than as higher versus lower "government spending."

Looking at the problem in this way helps to show how misguided it is to assume that progressive fiscal systems must have graduated marginal rates. A goal of keeping poorer people's marginal rates lower than those of richer people, without regard to the size of the cash grant at the bottom, completely ignores one of the two key distributional variables. Why should the marginal rates that happen to be imposed at the middle and top of the income distribution have any bearing on how one resolves the trade-off at the bottom between providing an adequate minimum and avoiding excessive work disincentives?

## Actual Marginal Rates in the U.S. Fiscal System for Poor and Near-Poor Individuals

The marginal rates faced by poor and near-poor individuals are of interest even if one rejects the need for rate graduation. Marginal rates determine how much extra economic reward one gathers, after accounting for the effects on taxes and transfers, by reason of earning more. This, in turn, matters for both incentive and distributional reasons. It affects work effort insofar as people respond to economic rewards, and it determines the extent to which high earners do better than low earners.

Unfortunately, the marginal rates that poor and near-poor individuals face are hard either to determine or to summarize concisely for a number of different reasons, including the following:

1) **Interstate variations:** Programs that aid the poor, although subject to extensive federal law and regulation, are in many key respects (including benefit levels and phase-out rates) set at the state level. As a result, there are at least fifty different sets of marginal rate structures that a given household could face, depending on where it is situated, and even more to the extent that there is intrastate variation between localities.

2) **Different household types:** Benefits are highly sensitive to household characteristics, such as the number of adults and/or children. In general, aid is far more generous to poor households with children than to those without. Given the belief that rapid phase-out is necessary, this causes households with children, though treated more favorably, to face much higher marginal rates, since much larger benefits are being phased out over what remains a compressed income range.

3) **Variation in program design:** Even when different programs are designed in similar ways – for example, to increase benefits with the number of dependent children, or to phase out benefits as income rises – there are often significant differences in their details, reflecting the fact that they may have been separately designed by different people at different times. Thus, such important details as who is included in a given household and how income or assets are measured may vary across the programs, leading to even more of an individualized polyglot of rate structures.

4) **Differences in take-up or participation rates:** Eligible individuals often do not participate in a given program, whether owing to lack of information, discouragement by procedural hurdles, or simply personal preference. In addition, income-conditioned federal housing subsidies, which can provide substantial benefits, are rationed, with the consequence that not all equally eligible households get them (Shaviro 1999, 1194). Nonparticipation in a program lowers not only one's benefit but also one's marginal rate in the phase-out range.

5) **Accrual of Social Security benefits:** While Social Security payroll taxes, which have no exemption for low earners, are among the positive inputs to marginal rates, Social Security benefits are in effect a wage subsidy. Retirement benefits generally increase with earnings

that were subject to the Social Security tax. Should we therefore *not* include the full Social Security payroll tax when determining low earners' marginal rates, at least for earning years that are likely to be among the earner's top thirty-five? In part, this depends on whether we are interested, for a given purpose, in actual net taxes paid on a lifetime basis, or in the perceived marginal rates that people use when making labor supply decisions. When we are interested in perceived rates, there is an argument for ignoring the accrual of retirement benefits, on the view that people generally do not understand it (Kotlikoff and Sachs 1997, 17). Or they may apply too high a discount rate, reflecting the myopic lack of concern about one's retirement resources that is a key reason for our having Social Security to begin with. But distributional outcomes depend on actual, not perceived, tax rates.

6) **Other misperceptions:** The question of how perceived marginal rates compare to actual ones is not limited to Social Security. For many benefits, most people probably lack any detailed understanding of how the income phase-outs work. This could cause perceived marginal rates to be either higher or lower than actual ones. For example, perceived rates might be higher when people mistakenly believe that they will lose Medicaid benefits immediately upon phasing out of TANF, rather than after a twelve-month delay. Or, going the other way, they "may not recognize the work incentives built into the EITC, since nearly all receive their payments as a lump sum based on their work during the prior year" (Coe et al. 1998, 6).

7) **The choice of income range for measuring marginal rates:** Marginal rate tables typically show the extra net tax associated with each extra dollar of earnings. What really matters, however, for both incentive and distributional purposes, is the set of choices that people actually face. Thus, suppose that one's only work options were to spend the entire year either in a part-time job that paid the federal minimum-wage (currently $5.15 per hour) for twenty-five hours per week, or in a full-time job that paid the same hourly rate for forty hours. One's only choices, therefore, assuming a fifty-week work year, would be to earn zero, $6,437.50, or $10,300. Under these circumstances, only the marginal rates computed by comparing the three possible end points

would matter, as opposed to those for any given extra dollar between the end points.

While this example may be atypically restrictive, workers often do not have the full range of dollar-by-dollar choice that typically is portrayed on economists' labor supply graphs. Job opportunities may be limited, and may involve weekly or annual time requirements that are not freely negotiable. Thus, if work choices tend to group at particular broad margins, such as those between full-time and half-time minimum wage work, attention should focus on the marginal rates that apply to these broad ranges, and the dollar-by-dollar picture may not really be what matters.

8) **The choice of time period for measuring marginal rates:** A final difficulty in determining relevant marginal rates concerns the choice of time period. Thus, consider the rule under which one may lose Medicaid benefits twelve months after leaving the welfare rolls. A rational and well-informed worker would disregard this future loss of benefits if she did not expect to be off welfare for the full twelve months. Suppose, however, that she is considering a significant life change that might keep her permanently off Medicaid once the grace period has passed. Under these circumstances, the pending loss of what may be extremely valuable health care benefits (especially if she has several children and her employer would not offer health insurance coverage) may be important despite the grace period. The time frame people use is hard to discern, however.

Despite all these issues, several studies have tried to measure the marginal rates that low-income households face. The general pattern is to find low rates at the very bottom, which rapidly become extremely high, commonly exceeding 70 percent or even 100 percent over significant ranges, and that may not decline to more normal levels until well past the official poverty line (see Shaviro 1999; Giannarelli and Steuerle 1995).

Owing to a lack of integrated data concerning the application of both tax and transfer programs, marginal rate studies have generally relied on applying the rules on the books to actual or simulated households. In 2005, however, Stephen Holt, making use of integrated data from Wisconsin, presented a study, based on extensive data from actual poor and near-poor households, that is the first of its kind.

The "good" news from the study, such as it is, is that marginal rates for low-income households often fall short of the stratospheric levels suggested by simulations, due to widespread nonparticipation by poor households in benefit programs for which they are likely to be eligible, eliminating the effect of the phase-outs. Thus, consider single parents with two children and incomes under $18,000, who were highly likely to be eligible for all five of the income-support programs in the study (TANF, food stamps, Medicaid, and Wisconsin's distinctive health insurance and subsidized child-care programs). Within this population, 8 percent participated in none of the programs, and fewer than a third participated in more than three (Holt 2005, 5).

Needless to say, nonparticipation by eligible households is not actually good news, if they have been made eligible for a reason. Even wholly voluntary nonparticipation, such as out of a sense of self-reliance, can have effects on children who could not really have decided to opt out. It is even less benign when it results from administrative obstacles, lack of information, or fear of stigma associated with being a claimant. Where broader participation is not considered desirable, curtailing eligibility would be a more straightforward way of accomplishing it.

For households that participate in all of the transfer programs, the resulting overall marginal rates through the phase-out ranges can be staggering. Consider, for example, a single parent with two children who participates in all five of Wisconsin's programs, as well as claiming the federal and Wisconsin EITCs, and whose annual income increases from $15,000 to $35,000. This is an example of what we might ordinarily think of as escaping poverty through hard work and self-improvement. Such an increase in income would result if the single parent moved from a full-time job (defined as 2,000 hours a year) paying $7.50 per hour to one paying $17.50 per hour. According to the Wisconsin data (Holt 2005, D-2), this would result in no net increase in the household's net disposable income. In other words, the marginal tax rate for such a household, for the range from $15,000 to $35,000 as a whole, is 100 percent if the parent takes care to participate in all relief programs for which the household is eligible. Results are similar for other households at typical margins.[4]

These results pertain only to one state, and would probably be less dire, from the marginal-rate standpoint, in states that offer less generous benefits than Wisconsin. In at least one respect, however, Wisconsin's marginal rates on poor and near-poor households may be unusually low. Wisconsin mitigates the marginal-rate effect of losing Medicaid benefits when one's income rises above the threshold by offering more gradually phased-out income-conditioned health insurance for children.

Insofar as the Wisconsin data is nationally representative, however, it is clear that, when they participate in multiple programs that are meant to help them, poor and near-poor households may face marginal rates that far exceed acceptable levels. The effect on behavior remains uncertain, given that a lot of the marginal-rate effects are hard for people to figure out. However, empirical studies suggest that poor households do indeed respond to economic incentives created by the fiscal system.[5] People might respond even without understanding how all the rules work if they observe, for example, that hard-working neighbors do not seem to be doing much better than those who work less.

Why do we have marginal rates in the neighborhood of 100 percent across broad swathes of income in the lower ranges, when almost no one would openly advocate such rates? Fiscal language is unlikely to be the sole cause. The fact that so many different programs, even just on the transfer side, are designed and operated separately without full coordination may also play a role. In addition, there is a political explanation for the pattern, if those on the very bottom of the economic ladder are the most appealing cases for support and voters are reluctant to pay more in order to help those who are just a bit higher up. Lowering marginal rates for people who are beginning to escape poverty would require either giving smaller grants at the bottom or raising marginal rates for people above the near-poor income level. Nonetheless, given the awkwardness of openly and explicitly imposing marginal rates anywhere near to 100 percent, it seems likely that a more integrated view of taxes and transfers, both in general and for purposes of assessing marginal rates, would make the existing rate structure harder to maintain.

## What Should the Marginal Rate Structure Look Like?

So far, we have seen that (1) marginal rates need not be graduated in order for the fiscal system to be progressive, but that (2) in practice they often are much too high for poor people who participate in multiple programs. The latter point, however, is intuitively the more salient. Marginal rates approaching or exceeding 100 percent are easy to dislike. On the former point, however, even if marginal rates do not *have* to be graduated in order for the system to be progressive, this does not tell us whether or not they *should* be graduated.

Nearly all people favor – or think they favor – either graduated or flat marginal rates. And even (though not exclusively) among people who say they favor flat rates, it is common to agree that the marginal rate ought to be zero at the very lowest income levels (for example, at the levels needed to purchase basic necessities). So it is worth exploring briefly why marginal rates not only need not be, but possibly should not be, graduated even if one favors significant redistribution from richer to poorer individuals.

Those who support rate graduation, and who have simply failed to appreciate the benefit phase-out component of actual marginal rates, often base the argument for it on declining marginal utility, or the point that, the more money you have, the less each dollar affects your well-being. Thus, suppose that both Bill Gates and a single mother who has two children and is working at a minimum-wage job were to be taxed at 30 percent. The fact that losing thirty cents out of every extra dollar of income would have a greater negative impact on the single mother and her family (even if they are getting cash grants) than on Bill Gates and his family provides a reason for favoring rate graduation.

There is a countervailing factor, however, first brought to light in the Nobel Prize–winning work of economist James Mirrlees (1971). Everyone, and not just poor people, is subject to the tax rate at low-income brackets. The overall tax paid by Bill Gates, for example, depends on the marginal rates that apply to each dollar of his income, from the first to the last. Having a low marginal rate in lower-income brackets, therefore, has a huge revenue impact. But it has a relatively small distortionary impact on behavior, because people in higher brackets face a different set of incentives at the margin. If I am earning $1 million, for example, none of the alternative payoffs I may consider is likely to be affected by the marginal tax rate for income levels under several hundred thousand dollars.

Inquiry into optimal rate structures, given these sorts of considerations, has prompted an entire genre in public economics research, known as the optimal income tax literature (see Slemrod 1990, 163–166). While this literature, not surprisingly, yields varying results, it often finds that "optimal marginal tax rates will be high at the bottom of the income scale (and possibly higher than at middle or upper levels of income)" (Kaplow 2005, 8). High at the bottom does not, however, mean approaching 100 percent. Rather, low-income marginal rates tend to be in the 40 to 60 percent range, although some specifications lead to their being below 30 percent or above 80 percent (ibid.).

In sum, therefore, to say that marginal rates ought generally to be graduated is a bit like prescribing penicillin before examining the patient. Marginal rates are a technical detail, albeit an important one, in designing the fiscal system, and are best evaluated in combination with other features, such as the transfers available at the bottom, as well as the tax base to which the rates apply. Rates approaching 100 percent are unlikely to be desirable at any margin or range where significant numbers of people are actually making work decisions. However, relative rates, which is the concern raised by interest in rate graduation, are of little independent interest, other than as a technical design detail.

## Summary

Marginal rates are frequently analyzed based solely on taxes, without regard to benefit phase-outs that have exactly the same incentive and distributional effects as increasing positive taxes. In part, this myopia reflects the differing professional specializations of income tax and welfare experts, along with the difficulty of determining the marginal rate effects of programs having differing tax or phase-out bases and that are subject to significant interstate variation. It also, however, reflects the notion, rooted in our current fiscal language, that "taxes" and "spending" are fundamentally different.

Proposals to adopt an explicitly integrated fiscal system are often called "demogrant" or "negative income tax" proposals. These proposals appear to have no chance of enactment, in part because of their history but also because many people are uncomfortable with the notion of handing out universal and unconditional cash grants. The question of who should get income support, however, is distinct from that of how we should think about marginal rates. Cash grants can be conditional or selective, just as welfare benefits can be offered to everyone. The case for integrated thinking about the fiscal system has no necessary implications for the policies we should follow. It just permits better understanding of any given set of policies.

# PART 4

# CONCLUSION

*Could we change our attitude, we should not only see life differently, but life itself would come to be different.*

– Katherine Mansfield

# 10

## Some Modest Proposals

*Glendower: I can call spirits from the vasty deep.*
*Hotspur: Why, so can I, and so can any man / But will they come when*
*you do call for them?*

— From Shakespeare's *Henry IV, Part 1*

*When you see a fork in the road, take it.*

— Yogi Berra

Our current fiscal language, which rests on the basic concepts of "taxes" and "spending" plus their arithmetical comparison to determine the annual budget deficit or surplus, has served us poorly. The most obvious and well-known problem is the shortsightedness of an annual budget measure. This one came home to roost most disastrously in 2001, when four years of budget surpluses encouraged the collapse of fiscal discipline.

The problems with the terms "taxes" and "spending" may be even more serious, although less widely recognized. Mistakenly using them as if they had economic substance has yielded two distinct kinds of harm. First, it has deformed policy in a number of realms, ranging from a thumb on the scale in favor of using tax expenditures to the creation of welfare policies with harsh poverty traps that no one really wants.

Second, illusions concerning the economic significance of taxes and spending as categories have helped to raise the risk of government default, by encouraging antigovernment conservatives to follow a "starve the beast" strategy of continually cutting taxes in the face of an enormous fiscal gap. Simplistic notions that "tax cuts" followed by "spending cuts" must make the government smaller have encouraged this economically risky strategy. If principled small-government conservatives had focused instead on the distributional effects of cutting taxes for today's seniors in exchange for raising them on future generations, and on the allocative effects of creating unequal tax rates over time and heightening the risk of default, they might have been considerably more leery of this strategy.

The continued use of the terms "taxes" and "spending" cannot be avoided. Nor should it be, given that in many cases it communicates information. For example, if one suggests "raising taxes" to help reduce the fiscal gap, most people will have a pretty clear idea of what this might mean. Most likely, it refers to a laundry list of items such as the following: raising income tax rates, broadening the income tax base, increasing the payroll tax, adding a consumption tax, keeping or expanding the estate and gift tax, raising gasoline or excise taxes, and perhaps enacting some new instrument such as a carbon or pollution tax. While handy labels for laundry lists are convenient, we must avoid confusing them with more fundamental categories, such as distribution and allocation policy.

In thinking about distribution policy through the fiscal system, a good first step would be amalgamating transfer programs, such as Social Security, Medicare, and various forms of aid to the poor, to distributional taxes such as the income tax. Net taxes, not gross taxes, should be the main category for thinking about distribution, whether one's interest lies in progressivity or in the treatment of different generations. In thinking about allocation policy through the fiscal system, a good first step would be to treat clear tax expenditures as equivalent to direct spending. In addition, transfers should be set aside from other "spending" unless, like Medicare and Medicaid, they are tied to specific goods and services.

These ideas can remain vague when the idea is simply to suggest better ways of thinking about fiscal issues. We need greater specificity, however, when the issue is designing budget rules, or specifications for official data and estimates. To this end, I propose the following as starting points for further debate:

1) **Super-majority requirement for legislation that would lose money on balance over a one-year, five-year, or ten-year period:** Senator Lieberman's Honest Government Accounting Act proposal, discussed in Chapter 6, would require 60 percent approval in both the House and the Senate for any tax or entitlement legislation that would increase the deficit or reduce the surplus in the current fiscal year or over a five-year or ten-year period. This makes considerable sense, although conceivably one might drop the five-year rule.

Could this rule be extended to apply as well to increases in particular categories of discretionary spending? The technical problem here is deciding on the category for a given item, presumably setting this in general terms rather than treating each item as its own category. Thus, building a new bridge would not be an increase if expenditures on all bridges were not rising above the permitted benchmark. If distinct categories could be devised and reasonably enforced, one might define an increase as occurring whenever an enactment in a given category would raise the total for that category above the previous year's number, adjusted upward for inflation or perhaps GDP growth.

For purposes of this rule, along with all other budgetary rules to be discussed, deferred discontinuous changes, or those that arise in future years without being phased in at a steady rate, would be disregarded if they made money for the government. Under this rule, the sunset for the 2001 tax cuts would have been ignored. On the other hand, a tax increase that was phased in at a steady rate – say, 20 percent per year, starting immediately, until it was fully effective in five years – would be included. A further important general feature would be attempting to give the official estimators some degree of independence from direct political control.

2) **Super-majority requirement for legislation that would lose money on balance over the next fifty years and/or the infinite horizon:** This proposal likewise echoes a provision in the Lieberman bill, which would apply both a seventy-five-year period and the infinite horizon. Despite the analytical arguments, discussed in Chapter 5, for infinite-horizon perspectives, this budgetary rule would not be seriously compromised by using only a finite period of seventy-five or even fifty years. Even if I am right that estimates for programs such as Social Security or Medicare should be made on an infinite-horizon basis, the main political dangers that this rule attempts to counter are probably more short-term. Politicians are unlikely to get a great deal of mileage out of proposals that would "explode" more than fifty years down the road.

The Lieberman bill would limit this rule to tax and entitlement legislation. Here the limitation is less unsatisfying than under the first budgetary rule, since purported current year provision for discretionary spending more than ten years out might have little meaning anyway. One would, however, want to cover other programs that involved similar long-term commitments.

Again as in the Lieberman bill, this requirement could be extended to legislative proposals by the president, as could the next few proposals I discuss. While compliance would be unenforceable, the requirement might increase public pressure on presidents to suggest financing for costly proposals.

3) **Require distributional estimates by income group for significant tax and transfer legislation:** Until recently, the Treasury Department and the Joint Congressional Committee on Taxation regularly prepared distributional tables showing the estimated impact of major proposed tax legislation by income group. This practice ought to be restored. Revisions to the estimates, beyond the obvious one of extending them to include transfer programs, might involve providing lifetime as well as annual measures, and stating annual or lifetime effects in dollar terms for the average member of each income group.

4) **Require estimates of the impact of all significant tax and transfer legislation on future generations:** This could be done in terms of both lifetime net tax rates and lifetime net taxes, using the

assumption that all increases in the fiscal gap will be borne by future generations.

5) **Require additional long-term estimates in the president's annual budget statement:** These could include generational accounting estimates, along with estimates of the fiscal gap over the next fifty years and the infinite horizon. The long-term fiscal gap estimates, like those that have for many years been released annually by the Social Security and Medicare trustees, could include multiple scenarios – for example, high, low, and intermediate estimates.

6) **Social Security and Medicare estimates:** As under recent practice, these could be required to include infinite-horizon as well as seventy-five-year estimates. (Or, as a gesture to placate those leery of long-term estimates, the estimates might be revised to fifty-year and infinite horizon.) For the portions of Medicare that rely on general financing rather than on dedicated payroll tax revenues, the programmatic fiscal gap could be estimated based on the assumption that these programs' current percentage share of general revenues will remain fixed.

7) **Current-law baselines for future Social Security and Medicare taxes and benefits:** Given the political difficulty of enacting changes that are defined as benefit cuts or tax increases, current law for Social Security and Medicare could be revised in order to make the programs grow less rapidly and/or to provide for automatic payroll tax increases that keep pace with benefit growth. This would convert the political problem, so far as the baseline change was concerned, into a one-time event rather than one to be faced repeatedly.

8) **Revise tax expenditure estimates to provide better information:** Official tax expenditure estimates should be revised to do the following: (a) use "pure" Haig–Simons income tax and consumption tax baselines, in lieu of the current reliance on a "normal income tax structure"; (b) compute tax penalties as well as tax expenditures; and (c) have separate listings for structural departures from the baselines (such as the realization requirement), other clear departures, and arguable departures.

9) **Marginal tax rate estimates that take account of benefit phase-outs:** The Treasury Department and Congress should be

required to prepare representative estimates of the marginal tax rates for different types of households among the poor, taking account of all phase-outs of means-tested benefits. These estimates might be done both on the basis of typical participation rates in the various programs, and under the assumption of full participation to the extent of eligibility. One way to do this, given interstate variations in the programs, would be to select one representative state each among those with high benefits, intermediate benefits, and low benefits. The choice of states might be required to change annually.

10) **Creation of a bipartisan commission to propose plans that would reduce the fiscal gap:** The Lieberman bill would require the appointment of a special commission that would be charged with proposing a set of alternative plans for greatly reducing the fiscal gap. Appointees would be named in various proportions by the president, several Cabinet officials, and certain legislators in each party.

While the commission proposed by the Lieberman bill would ostensibly be bipartisan, in fact it would be Republican-dominated if appointed while Republicans continue to control the White House and both houses of Congress (Kogan 2005b). Fifty-fifty bipartisanship, without regard to the control of particular institutions, would be better given the political need for proposals that both parties could embrace. There is little reason to name any such commission until the leaderships of both parties are clearly committed to restoring fiscal responsibility.

★   ★   ★

When half of Rome burned in 64 A.D., the Emperor Nero was accused not just of fiddling, but of having actually set the fires himself. Whether or not these charges were true, U.S. political leaders now seem determined to follow Nero's reputed example when setting budget policy. They dicker with trivial deficit reduction packages, and then on a regular basis stoke the fire by passing much larger tax cuts, while the long-term budget picture keeps getting worse. They know what is happening, as do the voters. Our long-term fiscal problems, resulting from the recent tax cuts and spending growth plus the unsustainable, demographically driven growth of Social Security and Medicare, are common knowledge. Yet the only thing our political leaders seem to want to do about the problems is make them worse. And voters, however skeptical and disaffected, are not demanding greater fiscal responsibility from anyone.

That the United States should face *any* threat of a calamitous fiscal default and collapse of the dollar is preposterous. We are rich and productive enough that only gross fiscal irresponsibility, continued for a long time and with no evident prospect of correcting itself, could lead us there. The current political climate for budgetary policy is not encouraging, however. Even the simple idea that if you are in a hole, the first thing to do is stop digging, seems out of reach.

Fiscal language can only do so much to encourage a course correction before it is too late to head off adverse consequences. Restoring bipartisanship is at least as important, and this may depend in part on changes in certain political factors, such as gerrymandering and low voter turn-out, that affect the incentive to seek the center. But improving our fiscal language would be a start.

# Notes

## Chapter 2. Taxes, Spending, and the Size of Government

1. See, e.g., Nagel and Murphy (2002, 26, 76, 88), asking whether the state's role should be "limit[ed] to . . . the protection of [basic] entitlements and other rights," discussing the "public-private division," and discussing "redistribution," evidently relative to the pre-intervention distribution of wealth.

2. Prior to the final 2003 enactments, it was estimated that, in principle, the fiscal gap could be eliminated by (a) raising federal income tax collections by 68.5 percent, (b) raising payroll tax collections by 94 percent, (c) cutting discretionary spending by 104.1 percent (which is mathematically impossible and also would imply no defense budget), or (d) cutting Social Security and Medicare outlays by 45.3 percent (Gokhale and Smetters 2003, 36).

3. A second allocative complaint is that the payroll tax discourages work. Commentators mainly agree that, in part because the linkage between Social Security taxes and benefits is so hard to figure out, "most contributors are likely to view the system's . . . payroll tax as a pure tax" (Kotlikoff and Sachs 1997, 16–17). Still, the picture is very different than it would be if these same taxes were paying for government production of specific goods and services, rather than for cash grants. Moreover, to the extent that workers *do* realize they are earning benefits at the same time as they pay the tax, cutting benefits might have effects similar to those of a straightforward tax increase, by conveying the message that even apparently promised benefits are liable to be cut.

## Chapter 3. Fun and Games with Budget Deficits

1. To keep things simple, I assume for this purpose that printing money is tantamount to debt issuance.

2. Five- and ten-year deficit forecasts are typically presented without any discounting for the later years in the measure.

## Notes

3. Ironically, lease accounting offers a more economically accurate way of accounting for military airplanes than treating the entire purchase price as an expense in the year of sale. Under lease accounting, the budget is charged each year for the cost of that year's usage. Extending this arguably correct treatment to an airplane that the government purchases would require allowing annual deductions for depreciation, in lieu of deducting the purchase price in year one. This is how companies generally account for asset purchases both in their financial records and for federal income tax purposes. "Capital budgeting," with amortization of government expenditures over their useful lives, has therefore been proposed by economists such as Robert Eisner, and resisted mainly on the ground that Congress would grossly abuse it.

### Chapter 4. What Are We Talking about When We Talk about Budget Deficits?

1. Since I am borrowing Richard Musgrave's distinction between the distributional and allocative branches of government, I should note that he attributes Keynesian countercyclical policy to a third notional branch of government, charged with stabilization policy. For convenience, I instead group this function with allocation, on the view that it affects the level and use of society's resources.
2. Similarly, the principle of tax smoothing, discussed in Chapter 2, supports raising taxes more modestly now so that they will not have to go up more steeply in the future.

### Chapter 5. Long-Term Measures in Lieu of the Budget Deficit

1. I will not here discuss technical measurement issues that could have major effects on GA's findings. Examples include determining which government programs to include, how to measure the incidence of benefit or burden, and what discount rate should be used in determining the present value of projected future cash flows. Important though these issues are, they do not affect the bottom line question of whether, at least for analytical purposes, *some* form of GA should be used.
2. Relatedly, Gokhale and Smetters (2003, 11) propose a measure of "generational imbalance" (GI), which they define as the present value of remaining outlays to current generations, minus the present value of remaining taxes to be paid by current generations (along with government assets). One can then measure how GI changes if one replaces Policy A with Policy B, thereby providing my proposed measure. Gokhale and Smetters state that, while the GI can be computed for programs, such as Social Security and Medicare, that provide cash to or on behalf of specific beneficiaries, it cannot be computed for government policy as a whole because "the benefits of outlays (such as spending on national defense or public infrastructure) cannot easily

be allocated to different generations. . . . Only the revenue side of the rest-of-government's budget may be so attributed" (13). This strikes me as a bit overscrupulous. So long as we understand the limitations of what we are doing, there is nothing wrong with a purely fiscal measure that overlooks the value of in-kind benefits.

3. Counting interest outlays on the national debt would amount to double-counting in a present-value sense, since the principal amount of the debt has already been included and paying interest expense perpetually would be economically equivalent to paying back the principal.

4. More specifically, the Auerbach (1994) flow measure requires that the specified increase in the government's net inflows keep current government debt constant as a percentage of GDP. The idea here is that a constantly increasing debt-to-GDP ratio is unsustainable. See Auerbach 1994, 166–173; Auerbach, Gale, and Orszag 2002, 1648.

5. There are nonetheless those, such as the economist Laurence Kotlikoff, who argue that official projections are frequently too optimistic from a fiscal standpoint. One recourse they have is to prepare and disseminate their own estimates.

6. Making this measure a bit perplexing or counterintuitive is the fact that the present value of the GDP base keeps increasing over time, barring new information. Thus, consider the perspective of 2005, when Gokhale and Smetters (2005) estimated that, assuming constant information, the present value of the GDP base would have increased to $772.3 trillion. While the GDP base therefore superficially had increased, it has nonetheless had shrunk in time-consistent terms by 1.5 percent, as previously stated. After all, the passage of time, causing future years' GDP to have greater present value than previously, did not change the tax increases and benefit cuts for those periods that foreseeably were necessary as of mid-2004 if nothing was done in the interim. Or, to put it another way, the fiscal gap likewise grew in present value with the passage of a year's time (from $63.2 trillion to $65.9 trillion), and yet it had not had a piece lopped off it (like 2004 GDP from the GDP base), since nothing was done in 2004 to address it.

## Chapter 6. Fiscal Gap Politics

1. Part B of Medicare was not specifically financed, being based on general revenues that were not increased by reason of the enactment. However, the projections at the time for Part B of Medicare were relatively small.

2. For just a small sampling of recent literature, see Shaviro 2004; Shaviro 2000; Rivlin and Sawhill 2004; Kotlikoff and Burns 2004; Diamond and Orszag 2004; and Auerbach, Gale, and Orszag 2002.

3. Deficits were roughly 30 percent lower for the years from 1987 through 1989 than immediately before or after (Shaviro 1997, 253). Analysts dispute,

however, whether GRH was the cause or merely signaled Congress's seriousness about the problem at the time (see Gramlich 1990).

## Chapter 7. Benign Fictions? Describing Social Security and Medicare

1. See Nataraj and Shoven 2004, 1 ("attempts to balance the Unified Budget while the trust funds were generating surpluses has led to increased government spending and personal and corporate income tax cuts within the rest of the federal government"); and Bosworth and Burtless 2004 (finding similar results for foreign governments but not for U.S. state governments).
2. On Rove's use of the term "privatization," see <http://archives.cnn.com/2000/ALLPOLITICS/stories/08/13/talk.wrap/>. On its use by Norquist and Moore, see Noah 2002a.
3. See <http://www.whitehouse.gov/news/releases/2004/12/20041216-2.html>.
4. See, e.g., <http://www.forbes.com/business/healthcare/feeds/ap/2005/02/21/ap1839523.html>; <http://www.silive.com/news/advance/index.ssf?/base/news/1107355589298600.xml>; and Castelli 2005.

## Chapter 8. Tax Expenditures

1. Public Law No. 93–344, 88 Stat. 297 (July 12, 1974). The German definition, though carrying less political freight, was not significantly different, apart from being terser. A 1970 law defining "tax concessions" that must be estimated for purposes of comparison with direct spending specified that they are "special exceptions to the general tax norm, which result in shortfalls in receipts for the public sector (Shannon 1986, 205).
2. For example, allowing tax-free savings accounts, exclusion of unrealized gains, and expensing for some capital outlays by businesses are all consumption-style features of our actual "income" tax.
3. As an additional detail, I have elsewhere suggested also including a separate listing for "proxy" departures from the baseline that clearly are incorrect considered in isolation, but that might be viewed as offsetting the failure to measure other items properly (Shaviro 2004d). An example would be disallowing investment interest deductions on the view that the taxpayer may have untaxed net investment income, such as from appreciated assets. I ignore this issue here to keep things simple.

## Chapter 9. Welfare, Cash Grants, and Marginal Rates

1. In-kind benefits could be provided without requiring that Bill Gates get food stamps. For example, in-kind benefits could gradually be scaled back, with the lost portion being converted into cash, as income increased, with no effect on

the marginal tax rate (which could be determined separately) except insofar as the in-kind benefits were not equated by recipients with their cash value.

2. In principle, the welfare description can be just as flexible as the cash grant description. Suppose that the best marginal-rate structure in the earlier example would involve a 50 percent marginal rate on the first $30,000 of income and a flat 38 percent rate above that. All we would need do to get there under the welfare description is to say that the $15,000 maximum benefit should not be fully phased out until income reaches $30,000, and that $30,000 should also be the income tax exemption amount. Other combinations of the phase-out rate and the income tax marginal rate could work identically, since an increase to either rate could be offset by reducing the other rate. The hard part is getting to the right answer from an inquiry that starts by asking who should get welfare benefits, rather than by asking what the marginal rate structure should look like.

3. There might also be indirect budgetary effects by reason of changes in people's work decisions.

4. The marginal rate is roughly 100 percent for a single-parent household with one child when its income increases from $20,000 to $30,000 (Holt 2005, D-4), and for a two-parent, two-child household when its income increases from $20,000 to $35,000 (D-5).

5. See, e.g., Eissa and Hoynes 2004; Meyer and Rosenbaum 2000.

# Bibliography

Aaron, Henry J., Alan S. Blinder, Alicia H. Munnell, and Peter R. Orszag. 2001. "Perspectives on the Draft Interim Report of the President's Commission to Strengthen Social Security." Washington, DC: Center on Budget and Policy Priorities and The Century Foundation, July 11.

Ackerman, Jan. 1993. "Forked Tongues Prevail on High; Pentagon Gets Annual Doublespeak Award from Teachers Group." *Pittsburgh Post-Gazette*, November 22, p. B-1.

Alesina, Alberto, and Allan Drazen. 1991. "Why Are Stabilizations Delayed?" *American Review* 82: 1170–1188.

Alesina, Alberto, and Roberto Perotti. 1995. "Political Economy of Budget Deficits." Washington, DC: International Monetary Fund.

Alesina, Alberto, and Guido Tabellini. 1990. "A Positive Theory of Fiscal Deficits and Government Debt." *Review of Economic Studies* 57: 403–414.

Allen, Mike. 2005. "Semantics Shape Social Security Debate: Democrats Assail 'Crisis' While GOP Gives 'Privatization' a 'Personal' Twist." *Washington Post*, January 23, p. A-4.

Andreoni, James. 1989. "Giving with Impure Altruism: Applications to Charity and Ricardian Equivalence." *Journal of Political Economy* 97: 1447.

Andrews, William D. 1974. "A Consumption-Type or Cash-Flow Personal Income Tax." *Harvard Law Review* 87: 1113–1188.

Andrews, William D. 1972. "Personal Deductions in an Ideal Income Tax." *Harvard Law Review* 86: 309–385.

# Bibliography

Antos, Joseph, and Jagadeesh Gokhale. 2003. "The Cost of Adding a Pre-scription Drug Benefit to Medicare." Testimony to the Subcommittee on Human Rights and Wellness, July 17. Available online at <http://www.aei.org/news/filter.,newsID.18039/news_detail.asp>.

Associated Press. 2005. "Parties Hope to Win on Social Security." February 21. Available on-line at <http://www.forbes.com/business/healthcare/feeds/ap/2005/02/21/ap1839523.html>.

Auerbach, Alan J. 2004. "Budget Windows, Sunsets and Fiscal Control." Cambridge, MA: National Bureau of Economic Research Working Paper No. 10694.

Auerbach, Alan J. 2003. "Is There a Role for Discretionary Fiscal Policy?" In Federal Reserve Bank of Kansas City. *Rethinking Stabilization Policy*, 109–150.

Auerbach, Alan J. 1994. "The U.S. Fiscal Problem: Where We Are, How We Got Here, and Where We're Going." In *NBER Macroeconomics Annual* 9: 1994.

Auerbach, Alan J., William G. Gale, and Peter R. Orszag. 2004. "Sources of the Long-Term Fiscal Gap." *Tax Notes* 103: 1049.

Auerbach, Alan J., William G. Gale, and Peter R. Orszag. 2002. "The Budget Outlook and Options for Fiscal Policy." *Tax Notes* 95: 1639.

Auerbach, Alan J., and Kevin Hassett. 2002. "Optimal Long-Run Fiscal Policy: Constraints, Preferences and the Resolution of Uncertainty." Cambridge, MA: National Bureau of Economic Research Working Paper No. 9132.

Auerbach, Alan J., and Philip Oreopoulos. 1999. "Analyzing the Fiscal Impact of U.S. Immigration." *American Economic Review* 89, Part 2, Papers and Proceedings, 176–180.

Baird, Douglas G., Robert H. Gertner, and Randal C. Picker. 1994. *Game Theory and the Law*. Cambridge, MA: Harvard University Press.

Ball, Laurence, and N. Gregory Mankiw. 1995. "What Do Budget Deficits Do?" In *Budget Deficits and Debt: Issues and Options*. Kansas City: Federal Reserve Bank of Kansas City, pp. 95–119.

Bandow, Doug. 2004. "The Conservative Case for Voting Democratic." *Fortune*, May 3.

Birnbaum, Jeffrey H. 2005. "Private-Account Concept Grew from Obscure Roots." *Washington Post*, Februrary 22, p. A-1.

Birnbaum, Jeffrey H., and Alan S. Murray. 1987. *Showdown at Gucci Gulch: Lawmakers, Lobbyists, and the Unlikely Triumph of Tax Reform*. New York: Random House.

Bittker, Boris I. 1969. "Accounting for Federal 'Tax Subsidies' in the National Budget. *National Tax Journal* 22: 244.

Bittker, Boris I. 1967. "A 'Comprehensive Tax Base' as a Goal of Income Tax Reform." *Harvard Law Review* 80: 925–985.

Blinder, Alan S., and Harvey S. Rosen. 1985. "Notches." *American Economic Review* 75: 736–747.

Block, Fred. 2001. "Why Pay Bill Gates?" In Phillipe Van Parijs, *What's Wrong with a Free Lunch?* (ed. Joshua Cohen and Joel Rogers). Boston: Beacon Press.

Blum, Walter J., and Harry Kalven, Jr. 1953. *The Uneasy Case for Progressive Taxation.* Chicago: University of Chicago Press.

Boards of Trustees of the Federal Hospital Insurance and Federal Supplementary Medical Insurance Trust Funds. 2005. *2005 Annual Report.*

Bosworth, Barry P. and Gary Burtless. 2004. *Pension Reform and Saving.* Washington, DC: Brookings Institution Press.

Bradford, David F. 2003. "Reforming Budgetary Language." In Ssjibren Cnossen and Hans-Werner Sinn (eds.), *Public Finance and Public Policy in the New Century.* Cambridge, MA: MIT Press, pp. 93–115.

Bradford, David F., and Daniel Shaviro. 2000. "The Economics of Vouchers." In C. Eugene Steuerle, Van Doorn Ooms, George Peterson, and Robert D. Reischauer (eds.), *Vouchers and the Provision of Public Services.* Washington, DC: Brookings Institution Press.

Bradford, David F., and the U.S. Treasury Tax Policy Staff. 1984. *Blueprints for Basic Tax Reform*, 2d ed. Stanford, CA: Hoover Institution Press.

Buchanan, James, and Richard Wagner. 1977. *Democracy in Deficit: The Political Legacy of Lord Keynes.* New York: Academic Press.

Buchanan, Neil. 2005. "Social Security, Generational Justice, and Long-Term Deficits." *Tax Law Review* 58: 275.

Coe, Norma B., Gregory Acs, Robert I. Lerman, and Keith Watson. 1998. "Does Work Pay? A Summary of the Work Incentives under TANF." Washington, DC: The Urban Institute.

Confirmation of Office of Management and Budget Director, 1989: Before the Senate Governmental Affairs Committee, 101st. Cong., 1st Sess. (1989). Statement of OMB director designate Richard Darman.

Congressional Budget Office. 2003. *The Long-Term Budget Outlook.* Washington, D.C.: Congress of the United States, Congressional Budget Office, December.

Derthick, Martha. 1979. *Policymaking for Social Security.* Washington, DC: The Brookings Institution.

# Bibliography

Diamond, Peter A., and Orszag, Peter R. 2004. *Saving Social Security: A Balanced Approach*. Washington, DC: Brookings Institution Press.

Downs, Anthony. 1957. *An Economic Theory of Democracy*. New York: Harper Collins Publishers.

Eisner, Robert. 1994. *The Misunderstood Economy: What Counts and How to Count It*. Boston: Harvard Business School Press.

Eisner, Robert. 1986. *How Real Is the Federal Deficit?* New York: Free Press.

Eissa, Nada, and Hilary Hoynes. 2004. "Behavioral Responses to Taxes: Lessons from the EITC and Labor Supply." Washington, DC: National Bureau of Economic Research Working Paper No. 11729.

Farkas, Steve, and Jean Johnson, with Ali Bers and Ann Duffet. 1997. *Miles to Go: A Status Report on Americans' Plans for Retirement*. Washington, DC: Public Agenda.

Farrell, John Aloysius. 2003. "Rancor Becomes Top D.C. Export, GOP Leads Charge in Ideological War." *Denver Post*, May 26, p. A-1.

Feldstein, Martin. 1974. "Social Security, Induced Retirement, and Aggregate Capital Accumulation." *Journal of Political Economy* 82: 75–95.

Ferrara, Peter J. 1980. *Social Security: The Inherent Contradiction*. Washington, DC: Cato Institute Press.

Firestone, David. 2003. "DeLay Rebuffs Move to Restore Lost Tax Credit." *New York Times*, June 4, p. A-1.

Forman, Jonathan Barry. 1986. "Origins of the Tax Expenditure Budget." *Tax Notes* 30: 537.

Fried, Barbara H. 1999. "The Puzzling Case for Proportionate Taxation." *Chapman Law Review* 2: 157.

Friedman, Milton. 2003. "What Every American Wants." *Wall Street Journal*, January 15, p. A-10.

Friedman, Milton. 1999. "Social Security Socialism." *Wall Street Journal*, January 26, p. A-18.

Friedman, Milton. 1984. "The Taxes Called Deficits." *Wall Street Journal*, April 26, section 1, p. 28.

Friedman, Milton. 1962. *Capitalism and Freedom*. Chicago: University of Chicago Press.

Furchtgott-Roth, Diana. 1995. "Abuses of Distribution Tables in Tax Policy." *Tax Notes* 69: 1414.

Gale, William G., and Brennan Kelly. 2004. "The 'No New Taxes' Pledge." Brookings Institution and Tax Policy Center, available online at <http://www.brookings.edu/views/papers/gale/20040604.htm>.

Gale, William G., and Peter R. Orszag. 2004. "Bush Administration Tax Policy: Starving the Beast?" *Tax Notes* 102: 999.

Gale, William G., and Peter R. Orszag. 2003a. "Sunsets in the Tax Code." *Tax Notes* 99: 1553.

Gale, William G., and Peter R. Orszag. 2003b. "The Economic Effects of Long-Term Fiscal Discipline." Washington, DC: Urban-Brookings Tax Policy Center Discussion Paper No. 8, April.

Giannarelli, Linda, and Eugene Steuerle. 1995. "The Twice-Poverty Trap Faced by AFDC Recipients." Washington, DC: The Urban Institute.

Gokhale, Jagadeesh, and Kent Smetters. 2005. "Measuring Social Security's Financial Problems." Cambridge, MA: National Bureau of Economic Research Working Paper No. 11060.

Gokhale, Jagadeesh, and Kent Smetters. 2003. *Fiscal and Generational Imbalances: New Budget Measures for New Budget Priorities.* Washington, DC: AEI Press.

Graetz, Michael J. 1995. "Distribution Tables, Tax Legislation, and the Illusion of Precision." In David F. Bradford (ed.), *Distributional Analysis of Tax Policy.* Washington, DC: AEI Press.

Gramlich, Edward M. 1990. "U.S. Federal Budget Deficits and Gramm-Rudman-Hollings." *American Economic Review* 80: 75.

Greenhouse, Steven. 1993. "Clinton's Economic Plan: Seeing Figures, Two Sides Calculate Clinton's Math." *New York Times*, February 22, p. A-14.

Gross, Daniel. 2003. "How to Make the Deficit Look Smaller Than It Is." *New York Times*, November 23, section 3, p. 4.

Gruber, Jonathan. 2004. *Public Finance and Public Policy.* New York: Worth Publishers.

Hacker, Jacob S., and Paul Pierson. 2005. *Off Center: The Republican Revolution and the Erosion of American Democracy.* New Haven, CT: Yale University Press.

Hayek, F. A. 1944. *The Road to Serfdom.* Chicago: University of Chicago Press. [Fiftieth Anniversary Edition, 1994.]

Himelfarb, Richard. 1995. *Catastrophic Politics: The Rise and Fall of the Medicare Catastrophic Coverage Act of 1988.* University Park: Pennsylvania State University Press.

Holmes, Stephen, and Cass R. Sunstein. 1999. *The Cost of Rights: Why Liberty Depends on Taxes.* New York: Norton.

Holt, Stephen D. 2005. "Making Work *Really* Pay: Income Support and Marginal Effective Tax Rates Among Low-Income Working Households." Washington, DC: American Tax Policy Institute.

# Bibliography

Hotelling, Harold. 1929. "Stability in Competition." *Economic Journal* 35: 41–57.

Jackson, Howell E. 2004. "Accounting for Social Security and Its Reform." *Harvard Journal on Legislation* 41: 59.

Jehl, Douglas. 2003. "Air Force Pursued Boeing Deal Despite Concerns of Rumsfeld." *New York Times*, December 6, p. A-3.

Kahneman, Daniel, et al. 1991. "Anomalies: The Endowment Effect, Loss Aversion, and Status Quo Bias." *Journal of Economic Perspectives* 5: 193.

Kamin, David, and Richard Kogan. 2005. "The Administration's Misleading $600 Billion Estimate of the Cost of Waiting to Act on Social Security." Washington, DC: Center on Budget and Policy Priorities, February 2.

Kaplow, Louis. 2005. "Optimal Income Transfers." Unpublished manuscript.

Kogan, Richard. 2005a. "Bill Illuminating Long-Term Budget Problems Would Provide Both Important Information and Misleading Information." Washington, DC: Center on Budget and Policy Priorities.

Kogan, Richard. 2005b. "Budget Process Changes Required by the 'Honest Government Accounting Act.'" Washington, DC: Center on Budget and Policy Priorities.

Kotlikoff, Laurence J. 2001. "The Coming Generational Storm." Unpublished manuscript.

Kotlikoff, Laurence J. 1992. *Generational Accounting: Knowing Who Pays, and When, for What We Spend*. New York: The Free Press.

Kotlikoff, Laurence J., and Scott Burns. 2004. *The Coming Generational Storm: What You Need to Know about America's Economic Future*. Cambridge, MA: MIT Press.

Kotlikoff, Laurence J., and Jeffrey Sachs. 1997. "It's High Time to Privatize." *Brookings Review* 15: 16.

Krugman, Paul. 2005a. "A Gut Punch to the Middle." *New York Times*, May 2, p. A-21.

Krugman, Paul. 2005b. "The $600 Billion Man." *New York Times*. May 15, p. A-25.

Lakoff, George. 2004. *Don't Think of an Elephant: Know Your Values and Frame the Debate*. White River Junction, VT: Chelsea Green Publishing.

Lakoff, George. 2002. *Moral Politics: How Liberals and Conservatives Think*. Chicago: University of Chicago Press.

Lang, Thomas. 2005. "Spin Buster." *Columbia Journalism Review*, January 25, available online at <http://www.cjrdaily.org/archives/001264.asp>.

Locke, John 1952. *Second Treatise On Government*. New York: Liberal Arts Press.

Martinez, Gebe. 2005. "Language Could Chart the Course of Social Security; Both Parties Are Carefully Choosing Words in Hopes of Swaying the Public." *Houston Chronicle*, February 2, p. A-8.

McCaffery, Edward J., and Jonathan Baron. 2005. "Tax Policy in an Era of Rising Inequality: The Political Psychology of Redistribution." *UCLA Law Review* 52: 1745–1792.

Meyer, Bruce D., and Dan T. Rosenbaum. 2000. "Making Single Mothers Work: Recent Tax and Welfare Policy and Its Effects." Cambridge, MA: National Bureau of Economic Research Working Paper No. 7491.

Mikesell, John L. 2003. "The Normal States Sales Tax: The Vision Revealed in State Tax Expenditure Budgets." *State Tax Today* 2003: 66–4.

Miron, Jeffrey A., and David N. Weil. 1997. "The Genesis and Evolution of Social Security." NBER Working Paper No. 5949.

Mirrlees, James. 1971. "An Exploration in the Theory of Optimum Income Taxation." 38 Review of Economic Studies 175–208.

Moynihan, Daniel Patrick. 1973. *The Politics of a Guaranteed Income: The Nixon Administration and the Family Assistance Plan*. New York: Random House.

Mueller, Dennis C. 1989. *Public Choice II*. Cambridge, UK: Cambridge University Press.

Munnell, Alicia H., and Mauricio Soto. 2005. "What Does Price Indexing Mean for Social Security?" Boston, MA.: Center for Retirement Research at Boston College, January, No. 14.

Murphy, Liam, and Thomas Nagel. 2002. *The Myth of Ownership: Taxes and Justice*. New York: Oxford University Press.

Musgrave, Richard A. 1959. *The Theory of Public Finance: A Study in Political Economy*. New York: McGraw-Hill Book Company, Inc.

Nataraj, Sita, and John B. Shoven. 2004. "Has the Unified Budget Undermined the Federal Government Trust Funds?" Unpublished manuscript.

*New York Times* Editorial. 2005. "Shameless Photo-Op." *New York Times*, April 7, p. A-22.

Noah, Timothy. 2002. "Who Said Anything about Privatizing Social Security?" September 6. Available online at <http://slate.msn.com/?id=2070573>.

# Bibliography

Olson, Mancur. 1965. *The Logic of Collective Action: Public Goods and the Theory of Groups*. Cambridge, MA: Harvard University Press.

Organization for Economic Co-operation and Development. 1996. *Tax Expenditures: Recent Experiences*. Washington, DC: OECD Publications and Information Center.

Penner, Rudolph G., and C. Eugene Steuerle. 2004. "Budget Rules." *National Tax Journal* 57: 547–557.

Persson, Torsten, and Lars E. O. Svensson. 1989. "Why a Stubborn Conservative Would Run a Deficit: Policy with Time-Inconsistent Preferences." *Quarterly Journal of Economics* 104 (May): 325–345.

Ponnuru, Ramesh. 2002. "The P Word." *National Review*, September 4. Available on-line at <http://www.nationalreview.com/ponnuru/ponnuru090402.asp>.

Reinhardt, Uwe T. 2000. "Health Care for the Aging Baby Boom: Lessons from Abroad." *Journal of Economic Perspectives* 14: 71.

Ricardo, David. 1996 ed. *Principles of Political Economy and Taxation*. Amherst, NY: Prometheus Books.

Ricardo, David. 1951 ed. *The Works and Correspondence of David Ricardo*, ed. Piero Sraffa. Cambridge: Cambridge University Press for the Royal Economic Society.

Rivlin, Alice M., and Isabel Sawhill (eds.). 2004. *Restoring Fiscal Sanity: How to Balance the Budget*. Washington, DC: Brookings Institution.

Robinson, James W. (ed.). 1992. *Ross Perot Speaks Out*. Rocklin, CA: Prima Publishing.

Rosen, Harvey S. 1999. *Public Finance*. New York: McGraw-Hill.

Rubin, Robert E., Peter R. Orszag, and Allen Sinai. 2004. "Sustained Budget Deficits: Longer-Run U.S. Economic Performance and the Risk of Financial and Fiscal Disarray." Paper presented at the AEA-NAEFA Joint Session, Allied Social Science Associations Annual Meetings, The Andrew Brimmer Policy Forum, "National Economic and Financial Policies for Growth and Stability," January 4, San Diego, CA.

Samuelson, Paul A. 1958. "An Exact Consumption-Loan Model of Interest with or without the Social Contrivance of Money." *Journal of Political Economy* 66: 467–482.

Savage, James D. 1988. *Balanced Budgets And American Politics*. Ithaca, NY: Cornell University Press.

Schlesinger, Arthur M. 1959. *The Age of Roosevelt*, vol. 2: *The Coming of the New Deal*. New York: Houghton Mifflin.

Shafroth, Frank. 2003. "Dissaving Grace." *State Tax Notes* 30: 797–800.

Shannon, Harry A. 1986. "The Tax Expenditure Concept in the United States and Germany: A Comparison." *Tax Notes* 33: 201.

Shaviro, Daniel. 2005. "A Blueprint for Future Tax Reform? Evaluating the Reform Panel's Report." *Tax Notes* 109 (November 7): 827–835.

Shaviro, Daniel N. 2004. *Who Should Pay for Medicare?* Chicago: University of Chicago Press.

Shaviro, Daniel. 2002. "The Growing U.S. Fiscal Gap." *World Economics Journal* 3(1) (October–December): 1–8.

Shaviro, Daniel N. 2000. *Making Sense of Social Security Reform*. Chicago: University of Chicago Press.

Shaviro, Daniel N. 1999. "Effective Marginal Tax Rates on Low-Income Households." *Tax Notes* 84: 1191–1200.

Shaviro, Daniel N. 1997. *Do Deficits Matter?* Chicago: University of Chicago Press.

Simons, Henry C. 1938. *Personal Income Taxation*. Chicago: University of Chicago Press.

Slemrod, Joel. 1990. "Optimal Taxation and Optimal Tax Systems." *Journal of Economic Perspectives* 4: 157–178.

Smetters, Kent. 2003. "Is the Social Security Trust Fund Worth Anything?" Cambridge, MA: National Bureau of Economic Research Working Paper No. 9845.

Smithies, Arthur. 1941. "Optimal Location in Spatial Competition." *Journal of Political Economy* 49: 423–439.

Stein, Herbert. 1996. *The Fiscal Revolution in America: Policy in Pursuit of Reality*. Washington, DC: AEI Press.

Steuerle, Eugene. 2003. "Can the Progressivity of Tax Changes Be Measured in Isolation?" *Tax Notes* 100: 1187–1188.

Stevenson, Richard W. 2001. "Declining Surplus Renews Debate Over the Budget Outlook." *New York Times*, July 12, p. A-20.

Stigler, George. 1946. "The Economics Of Minimum Wage Legislation." *American Economic Review* 36: 358.

Suellentrop, Chris. 2003. "Grover Norquist: The Republican Party's Prophet of Permanence." *Slate magazine*, July 7, <http://slate.msn.com/id/2085277>.

Sullivan, Martin A. 2003. "The Decline and Fall of Distribution Analysis." *Tax Notes* 99: 1869–1873.

# Bibliography

Sullivan, Martin A. 2000. "Tax Expenditure Budgets: Now More Than Ever." *Tax Notes* 86: 1187.

Sunstein, Cass R. 2000. "Introduction." In Cass R. Sunstein (ed.), *Behavioral Law and Economics*. Cambridge: Cambridge University Press.

Surrey, Stanley S. 1973. *Pathways to Tax Reform*. Cambridge, MA: Harvard University Press.

Surrey, Stanley S. 1957. "The Congress and the Tax Lobbyists – How Special Tax Provisions Get Enacted." *Harvard Law Review* 70: 1145.

Surrey, Stanley S. 1953. "Our Schizophrenic Income Tax." The Stanley S. Surrey Papers, Harvard Law School Library, Modern Manuscript Division, Box 23, Folder 7.

Surrey, Stanley S., and Paul McDaniel. 1985. *Tax Expenditures*. Cambridge, MA: Harvard University Press.

Suskind, Ron. 2004a. *The Price of Loyalty: George W. Bush, the White House, and the Education of Paul O'Neill*. New York: Simon & Schuster.

Suskind, Ron. 2004b. "Without a Doubt." *New York Times Magazine*, October 17, p. 44.

Suskind, Ron. 2003. "Why Are These Men Laughing?" *Esquire* 139: 96–105.

Tabellini, Guido, and Alberto Alesina. 1990. "Voting on the Budget Deficit." *American Economic Review* 80: 37–49.

Thaler, Richard. 1991. "Toward a Positive Theory of Consumer Choice." In Richard Thaler (ed.), *Quasi Rational Economics*. New York: Russell Sage Foundation.

Thuronyi, Victor. 1988. "Tax Expenditures: A Reassessment." *Duke Law Journal* 1988: 1155.

Tierney, John. 2005. "Can Anyone Unseat F.D.R.?" *New York Times*, January 23, section 4, p. 1.

Tobin, James, Joseph A. Pechman, and Peter M. Mieszkowski. 1967. "Is a Negative Income Tax Practical?" *Yale Law Journal* 77: 1–27.

Tsongas, Paul. 1991. *A Call To Economic Arms: Forging A New American Mandate*. Boston: Tsongas Committee.

United States Treasury Department. 2003. "Analytical Perspectives, Budget of the United States Government for Fiscal Year 2003." Washington, DC: U.S. Treasury Department.

*Washington Post*. 2005. "Transcript of Bush Interview." January 16. Available online at <http://www.washingtonpost.com/wp-dyn/articles/A12570–2005Jan15.html>.

Weisbach, David A., and Jacob Nussim. 2004. "The Integration of Tax and Spending Programs" *Yale Law Journal* 113: 995.

Weisman, Jonathan. 2004. "Senate Passes Corporate Tax Bill." *Washington Post*, October 12, p. A-1.

White, Joseph, and Aaron Wildavsky. 1989. *The Deficit and the Public Interest: The Search for Responsible Budgeting in the 1980s*. Berkeley: University of California Press.

Zitner, Aaron. 1997. "Longtime Fears on Deficit Begin to Fade." *Boston Globe*, May 3, p. A-1.

# Index

# Index

# Index

# Index

# Index